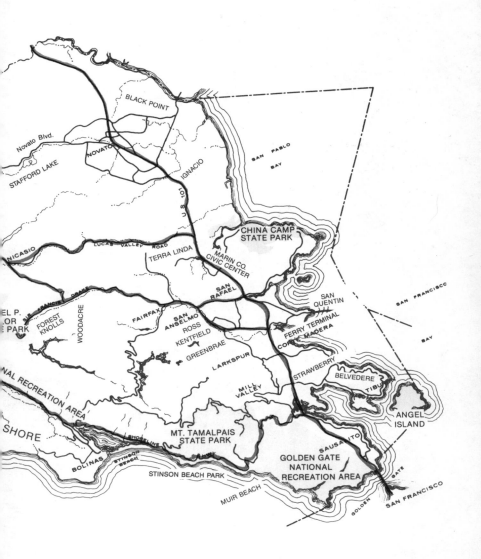

*Making the Most of MARIN*

Cover photos by Patricia Arrigoni: Golden Gate Bridge from the top of the South Tower looking north to Marin; Wild flowers; Angel Island; Ten Mile Beach, Harbor seal at the California Marine Mammal Center, Fort Cronkhite; Sea grass at Stinson Beach; Racing sailboat from Australia competes on San Francisco Bay; Muir Woods National Monument.

Back cover: Golden Gate Ferries at the Larkspur Ferry Terminal; Lyford House in Tiburon; Lisa Boyajian Moon relaxes at her parents home in Ross with Mt. Tamalpais in the background.

All photos in the book were taken by the author unless otherwise acknowledged.

Printed in the United States of America.

# MAKING THE MOST OF
# MARIN

## A best selling guide to the most stunning county on the California coast.

## by Patricia Arrigoni

Revised 1990 Edition

Travel Publishers Int.

*To Peter*

---

Copyright © 1981 and © 1990 by Patricia Arrigoni.
First Printing, 1981
Second printing, completely revised, 1990
All rights reserved.

Published by Travel Publishers International
P.O. Box 1030, Fairfax, California 94930

**Library of Congress Cataloging-in-Publication Data**

Arrigoni, Patricia
   Making the most of Marin: a best selling guide to the most
stunning county on the California coast / by Patricia Arrigoni.
      p.      cm.
   Includes bibliographical references.
   ISBN 0-9625468-9-5 : $15.95
   1. Marin County (Calif.)—Description and travel—Guide-books.
   2. Marin County (Calif.)—History, Local. I. Title
F868.M3A77 1990
917.94'620453—dc20
                                              90-10895
                                              CIP

Book design by Robert and Kayla Van Norman
   /Van Norman Associates
Cover design by Joe Di Vincenzo
Edited by Diane Van Renselaar

# Contents

## DISCLAIMER

*Making the Most of Marin* is designed to provide information in regard to Marin County, California. It is not the purpose of this book to supply all information available on the subject. You are urged to read other material listed in the section, "Further Reading on Marin."

Every effort has been made to make this book as accurate as possible, however, there may be mistakes. Please consider this text as a general guide and not as the ultimate source of everything on Marin.

The purpose of this book is to educate and entertain. The author and Travel Publishers International shall have neither liability nor responsibility to any person or entity with respect to any loss or damage caused or alleged to be caused, directly or indirectly by the information contained in this book.

If you do not wish to be bound by the above, you may return this book to the publisher for a full refund.

*Making the Most of MARIN*

# Introduction

**M**arin County has been the vacation playland of San Francisco residents since ferryboats first brought visitors across the bay to its pristine shores in the second half of the nineteenth century. When the summer fog poured through the Golden Gate and settled over the city, San Franciscans headed north to the warm, sunny hills and valleys of Marin. From the ferry landings at Sausalito and Tiburon, they would board trains or stagecoaches and head for Mill Valley to hike on the trails of Mt. Tamalpais, or to ride "the crookedest railroad in the world" to the mountain's summit and then glide down to Muir Woods to gaze at the towering redwoods. The more hearty souls would go to tent camps at Stinson Beach, or to summer cottages in the San Geronimo Valley. Young people enjoyed the Rose Bowl dances in Larkspur or the Portuguese festivals in Sausalito. Lured by the natural beauty of the county, many of these San Franciscans eventually made their homes here.

Marin had originally been settled in the early 1800s by Spanish padres, who established a mission in San Rafael and set about converting the local Coast Miwok Indians. Large Mexican land grants divided up the rest of the land. Life on these ranchos was leisurely and comfortable. The pace quickened with the arrival of the railroad and ferries. Then, in 1906, refugees from the big San Francisco earthquake and fire began moving into Marin, increasing its population by sixty percent. Towns sprang up overnight. The Arrigoni family was part of this migration, arriving in 1907. My husband's grandfather, Dante Divita, settled in Manor (now Fairfax) where his descendants remain to this day.

With the opening of the Golden Gate Bridge in 1937, a new rush to Marin began. Tied now to the city, Marin grew into a suburban community. The new residents (an affluent, educated group with a high percentage of professional people and artists) shared with the early settlers an appreciation for the beauty of their county and a desire to preserve it. As Marin's population increased, adamant conservationists fought against exploitation of the land, with great success—the Pacific coastline is unspoiled, protected by thousands of acres of parkland; virgin redwood forests remain; West Marin is still rural; and open space borders developed areas.

Today, Marin County is one of the most beautiful places to live or visit. Millions of people come each year, attracted by the picturesque villages, extensive parkland, and also by a curiosity about the casual (and over-publicized) lifestyle of Marinites.

*Making the Most of Marin* is an insider's guide to the pleasures of our county—to the well-known places: the beaches, seaside villages, redwood forests, and the mountain; but also to little-known spots even residents may have missed: an earthquake trail, the new China Camp State Park, old forts and bunkers in the Headlands, historic Victorian homes, unique shops and restaurants, the best spots for clamming, even a place to learn hang-gliding. There are also historical sketches of Marin towns, based on extensive research and on interviews with descendants of Marin's pioneer families.

This updated edition of *Making the Most of Marin* is illustrated with all new photographs taken by the author, and some rare historical pictures of Marin shot in the 19th and early part of the 20th Centuries. All telephone numbers in Marin have a 415 area code.

*Old steam engine #498 (without its large diamond spark-attesting smoke stack), on top Mt. Tamalpais in the early 1900s. Note cable car.* Photo courtesy of Nancy Skinner.

# Golden Gate Bridge 1

## *A Miracle of Engineering*

The magnificent Golden Gate Bridge, linking San Francisco and Marin County, is an international symbol of the entire Bay Area and is one of the most visited attractions in the world. Its art deco design is one of essential simplicity, the graceful lines of a single suspended span running between two well-proportioned post-braced towers. Known poetically as the "Span of Gold," the bridge is actually painted a vivid orange-vermilion color called "International Orange."

Visitors gazing at its brilliant color and splendid artistic sweep can little guess at the swirl of controversy that preceded its construction. The Golden Gate Bridge District, consisting of San Francisco and five northern California counties, was formed in 1923 by the California legislature for the purpose of financing the building of the bridge by selling bonds totaling $35 million. For six years the district was dragged through various courts in an effort to prevent construction.

The Citizens Committee Against the Golden Gate Bridge Bonds argued that the bridge was physically and financially impossible, that it was an outrage, a wildcat scheme. Opponents screamed that a bridge would mar San Francisco's beautiful natural harbor entrance and destroy Sausalito's splendid isolation. Further, they argued that enemy bombing or gunfire could destroy the bridge and bottle up the harbor. Many worried about an earthquake. Others called it an economic crime, claiming that Marin was so sparsely settled it would not support sufficient traffic to allow a toll bridge to meet its financial obligations.

Despite all the controversy, the District moved ahead. On August 15, 1929, Joseph B. Strauss of Strauss and Paine, Inc. of Chicago was hired as chief engineer.

Strauss recommended a single suspension bridge, which he felt would be effective in resisting irregular and turbulent wind forces as well as earthquake movements. His theory proved correct and the bridge has withstood severe storms; winds blowing 50 mph have swayed the bridge laterally 4.9 feet, and vertically up to 2 feet, without damage. On December 1, 1951, a record wind was recorded of 69 mph.

Actual designing of the bridge took place in Chicago. Irving F. Marrow, a consulting architect, is credited with the details of the architectural design which allows motorists to enjoy the spectacular views while driving across the bridge. Clifford E. Paine, the engineer in charge of the designing staff, interpreted Strauss's ideas and, while keeping a low profile, ensured the success of the project.

Construction began January 5, 1933 with a ground breaking ceremony at Crissy Field adjacent to the bridge site in San Francisco. Even the United States fleet participated in the celebrations. Citizens cheered the opening up of thousands of jobs during the heart of the Depression.

The bridge progressed steadily across the mile-long expanse for the next four years. Before it was completed, however, eleven men had lost their lives; ten in a single accident when the stripping scaffold of a painting contractor gave way and fell, destroying 2,100 feet of safety net. Other nets saved the lives of nineteen men, who formed a club called the "Halfway to Hell Club" in commemoration of their miraculous survival of close calls.

The completed bridge was truly a miracle of structural design. Its total length, including approach structures, is 8,981 feet; its width is 90 feet between cables and can accommodate six lanes of traffic. The height of the towers is 746 feet, and the clearance above low tide is 220 feet.

On May 27, 1937, a huge celebration was held to open the "Span of Gold." Pedestrians crossed the bridge that day; vehicular traffic began the next day and has continued ever since except for the bridge's 50th birthday party held May 24, 1987.

Estimates of 250,000 people jammed the bridge for an historic dawnwalk causing the span to temporarily flatten out. Another 500,000 celebrators were in the Presidio and Toll Plaza area as

*Crowds gather for the 50th Birthday of the Golden Gate Bridge, May 24, 1987.*

well as north of the bridge attempting to get on for the Bridge Walk.

Over one million joined in the general festivities which included concerts, a cavalcade of antique cars, a Golden Regatta parade of vintage boats, a fly-over of old airplanes, and finally a spectacular fireworks display with a 4,000 foot long waterfall suspended between bridge towers.

The finale to the bridge's party was the permanent lighting of the two 746-foot towers. This subtle lighting of the Golden Gate Bridge and the bright lights spanning the Bay Bridge have added a glittering new dimension to the San Francisco Bay scene at night.

Most people see the Golden Gate Bridge from their cars on the mile-and-a-half drive across the bridge to Marin. There is no toll driving north on Highway 101; upon returning to San Francisco to the south, the toll is $2.00. But if you feel adventurous, you can walk, jog, or bicycle across the bridge. It is a unique experience.

The east sidewalk, facing San Francisco, is open all daylight hours; the west side is open only for bicycles on weekends and holidays. There is no toll for walking or bicycling across the bridge. Bicycles must be walked around the towers. Be sure to bring a sweater, for the winds are usually strong and the air chilly, especially when the fog rolls in.

You may park your car on the east side of the San Francisco Toll Plaza. Meters cost $.25 per 30 minutes with a two-hour maximum. A pedestrian and vehicle underpass runs under the Toll Plaza to the administration building of the Golden Gate Bridge, Highway and Transportation District where you may pick up bus and ferry schedules plus other information on the bridge.

Begin your walk at the small park on the east side of the Toll Plaza. A statue of Joseph B. Strauss, the engineer of the bridge, is situated amid benches and flower gardens. Restrooms (with wheelchair access) and a gift shop are in a round building adjoining the park. You may notice brick walkways decorated with people's names. 90,000 bricks were sold for $30 to $75 each after the bridge party with 15% of the proceeds going to Friends of the Golden Gate Bridge to help pay off the party debt.

Historic Fort Point is just below the bridge and can be reached by driving or hiking down. Constructed from 1853 to 1861, the fort at one time housed 600 soldiers; its cannons could fire 65-pound balls for a distance of two miles. The water that swirls below is a popular, though dangerous, surfing and fishing area. The fort is open daily from 10:00 A.M. to 5:00 P.M. Wear something warm for your visit. You will see that the rangers are usually dressed in heavy parkas and gloves. Phone the Fort Army Museum at 921-8193 for more information.

As you start across the bridge, look down for a bird's-eye view of old Fort Point.

The first, or south, sixty-five-story bridge tower houses a service elevator that goes clear to the top. At the tower's base is a plaque dedicated to the engineers and directors of the District in celebration of the bridge's "Silver Anniversary" in 1962. The tower also houses airplane beacon lights and foghorns.

Halfway across the bridge is the "mid-span" emergency telephone with an old-fashioned receiver and crank for ringing the bell. In this area, two foghorns, called diaphones, guide ships safely through the main channel.

The view is breathtaking. Below are the rushing waters of San Francisco Bay dotted with sailboats, motor yachts, heavy tankers, and cruise ships. Beyond is the panorama of the San Francisco skyline, the Bay Bridge, Treasure Island, Alcatraz, the cities of the East Bay, the Marin shoreline and headlands, and Angel Island.

*Golden Gate Bridge under construction. View from Crissy Field, October 1936.* Photo by Chas. Hiller. From the Archives of the Golden Gate Bridge, Highway & Transportation District.

The second or north tower marks the entrance to Marin County. Lime Point, a lighthouse whose construction in 1900 helped usher in the new century, is just below this tower. It has fully-automatic lights and foghorns. A little to the north are the perpendicular rocks called the Needles.

As you gaze across the waters of San Francisco Bay, you may wonder if Sir Francis Drake, the intrepid English pirate, navigator and explorer, did indeed find this secret harbor over four hundred years ago, in 1579. On March 8, 1975, a replica of his ship, the Golden Hinde, sailed under the bridge after a long and hazardous trip from Plymouth, England. The Golden Hinde was greeted on that memorable afternoon by hundreds of private yachts and sailboats, San Francisco fireboats spraying arcs of water, dignitaries from all over the Bay Area, and thousands of cheering people hang-

*Golden Gate Bridge under construction. View from San Francisco anchorage looking toward Marin, February 16, 1935.* From the Archives of the Golden Gate Bridge, Highway & Transporation District.

ing out of the windows of tall office buildings and standing along the shore.

In 1775, the Spanish packet San Carlos, under the command of Lieutenant Juan Manuel de Ayala, was recorded as the first European vessel to sail into the bay. On August 5, Ayala anchored off an area he called "Little Willows," or in Spanish, "Saucelito." Ayala left the next day to explore and survey the waters and became well acquainted with the coast Indians. He remained almost six weeks and made the first map of the area.

San Francisco Bay was originally a coastal valley developed by the Sacramento and San Joaquin rivers, which joined in what is now the Delta west of Stockton, passed through the Carquinez Straits, and flowed out to the Pacific Ocean. A gradually sinking coastline allowed ocean water to flood the valley, thus forming the bay.

In 1769, when the overland explorer Gaspar de Portola first gazed at the waters of San Francisco Bay, they covered 700 square miles, including the northern San Pablo Bay. The area has shrunk to about 400 square miles, but a strong Bay Conservation and Development Commission has been formed to protect what is left. The volume of water that flows in and ebbs out four times a day with the tides averages 1,250,000 acre feet.

At the end of the bridge you will arrive at Juan Manuel de Ayala Vista Point, a Roadside Ecological Viewing Area with a parking lot, restrooms, telephones, and, of course, spectacular views of the "City by the Bay." A plaque honoring the 400-year anniversary of Sir Francis Drake's landing in Marin is attached to a cross section of a huge coast redwood tree.

(If you are driving south on Highway 101 and would like to visit Vista Point before crossing the Golden Gate Bridge, exit at the Golden Gate National Recreational Area, drive a short distance, then turn right at the sign to "Forts Baker, Barry and Cronkhite." Instead of driving straight up the hill, turn left and proceed down to the parking lot. A pedestrian underpass leads to the observation area at Vista Point.)

Look away from San Francisco, and you will see the magnificent headlands to the west, the piers of Fort Baker below, a winding road leading to the town of Sausalito, and Highway 101 disappearing into a rainbow tunnel. You are in Marin.

# The Marin Headlands

# 2

Hidden Beaches, Sweeping Vistas

The Marin Headlands loom above the Golden Gate—fifteen square miles of coastal hills, valleys, steep cliffs and uninhabited shoreline. This area, once a strategic part of the United States coastal defense system, is now the heart of the Golden Gate National Recreation Area, of which approximately 42,600 acres are in Marin. Nowhere are there more spectacular, panoramic views of the ocean, the Golden Gate Bridge, and the dazzling city of San Francisco.

Visitors can explore the remains of the military bunkers that housed large coastal guns set up in defense of the Golden Gate from 1870 on, a period covering the Spanish-American War, World War I, and World War II. Old installations of brick and batteries of granite and concrete give silent evidence of the world of yesterday when a harbor could be defended by shooting a gun.

Now cracks appear, weeds grow, iron rusts, and cement crumbles. The land has returned to peaceful purposes, saved from urban sprawl by the powerful military which mercifully kept its wildness intact.

How miraculous to find this sprawling open space adjacent to a city the size of San Francisco. It is a place where wildflowers carpet the hills in a rainbow of color each spring. Here you will find orange poppies, blue and yellow lupine, red Indian paintbrush, and white flowering hemlock with tiny dots of red on the blossoms. Here also you can enjoy the pungent smell of eucalyptus mixed with the fragrance of sage. Wildlife is abundant and you may spy a doe with her tiny, spotted fawn grazing peacefully in the evening

*◄ The Golden Gate Bridge as seen from the Presidio Yacht Harbor in Sausalito.*

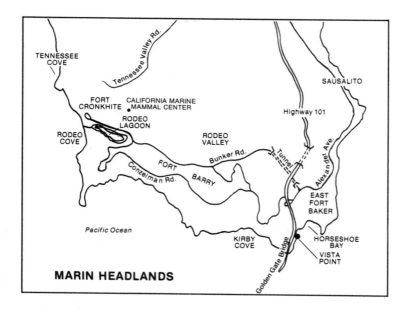

**MARIN HEADLANDS**

light, a family of raccoons, or an occasional fox.

Overhead a redwing blackbird flies slowly by, silhouetted against a setting sun. A Steller's jay screeches, and the sea gulls cry out as they swoop down on currents of wind along the cliffs.

Below, the waves race upward against the shore while white foamy water crashes over jagged rocks. The tide turns, the water recedes, and a tiny beach appears, inaccessible to all but the curlews, cormorants, and sanderlings racing on tiny legs along the edge of the water.

When the fog rolls in, the sharp line of the ridge disappears and all is silent except for the wind, the crashing of the surf, and a lonely warning from a distant foghorn.

Whether misty or clear, take time to visit the Marin headlands and explore the old gun batteries once so important to the defense of the bay.

From Vista Point, bear right at a sign that reads "San Francisco thru Underpass 1000'." Follow the gravel road down under the Golden Gate Bridge to Conzelman Road. Turn left, or downhill, and you will soon arrive at Fort Baker.

From Highway 101 north, take the Alexander Avenue exit (going south, take the last Sausalito exit) and follow signs for Forts Baker, Barry, and Cronkhite. A long one-way tunnel leads to the other forts. Turn right on Bunker Road to reach Fort Baker. (There is no sign until you drive through an underpass.)

Fort Baker was built on part of a Mexican land grant awarded to William A. Richardson, an English seaman, in 1838. It was called *Rancho Saucelito* and covered 19,000 acres. In 1886, the government purchased a large portion and developed the Lime Point Military Reservation on San Francisco Bay.

From this Fort Baker was carved out. Begun in 1897 as a harbor defense, the fort was named for a Civil War hero, Colonel Edward Dickinson Baker. Baker, a friend of Abraham Lincoln, fell in the Battle of Ball's Bluff, Virginia, in 1861. He had fought with Lincoln in the bloody Black Hawk War in 1832, and in the Mexican War with General Zachary Taylor in 1845.

Five gun emplacements at Fort Baker house Endicott cannons; rifle-barreled, armor-piercing guns named for the secretary of war. They were capable of shooting accurately for a range of twelve miles.

A sign at the entrance to the old fort reads, "Fort Baker, Sub Post of Presidio of San Francisco"; this is still true today. When the fort was active in coastal defense, several thousand men were stationed there.

The heart of the base is the picturesque parade ground surrounded by several well-kept, two-story white houses currently occupied by military personnel. Also located in this area are the headquarters of the 91st Division, U.S. Army Reserve Center, and the 6th Army Recruiting Brigade (Western).

In the southeast part of the base are the private Presidio Yacht Harbor and Horseshoe Bay, a good area for fishing. This is an excellent place to view the Golden Gate Bridge from another angle as it looms overhead.

After exploring Fort Baker, go on to Forts Barry and Cronkhite in the ocean-facing portion of the headlands by taking Bunker Road back to the one-way tunnel. The tunnel was built in 1918 (enlarged in the 1930s) and was used to haul guns to Fort Barry. Also named for an army hero, General William F. Barry, this strategic coastal defense base had battery emplacements for fifty guns.

In 1937, eighty-two acres north of Fort Barry were acquired for

a third fort named for General Albert Cronkhite. Sixteen-inch guns capable of firing thirty-two miles were installed here.

After World War II, missile installations for the Nike-Ajax and the Nike-Hercules were built in the Headlands. When these too became obsolete, they were removed, and the bases were gradually phased out. They all became part of the Golden Gate National Recreation Area in 1972.

At the entrance to the tunnel signs read: "6 minutes red light." There is no hiking or bicycling allowed. Enter when the light turns green, drive through the tunnel, and follow Bunker Road to Rodeo Lagoon. (At this writing in 1990, the tunnel is closed for repairs and entry to Fort Cronkhite is by Conzelman Road, the Sausalito exit off Highway 101.

Continue down to the lagoon, and you will see the ranger station on your right; it is open daily form 8:30 A.M. to 4:30 P.M. Here you can pick up maps of the roads and hiking trails.

In the future, the visitors center will move to the Fort Barry Chapel once used by the military for religious services. The chapel is located at the intersection of Bunker and Field roads.

One a major trail, called the Coast Trail, goes all the way north to the Point Reyes National Seashore. It is only recommended for reasonably experienced hikers as it is quite steep in parts.

Point Bonita Lighthouse, built in 1877, is a half-mile hike from the lighthouse parking lot located up Field Road. You may drive on up to the right and park for a magnificent view of the lighthouse, the Golden Gate Bridge, San Francisco, Rodeo Lagoon and the ranger station. The lighthouse is open from 12:30 P.M. to 4:00 P.M. on weekends. Guided walks are conducted at 1:00 P.M.

You may also hike to Kirby Cove from Battery Spenser, off Conzelman Road. The distance is one-and-a-half-miles, and you will be rewarded by a nice beach and good fishing area. The water here is cold for swimming averaging from 55 to 77 degrees.

Information is available at the Marin Headlands Ranger Station on camping facilities and on the nature walks conducted by the park rangers every Saturday and Sunday at 1:00 P.M. The station, open daily from 8:30 A.M. to 4:30 P.M., contains changing

◄ *The 1877 Point Bonita Lighthouse located in the Marin Headlands along the rugged Pacific Coast.*

cultural displays. For further information on the headlands including the lighthouse, call the ranger station at 331-1540.

Privies, including facilities for wheelchairs, are located just past the parking lot west of the headquarters. There are also benches and information bulletin boards where the number for the Emergency Park Police (556-7941), lists of birds and flora in the area, and places to hang glide are posted.

Across from the ranger station, a wooded bridge spans the tip of Rodeo Lagoon. The bridge leads to Rodeo Beach, Rodeo Cove, and the Pacific Ocean. Dogs need to be on leashes on South Rodeo Beach. This beach is a good spot for fishing but the strong currents, steep drop-off, and rip tides make it hazardous for swimming. Rock collectors can gather samples of jasper, carnelian, and agate.

To the south is Bird Island. From June to December, you may see large birds with six-and-one-half foot wingspans and summer plumage of dark brown feathers gliding gracefully over the waves, then diving with accelerated speed into the ocean. These birds are brown pelicans. Many observers feel the brown pelican resembles a prehistoric bird and, indeed, it is considered a rare and endangered species. DDT has weakened the eggs laid by the females, causing shells to crack and be destroyed before the chicks are ready to hatch. With DDT now illegal, the breeding success is beginning to increase. The birds nest in the Channel Islands off Santa Barbara and Baja California.

A pair of binoculars will help you get a good look at the Heerman's gulls, western gulls, and other sea birds found around Bird Island. Cormorants build round nests here of dried seaweed.

Several organizations are located in the Marin Headlands. The Headlands Institute, a member of the Yosemite National Institute (located 300 feet east of the visitor's center), conducts educational programs "directed toward the improvement of environmental perceptions and ethics." The Institute is set up for field studies, seminars, and conferences, and maintains a staff of around seven qualified instructors with degrees in natural science. Members of the public are welcome to drop by. (332-5771)

The YMCA Point Bonita Outdoor Center, up Field Road, will provide housing and food services to groups of over twenty people (the group must have an identifiable leader). Arrangements

*Bird Island sits just off Rodeo Beach at Fort Cronkhite.*

may be made for a regular class to stay at the Center and be taught by their own teacher.

The facilities—concrete barracks built for the Nike Missle Site, then remodeled for use by the National Guard—are also popular for church retreats, adult special interest group meetings, and outdoor education. The public may walk through to see the facilities but must make reservations in advance to stay overnight. (331-9622)

The California Marine Mammal Center is located in the old Nike missile site above the ranger station a little to the east in Fort Cronkhite. This unique institution founded in 1975 by Paul Maxwell, Lloyd Smalley and myself, is federally and state licensed to rehabilitate sick and injured marine mammals. It also conducts research, and provides a data bank of information.

The Center services an area covering 1,000 miles of coastline. Volunteers pick up orphaned and injured marine mammals and nurse them back to health.

Visitors may see a sea lion being nursed for respiration problems, an undernourished baby elephant seal or an abandoned

*The Golden Gate Hostel at Fort Barry.*

harbor seal pup being fed. The mammals are kept an average of six months before being released back to their native habitat. The Center has an admirable 60 to 70 percent survival rate and can accommodate up to 300 marine mammals in one year.

In 1989 the California Marine Mammal Center was named one of the 18 national winners of the President's Volunteer Action Award. A silver medal from President George Bush was presented at the White House to Peigin Barrett, Executive Director, and publicist Mary Jane Schramm on April 11. The Center handles 50,000 visitors a year.

The California Marine Mammal Center is open from 10:00 A.M. to 4:00 P.M. daily. There is no admission charge. (311-SEAL or 311-7325)

Overnight hikers in the headlands can make arrangements to spend the night in the Golden Gate Hostel (also called the Marin Headlands Hostel) in Fort Barry. It may be reached by turning uphill on Field Road off Bunker Road and following the well-marked directions. Guests here observe the international hostel customs which include no alcohol or pets, and smoking outside only. Guests should bring a sleeping bag, towel, food to prepare, and firewood if desired. They must also be willing to contribute to clean-up in the morning.

Facilities include sixty beds, a common room, family room, a spacious kitchen, and a coin-operated laundry room. Hostelers may check in until 10:00 P.M. Reservations must be made by mail and paid in advance. The cost is $6.50 per person per night with a limit of three nights in summer and five nights in winter. Along with payment, the manager suggests sending a self-addressed stamped envelope for confirmation. The address is: Building 941, Fort Barry, Sausalito, California 94965. Phone 331-2777 between 7:30 A.M. to 9:30 A.M. and 4:30 P.M. to 11:00 P.M.

For the most spectacular views of the Golden Gate and the bridge, take Conzelman Road (Sausalito exit off Highway 101), a long scenic road, which twists up the face of the headlands. You will usually see a variety of cameras set up along here as this is an extraordinary place to shoot photographs. There are old military bunkers to explore and picnic tables where you can enjoy a leisurely lunch. The road becomes one-way at the top, then continues down to Rodeo Lagoon.

Farther north in the headlands is Rodeo Valley, which was once slated to become a city of 30,000 people. To be called "Marincello," the city would have housed these thousands of people in as small a space as possible by the generous use of high rises. Today you may park your car where the gates of Marincello once proudly marked the road which led through Tennessee Valley to Rodeo Valley and the site for the new city. (Exit Highway 101 at Stinson Beach sign, which puts you on Shoreline Highway. Turn west on Tennessee Valley Road.)

It is a level one-and-a-half-mile hike from the parking area to the lovely beach at Tennessee Cove; or you may hike the Bobcat and Miwok Trails which both lead to Rodeo Valley.

Thomas Frouge, who owned a gigantic construction company in the East, picked this site to build his dream city. The proximity to San Francisco, plus the spectacular views, assured the city's success. Never mind the heavy winds and daily fog.

With the financial backing of the Gulf Oil Corporation, Frouge hired architects and lawyers who drew up the plans and contracts. When all was ready, a huge public relations campaign was launched.

*An old military building at Fort Baker.*

The developer rented space in an industrial building in Sausalito where he installed a model of the proposed city. Members of the Marin County Board of Supervisors and Planning Commission, city councilmen, and other VIPs were invited to a steak dinner and tour of the model. Like Peter Pan, one could view the miniature Marincello from above by crossing on a specially-constructed bridge.

Frouge gave his visitors glowing facts and figures based on the premise that population figures proved that so many thousands of new residents would be moving into Marin in a specified number of years. He contended that his city would be the best way to plan for this influx. The Board of Supervisors approved Frouge's plan.

Some conservationists in Marin circulated petitions against the hasty approval, and the city of Sausalito filed a lawsuit. But what really brought construction to a halt was a three-year legal battle beginning in 1967 between the Gulf Oil Corporation and Frouge. Then in January 1969 Frouge unexpectedly died, and the project died with him.

The Nature Conservancy finally bought the land from Gulf Oil in 1972, preserving it for a park, and it is now part of the Golden Gate National Recreation Area. So what was to have been a model city of thousands of inhabitants is preserved forever as a lovely open area of valleys, rolling hills, streams, and a quiet lagoon—a place of peace and natural beauty for all to enjoy.

# Sausalito

**3**

## *"Riviera of the West"*

Travelers visiting Sausalito for the first time often recognize the similarities to the exquisite French/Italian Rivera. Like Portofino on the Italian Mediterranean, Sausalito rises from the blue waters of Richardson Bay, an exclusive hillside community tucked in among oak, willow, and eucalyptus trees, with commanding views of glamorous yacht harbors and graceful sailboats. Flourishing gardens with rhododendrons, begonia, wisteria, honeysuckle, and magnolia grow in profusion all over the hills.

Sausalito affords even more impressive vistas than the Riviera including the long, graceful Bay Bridge which may be seen in a glow of shimmering sun, or floating in mist or fog. And there is the magnificent skyline of San Francisco, shining white during the day and diamond-like at night.

Visitors to Sausalito find no end to the pleasures in this little town. Shoppers delight in discovering the perfect gift among the international array of import stores, jewelry shops, art galleries, gift boutiques, and designer clothing establishments. History buffs can explore the old landmarks. A wide variety of excellent restaurants offer seafood, Italian, French, and Japanese food.

The most exciting way to arrive in Sausalito, short of your own forty-eight foot yacht, is by one of the Golden Gate Transit District ferryboats from San Francisco (982-8834). Visitors may take an early morning ferry over, spend the day, and return in the afternoon or evening as late as 7:20 P.M. and 6:10 P.M. weekends.

The ride itself is pure pleasure. Standing on deck with the wind in your hair, you can watch the city recede and the Marin hills

◄ *Plaza Vina del Mar in Sausalito. The elephants are from the 1915 San Francisco Panama Pacific International Exposition.*

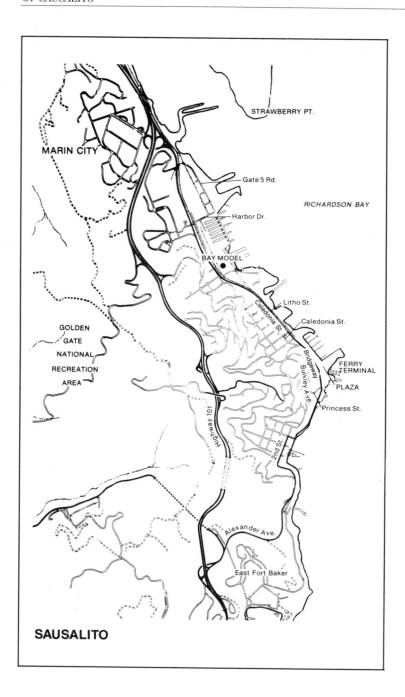

STRAWBERRY PT.

MARIN CITY

Gate 5 Rd.

RICHARDSON BAY

Harbor Dr.

BAY MODEL

Litho St.

Caledonia St.

Caledonia St.

GOLDEN
GATE
NATIONAL
RECREATION
AREA

Bridgeway

Bulkley Ave.

FERRY
TERMINAL

PLAZA

Princess St.

Highway 101

2nd St.

Alexander Ave.

East Fort Baker

SAUSALITO

gradually become a towering presence. If you prefer, you can stay below and have a drink and snack at the bar, relax, and look out the windows to watch the boats on the bay.

By automobile, driving north on Highway 101, exit at Alexander Avenue; driving south, take the Sausalito exit. Parking in town is tight and strictly policed, so be careful to watch your time. It is probably easier to use one of the large city-owned parking lots which cost $1.50 per hour the first two hours, and $1 thereafter with a maximum of $6 for 24 hours.

The principal street, which follows the shoreline, is Bridgeway, so called because it showed you the way to the Golden Gate Bridge which opened in 1937. Prior to that, it was called "Water Street". The south end of Bridgeway runs into Richardson and Second Street in an area that is known as Sausalito Old Town. A creek, fed by hillside springs, once flowed down the bay along what is now Main Street and provided fresh water for ships.

Around 1836, Mexican ships referred to the area as *El Puerto De Los Balleneros,* or "Whalers' Cove". It was a popular anchorage for several reasons: sailors claimed that the water found here stayed fresher for a longer period than any other found along the West Coast, the anchorage was sufficiently deep, the area was protected from westerly winds by Table Mountain to the northwest (now called Mt. Tamalpais), and wood was readily available.

In 1838, Captain William A. Richardson was awarded the 19,000-acre Mexican land grant called Sausalito, which in Spanish meant "little willow," and in 1841, he built an adobe house at what is now Pine and Bonita streets. As captain of the port, he acted as pilot to guide ships into the cove. He also owned the water supply, the source of wood, and collected all the Mexican anchorage fees. It was time of flourishing activity. Mexican schooners, Russian brigs, British man-of-war ships, and United States naval vessels anchored at Sausalito.

In 1868, Samuel R. Throckmorton, administrator of Richardson's land, sold 1,200 acres to the Sausalito Land and Ferry Company. That section of town was subdivided (including around 125 building lots which were in the bay), shares of stock were sold, and a steamer was chartered to ferry people back and forth to San Francisco. Hotels and homes were built, and by 1875, the narrow-gauge North Pacific Coast Railroad was serving the town.

*A traffic jam develops in the 1920s as cars line up for the auto ferry. Notice the trains on the right.* Courtesy of the Sausalito Historical Society.

A wharf and shops were built in the area where the ferries dock today, on land donated by the Land and Ferry Company.

Sausalito was on her way. By 1855 she had a new ferryboat, eight hotels, and a population of 1,500. The first issue of the *Sausalito News,* published February 12, 1885, reported that there were "two restauants, three blacksmith shops, two news agencies, one barber shop, one bakery, two boat houses, seven general merchandise houses and a very fair representation of saloons." The town had become a melting pot of English, Irish, Portuguese, Greeks, Norwegians, Germans, and Americans.

In 1887, the name of the town which was being misspelled, was changed to its present spelling by the United States Post Office, and in 1893, Sausalito voted to become an incorporated town. Civic improvements such as sidewalks, sewers, and streetlights were initiated.

By 1900, however, gambling interests had taken over, leaving the town wide open for all kinds of corruption. At least twenty-five saloons and as many poolrooms were in operation. The poolrooms were actually bookie joints which had been outlawed from San Francisco. Undesirable crowds flocked aboard the ferryboats on racing days and, reportedly, a "decent woman" had trouble getting past Water Street (Bridgeway). The area downtown smelled of stale beer, while the streets were full of mud. This situation lasted for about ten years until a reform political ticket was voted in.

As the railroad grew, Sausalito became a major ferry and rail terminal. It was here that all the Marin commuters left the suburban trains and boarded boats headed for San Francisco.

The completion of the Golden Gate Bridge in 1937 caused land values to soar in Marin though Sausalito was bypassed by the new highway. San Franciscans could now reach the county in ten to fifteen minutes.

By early 1941,the ferries had closed down and the trains stopped running as they could no longer compete with the bridge. Ferries used for public transportation would not be seen again in Sausalito until 1970 when the Golden Gate Bridge, Highway and Transportation District resumed this service.

During the Second World War, Sausalito became a shipbuilding center. The Maritime Commission condemned over two hundred acres of waterfront on north Bridgeway, rerouted the street and opened a shipyard, Marinship, which eventually employed 70,000 workers. The ferries were temporarily put back into use for the shipyard workers, who built fifteen Liberty ships, seventy-eight tankers, and twenty army invasion barges; outfitted three British coasters; and repaired twenty miscellaneous vessels. A total of ninety-three ships were launched. When the war ended, hundreds of new Sausalito residents were left behind.

In the 1950s, a community of houseboats was gradually established on Richardson Bay. These boats were occupied by artists, poets, and writers. Many were home-built creations of fascinating designs and materials which included wood from the deserted buildings of Marinship. Others were old ferryboats remodeled and divided into living sections. Sausalito became known as an artists' and writers' retreat.

Over the years, part of the floating boat community has become legitimate by complying with local codes such as electrical, water, and sewer hookups. Others remain renegades and periodically battle county officials over polluting the bay and other violations.

During the late 1970s, many handsome new houseboats, designed by architects and built by professional carpenters, were added to the community and occupied by doctors, lawyers, and other professionals. The socio-economics of the area changed as these people also learned to enjoy the shimmer of the sun on the water, the sight of a blue heron, or other shorebird feeding nearby, and the feel of a gentle rocking with the waves and tide.

To begin your tour of Old Sausalito, walk south along Bridgeway to Second Street and Main, where the fresh water creek once flowed into the bay. This area is called Hurricane Gulch as wind and fog whip through here regularly. The actual name was bestowed on the area around 1884 or 1886 when the Sausalito Bay Land Company was trying to promote the sale of land here with a summer picnic. The wind came up and blew the tablecloths, cutlery, and glasses right off the tables.

Hurricane Gulch is the location of the restaurant, the Chart House Valhalla. The actual address is 201 Bridgeway as the boardwalk running along the water is an extension of that street.

The building, constructed in 1893, was originally a German beer garden called "Walhalla," which is the German spelling for "Valhalla," a Scandinavian term meaning an abode where the souls of those who have fallen in battle are received by the god Odin. In this building, rooms were provided upstairs as a haven for seafaring men.

Water running down the hillside was piped through the building of the Walhalla and out the back into the casks and barrels of waiting boats. Sailors were supplied with liquor while they waited.

During Prohibition, the Walhalla became a center for bootlegging and was raided periodically by federal agents. When Marinship opened during World War II, the old building provided badly needed sleeping quarters.

In 1948 Sally Stanford, a former bootlegger and "lady of the house" in San Francisco, bought the Walhalla, changed the name to "Valhalla," and made it into a successful restaurant, decorating it with Victorian furniture, Tiffany lamps, and art nouveau pieces. Miss Stanford became involved in town politics and ran for city council six times before being elected in 1972. She served as mayor in 1976-77, and vice-mayor in 1979. Over the years she gained the respect of elected officials countywide, and in 1979, a street called "Stanford Way" was named in honor of the grande dame of Marin politics. Sally Stanford passed away February 4, 1982 at the age of 78.

From the Valhalla, follow the boardwalk past four wooden houses

*Sausalito children looking down at Central School in 1901.* Courtesy of the
Sausalito Historical Society.

and you will arrive at the house where Jack London was reported
to have lived (though the Sausalito Historical Society maintains
severe doubts about his residence). The house is situated on the
curve of Richardson and Bridgeway where London could watch
ferries ply the waters of San Francsico Bay. It is said this was
his inspiration for the novel *Sea Wolf,* published in 1904.

This whole area was once threatened by a wall of buildings when
a developer applied for a use permit to cover ten lots with apartments to be built right out over the water. Outraged citizens managed
to stop the construction and save the waterfront for the public.

Along stretches of open waterfront, as you walk north on
Bridgeway, you can see San Francisco, the Bay Bridge, Alcatraz,
Angel Island, and Belvedere Island. Benches have been placed
along here, while below the street level, a concrete walkway

(covered by water at high tide) has been provided for fishermen.

Across Bridgeway is Tiffany Beach Park which runs parallel to the street. It was named for the former city clerk, William Zobel Tiffany, who served the town for twenty-six years between 1913 and 1939. When he retired, his daughter Zelda continued in his job until 1944. The park features gardens and benches.

Proceeding along the waterfront, you will see a bronze sea lion statue just off shore. It was designed by the artist Al Sybrian, who liked to sketch the sea lions playing on the rocks in this area in the 1950s. The sea lions and brown pelicans can still be seen here, especially during the herring runs in the bay in January.

Sybrian's first sculpture, donated in 1955, stood four feet high and was made of concrete and haydite. It lasted eight years before cracking under the pressure of tides and floating debris. Because of its enormous popularity, funds were raised to replace the sea lion in bronze. The new sculpture was completed and placed here in 1966.

Up the hill from Bridgeway you will notice, almost hidden now among the trees, a large concrete and stonework retaining wall. It was built by William Randolph Hearst, who had planned to build a grand castle on the site. Hearst lived in a Queen Anne-style home called "Sea Point" located a little above and south of the wall foundation; at this time, he was the owner of the Piedmont Land and Cattle Company.

In 1890, Hearst donated a banner and carrying cart for the local Sea Point Chapter of the Native Sons of the Golden West to wheel through the streets of Sausalito during parades. This $1,000 contraption, with flag tassels of pure gold, is now on display at the Sausalito Historical Museum.

Around 1919, Hearst tore down Sea Point. Old-time Sausalito residents remember that he had been invited to leave town by a delegation of the husbands and fathers of the Hill. It seems William Hearst had a special lady friend he had installed at Sea Point, a striking blond whose presence offended the local matrons.

The town board of trustees, as the city council was called in those days, was more generous. On July 21, 1921, they wrote Hearst a letter requesting he return to Sausalito and build on his homesite. Hearst built his castle at San Simeon instead.

After passing Hearst's retaining wall, the next building you will see walking north is the old San Francisco Yacht Club at 558

Bridgeway which now houses Horizon's Restaurant, serving a continental cuisine. Constructed in 1897, the old building also was used at various times as a town meeting place, a bait and tackle shop, and an artist's studio. It was the second yacht club built on this site. The first burned in 1878, and divers have brought up fascinating artifacts from the original building, many of which are on display at the Sausalito Historical Society.

Shoppers may begin in earnest at this point. There are a variety of antique stores, interior decorating and clothing shops, the Venice Gourmet Boutique (an excellent deli), several restaurants and art galleries.

Princess Street marks the end of Old Town and the end of the sidewalk overlooking the water. Princess Street was named for the first ferry that came to Sausalito in 1868 and which made two trips daily to Meiggs Wharf in San Francisco.

The original landing site was a submarine net depot during World War II. It is now Yee Tock Chee Park, a tiny area containing several benches and a concrete platform for fishing. Look for a plaque with the inscription: "Yee Tock Chee Park. In loving memory of Willie Chee, November 1, 1891-March 2, 1975."

Yee Tock Chee was born in Canton, educated in China, and went to work in a Hong Kong shipyard at age sixteen. After a long steamer ride and a month in the old immigration center on Angel Island, he arrived in Sausalito in 1912. He went to work for Wing Low Ming in a tiny grocery store on Caledonia Street, delivering groceries in a two-wheeled horsecart. In 1919 he bought the business and is remembered with affection for carrying half of Sausalito on his books during the lean Depression years. He also loaned ferryboat fares to commuters short of cash and performed innumerable favors to his customers throughout World War II.

As you continue along Bridgeway, you will pass more shops, then a short street called El Portal adjacent to the Plaza Vina del Mar. This park, dating from 1904, was originally called Depot Park, but in 1960 was renamed Plaza Vina del Mar in honor of Sausalito's sister city in Chile. Its unique elephants and fountain were salvaged from the 1915 San Francisco-Panama Pacific International Exposition by the fountain's designer, architect William B. Faville, a Sausalito resident. It is a "Point of Historical Interest" for the State of California.

The elephants, which originally held 100-foot flagpoles of Oregon pine were designed by architects McKim, Meade and White of New York. In 1977, citizens of Sausalito donated nearly $16,000 to have the fountain completely refurbished by a skilled Italian craftsman, Eugene Mariani of the Western Art and Stone Company of Brisbane. The water of the fountain is turned on at 8:00 A.M. daily, a lovely, quiet time to visit.

There is also a drinking fountain at the western tip of the park which was dedicated in 1912 to Jacques Thomas. Thomas, a former Sausalito mayor, was instrumental in having the park, then part of the shoreline, filled in and donated to the city by the North Shore Railroad.

Just across Bridgeway from the park are steps leading up the hill. These steps will eventually bring you up to Bulkley Avenue.

At 810 Bridgeway is the elegant remodeled Casa Madrona Hotel which was built in 1885 as the private residence of William Gront Barrett, a wealthy Vermont-born lumber baron. The original house contained marble fireplaces, stained glass windows, brass chandeliers and elaborate wrought iron grillwork. In 1910 it was turned into a hotel and within the last few years, has been greatly enlarged.

Owner John Mays, who purchased the property in 1976, refurbished the old section of the hotel and added a 16-room addition so that the building now runs from Bulkley Avenue down to Bridgeway.

The part of Sausalito just described which includes the wharf, park, Bridgeway from Horizon's Restaurant to the Village Fair, up Princess Street on both sides, and up to the Alta Mira Hotel on Bulkley Avenue, is part of Sausalito's Historic District. A three-year effort finally resulted in recognition by the Secretary of the Department of Interior in Washington, D.C. in 1980, and protects the area for all time. Plans for remodeling any of the buildings in the Historic District must be submitted to the Sausalito Historical Landmarks Board. A Community Appearances Advisory Board gives final approvals.

On Anchor Street, off Bridgeway, just beyond the plaza, is Gabrielson Park where a two-ton, twenty-two-foot metal sculpture by Chilean artist, Sergio Castillo, is on display. On a sunny day, a carpet of sunbathing bodies will cover the entire park. Past Anchor on Bridgeway are public restrooms and telephones.

Continue on to the famous Village Fair at 777 Bridgeway. Built in 1924 as Mason's garage, this delightful hillside complex is now

*"The Pirate," a houseboat in Sausalito once owned by actor Stirling Hayden, was built in 1880.*

a shoppers' paradise. These shops offer such things as high-fashion clothing, cameras, a wide variety of imports, gifts, candles, hand-blown glass, bath accessories, jewelry, leather, antiques, Scandinavian clocks, artwork, lingerie, and imported coffee beans. The shops are connected by winding stairways and walks, with gardens and fountains. "Little Lombard," a replica of San Francisco's famous "crookedest street in the world," was a walkway made out of the parking garage ramp. In 1988, a remodeling of the entire structure turned the original ramp into brick stairs and waterfalls. A glass dome was built over the complex and an elevator installed.

Lunch or a snack may be enjoyed on the second floor with a superb view of Richardson Bay. A new restaurant has also been added to the third floor offering views of the bay and San Francisco. Restrooms are on the mezzanine.

Four-tenths of a mile past the Village Fair is Litho Street, where the city offices, library, and the Sausalito Historical Society are located in the old 1927 Sausalito Central School building. The school was remodeled and dedicated as the civic center in March 1975.

Take time to visit the Sausalito Historical Society Museum, founded by Jack Tracy, who can be found upstairs on Monday, Wednesday, and Saturday from 10:00 A.M. to 4:00 P.M. An entire hallway is filled with historic artifacts such as an old anchor, boats, a fog bell, and a permanent display of paintings done by Sausalito artists in the 1950s. There are currently two large rooms filled with interesting memorabilia and fascinating old photographs. You can pick up a free chamber of commerce map of Sausalito which includes a history of the city, an index to the city parks and playgrounds, a map of county bicycle trails, photographs, and ads from local establishments. There is no charge to visit the museum. (332-1005)

At the east end of Litho Street, along the waters of Richardson Bay, is the Earl F. Dunphy Park, dedicated in 1972 to a former mayor of Sausalito who is credited with four decades of dedicated public service. The two-acre Dunphy Park was the culmination of a long conservation battle in the 1960s. Developers bought up underwater lots totaling thirty-five acres off the waterfront and drew up plans to build a large development complex. Sausalito passed a bond issue to buy and establish the park in 1970, stopping this development. In 1971, volunteers were organized to plant a lawn and trees on an area of mudflats. The lovely white gazebo was designed by architect William Stephen Allen, a Sausalito resident, in 1976. Adjacent to the gazebo is a tall flagpole with the dedication: "Two Centuries of Freedom, Erected by the People of Sausalito, July 4, 1976."

Facilities at the park include benches, a picnic area, volleyball court, preschool children's playground, and a bocci ball court. There are also a small sandy beach, large grassy area, and a lovely view of the water, houseboats, sailboats, water birds, and the wonderful fresh smell of sea air. A new boat marina is planned on five acres south of the park.

Continue north of Dunphy Park another half-mile to 2100 Bridgeway where the United States Army Corps of Engineers has built an hydraulic scale-model of the entire San Francisco Bay and Delta in a building two acres in size. The model's purpose is to determine and analyze bay characteristics, behavior, and en-

*Sausalito around 1880. Caledonia Street runs from the foreground toward Hannon's Hill near Napa Street. The railroad trestle crosses Richardson Bay in the background. In the middle (left) is the old white adobe home of William Richardson.* Courtesy of the Sausalito Historical Society.

vironmental quality as affected by fill, pollution, fresh water flows, and problems of salt water intrusion into the Delta.

In 1980, the Corps of Engineers completely remodeled the bay model, adding an extensive visitor's center complete with ultramodern displays, a theater, multipurpose room, amphitheater, library, three overlooks of the model, and three sound-pods—banks of phones on which visitors may hear explanations of the model. Displays include exhibits about the sea, earthquakes, the evolution of man, the formation of the earth, and the beginning of life. The theater contains fifteen screens for projector slide shows.

The Bay and Delta Model is open Tuesday through Friday from 9:00 A.M. to 4:00 P.M.; holidays, 10:00 A.M. to 6:00 P.M. Groups may arrange conducted tours, and there is no charge. The actual running of the model is determined by the need to analyze a problem concerning the bay, so it is best to phone ahead to find out when it is operating. (332-3871)

The Sausalito Historical Society is setting up an exhibit on a 2500 square foot section of the Bay and Delta Model dedicated to Sausalito's "Marinship," a 210-acre shipyard which produced 93 ships (Liberty ships, oilers and tankers), in just three years during World War II.

A bonanza of artifacts from the "USNS Mission Santa Ynez," a tanker built in Marinship, will include a wide variety of displays such as charts, maps, life boats, the builder's plate, flags and life perservers.

Anchored at the U.S. Army Corps of Engineers dock adjacent to the Bay Model is the last of 225 steam schooners, the "Wapama." She was built in 1915 in Oregon and is being restored under the direction of the National Maritime Museum of San Francisco.

Continue north on Bridgeway to Harbor Drive, which is one-and-four-tenths miles north of the Village Fair. Turn right at the stoplight, proceed past the old Marinship mold loft building (now called the Industrial Center), then left on Gate 5 Road. During World War II, workers entered the shipyard here through guarded gates. It is now the area of the houseboat colony where several new piers have been built.

The famous Heath Ceramics is located at 400 Gate 5 Road. Heath manufactures ceramic tableware, decorative gift items, and architectural tiles. There are many bargains at their "Seconds Shop," which is open from 10:00 A.M. to 5:30 P.M. every day but holidays. Visitors may walk through the back part of the building and see how fine ceramics are made. Call 332-3732 for group tours.

To see the houseboat community, continue on Gate 5 Road, which becomes dirt and gravel, until you reach the Kappas Marina. A nostalgic sight here is the old ferry, the Vallejo (1879), where Jean Varda, a Greek artist, once lived and hosted flamboyant costume parties at which he often appeared as king.

Residents in this area do not appreciate people wandering about, and parking is strictly enforced with towing twenty-four hours a day. You may, however, see some attractive and unique houseboats farther north in the Yellow Ferry Harbor. Many are built of red-

*The ferryboat "Tamalpais," crosses San Francisco Bay around the turn of the century.* Courtesy of Nancy Skinner.

wood with stained glass windows, flower boxes, and hanging plants.

Just offshore of Sausalito is a palm-fringed, man-made island weighing 700 tons of floating concete. Built by Forbes Kadoo, it contains 14 luxury rooms, a bar, hot tub, waterfall and "sandy beach." Forbes runs tours and rents the island out for private parties, weddings, concerts and seminars. It can accommodate 50 people. For a Forbes Island tour, call 332-5727.

Above Bridgeway, the hills of Sausalito rise over six hundred feet and are covered with spacious old homes, hotels, and churches which contrast dramatically with the modern houses. To see some of this area walk up the steps across from Vina del Mar Plaza to Bulkley Avenue. Start at the First Presbyterian Church, built in a shingle style with an all-redwood interior. It dates from 1909 and was designed by the architect Ernest Coxhead. The address is 100 Bulkley.

Next stop by the famous Alta Mira Hotel at 125 Bulkley. Rebuilt in 1926 after a fire, the hotel is best-known for its Sunday brunch, served on a spacious deck overlooking the bay.

Another prime attraction of the original Sausalito is the Christ Episcopal Church, built in 1882 and located at Santa Rosa and San Carlos avenues. It is a shingle-style American Gothic design with an especially graceful bell tower and stained glass windows that date from the 1880s, memorial gifts of early Sausalito families. The center windows, installed in 1945, were designed by architect Arnold Constable.

Of special interest also is the Sausalito Woman's Club, 120 Central Avenue at San Carlos, designed by Julia Morgan and built in 1917. Morgan also designed a woman's club in Berkeley, buildings at the University of California at Berkeley, and the castle at San Simeon for William Randolph Hearst.

The Sausalito Woman's Club is a brown-shingled, split-level building with an all-redwood interior and French windows. It was Sausalito's first official landmark. Today it has a perfectly manicured lawn, brown picket fence, and brick walkways in front.

A fifteen-foot granite bench, affording a gorgeous view of Angel Island and the bay, can be found at Bulkley and Harrison avenues. It is called "Daniel O'Connell's Seat" in memory of the unoffical poet laureate of Sausalito and was installed by fellow members of the San Francisco Bohemian Club in 1901. In the walkway, there is a handsome three-leaf shamrock mosaic, added to celebrate O'Connell's Irish birth. A dedication reads:

*"In Memory Of Daniel O'Connell, Poet, 1849-1899."*

On February 2, 1988, Sausalito took on a second sister city in Japan. An inscription on display at the Historical Society reads:

*"Sakaide City, Japan. . .the founding city dates back over 300 years and is located on the island of Shikoku facing the inland sea. Mountains surround this city of 70,000. The 'Seto Ohashi' bridge, cost $3 billion, length 5.8 miles, will connect Sakaide, via islands to the mainland."*

The bridge was completed in 1988 and is the longest two-tiered bridge system in the world crossing five islands.

# Southern Marin

# 4

## From Bay to Mountain

## Marin City

As you leave Sausalito and the Marin Headlands and drive north on Highway 101, you will see Marin City on your left. The town began as a housing community for workers at Marinship during World War II. Now the old prefabricated community has been rebuilt into a small city of handsome apartments and single-family homes.

Marin City is the site of one of the most popular Bay Area flea markets. It is held most Saturdays and Sundays, beginning at 5:30 A.M. Bargain hunters flock from all over the Bay Area looking for everything from fresh-baked bread to flatwear and fur coats. Phone 332-1441 for more information.

Meanwhile there are plans to redevelop this area with hotels and retail complexes by the Marin City Development Corporation.

## Mill Valley

Nestled in the southeastern slopes of Mt. Tamalpais, Mill Valley has the charming look of a European mountain village. The town's public buildings and half-timbered shops are built among tall, stately redwood trees. Homes are hidden along the wooded slopes of the lower mountain.

The beauty and uniqueness of the town, as indeed all of Marin, has always attracted brilliantly talented people. Mill Valley's population includes many famous artists, writers, composers, and performers. Most residents take an active interest in their local government and have fought to keep the private, small-town flavor.

Mill Valley is located in the first Mexican land grant in Marin. Awarded to John Reed by Governor Figueroa in 1834 (some early records show his name as "Juan Read"), *Rancho Corte de Madera del Presidio* was an area that provided "cut wood for the Presidio." The grant was 8,878.82 acres and included what is now the Strawberry, Tiburon, Belvedere, and Corinthian peninsulas, as well as parts of Mill Valley, Corte Madera and Larkspur.

John Thomas Reed was born in Dublin, Ireland, in 1805, but left when he was fifteen years old on his uncle's ship to seek his fortune. Their voyage took them to Acapulco, Mexico, then on to California where they arrived in 1826. Reed turned twenty-one while visiting Los Angeles.

Traveling north, he took a liking to Sausalito and applied unsuccessfully for a grant of the *Rancho Saucelito*. He then moved on to Cotati in Sonoma County. Disaster overtook him there— Indians destroyed his crops and drove him off his land. From Sonoma he went to the mission in San Rafael where he became *mayordomo,* the manager.

Back in Sausalito in 1832, he lived in a wooden house near Old Town and established the first ferry on San Francisco Bay, a small boat that ran across the water irregularly to Yerba Buena, or what was later San Francisco.

Having applied for several land grants over the years, Reed finally became the recipient of the *Corte de Madera del Presidio* adjoining *Rancho Saucelito.* Here he erected the first sawmill in the county in 1836, planted orchards, put up fencing, and raised imported cattle. He married Senorita Hilaria Sanchez, daughter of the commander of the San Francisco Presidio, Don Jose Sanchez. They were married only eight years before Reed died of a "fever" at the early age of thirty-eight. He apparently had a sunstroke, and the friends who started bleeding him as a cure could not stem the flow of blood.

In 1856, Samuel Reading Throckmorton, a real estate dealer from San Francisco, bought *Rancho Saucelito* from Captain William Richardson. His land encompassed 19,000 acres to the west of

*John Reed's sawmill in Old Mill Park, Mill Valley.*

the *Corte de Madera del Presidio* Creek. A court decision in the late 1860s declared that it also included the site of the sawmill. The two grants were actually divided by a creek that flowed through what is now midtown Mill Valley and continued up Blithedale Canyon.

A 512-acre unclaimed pocket of land in the canyon, between the two grants, was homesteaded in 1873 by Dr. John Cushing, who built what became the fashionable and widely-known Blithedale Resort Hotel.

Captain Richardson's affairs in *Rancho Saucelito* had been in bad disarray when Throckmorton took them on. Throckmorton never was successful in clearing the major debts, and when he died in 1883, his daughter Susanna was forced to give up 3,790 acres to clear a $100,000 mortgage. The city of Mill Valley was eventually built on this land.

The Tamalpais Land and Water Company was formed to build the new town. Joseph Green Eastland, president of develop-

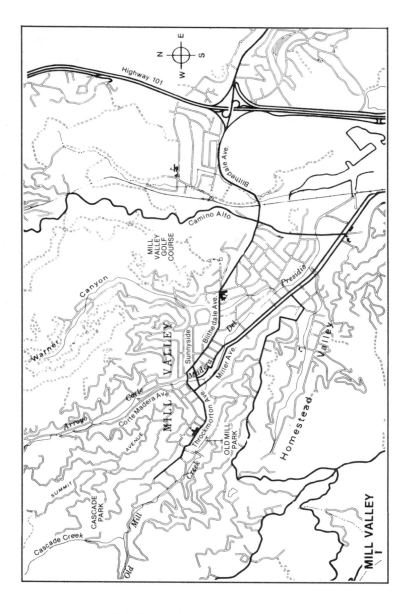

ment company, hired an engineer to survey the prospective town and persuaded the North Pacific Coast Railroad to run a spur line into the area. Train service began in 1890 and continued until 1941.

A successful auction for lots was held in May 1890 at a big picnic near the old sawmill site, where 3,000 prospective buyers purchased 200 acres of land. In 1892, the name of the town was changed to "Eastland" in honor of its most prominent citizen. The depot had a signboard with the new name placed over the old one, but residents still referred to their town as Mill Valley.

The town began as an area of summer homes for wealthy San Franciscans wanting to escape the summer fog. It grew in popularity in 1896 when a railroad was built to take sightseers up to the top of Mt. Tamalpais. Several resort hotels were constructed for the visitors who came from all over the world. (See Chapter 6 about the "Crookedest Railroad in the World.")

On September 1, 1900, the residents voted to incorporate and to reestablish the name of Mill Valley. A story persists to this day that on election day, pro-incorporation forces hired a man named Dan Slinky who, for $50 and a flask of whiskey, jumped off the 5:15 P.M. Marin-bound ferry San Rafael. This delayed commuters until the polls closed, assuring a victory for incorporation forces. Four years later, the post office dropped the name "Eastland" altogether.

As Mill Valley prospered, a few stores were built in the downtown area and the plank sidewalks were replaced with concrete. In 1906, refugees from the San Francisco earthquake and fire settled in Mill Valley, then called the "Switzerland of America." Population figures before the fire indicated there were around 900 residents. By 1910, the number had jumped to 2,891, and a library was built on Lovell Avenue.

One of Mill Valley's traditions is the Dipsea Foot Race, founded by athletes of the San Francisco Olympic Club in 1905. The race is 6.8 miles over tortuous terrain, starting in Mill Valley, continuing over Mt. Tamalpais to Stinson Beach, and originally ending at the Dipsea Inn. The Inn was located on a sandspit between Stinson Beach and the town of Bolinas. The race now ends in downtown Stinson Beach.

Rain dampened the first race, held November 19, 1905, so the following year it was moved up to October. Since then it has been moved up several times and is currently held in June because of fire hazards in late summer. Call the City of Mill Valley for the date, and be sure to go to Stinson Beach to watch the exciting finish and cheer the thousands of runners who cross the finish line after navigating long miles of treacherous mountain trails.

To get to Mill Valley, exit Highway 101 at the Mill Valley turnoff which is "Tiburon Blvd.-East Blithedale Avenue." Follow East Blithedale Avenue into the center of Mill Valley, a distance of 1.8 miles. At the Camino Alto intersection you will pass the Blithedale Plaza Shopping Center on the right.

The center of downtown Mill Valley is called Lytton Square, named for Lytton Barber, the city's first casualty of World War I. He died in Fort Lewis, Washington, a victim of the flu epidemic that struck the country in 1917-18.

Lytton Square is not a real square in the traditional sense, but a widening of Throckmorton Avenue, bordered on one side by half-timbered shops and the other by the old Northwestern Pacific Railroad depot, now the Depot Bookstore and Cafe. Next to the old depot is a tiny plaza made of red bricks with a round brick planter box and benches. It is dedicated to Richard Haitt who designed houses in the area. The plaque reads, "In Appreciation of His Services and His Love for Mill Valley."

In the center of Lytton Square are a stand of towering redwoods and beds of flowers. Interesting shops in the area include one for pets, coffee and tea, cameras, photo finishing, shoes, gourmet cookware, and culinary accessories.

A particular Mill Valley tradition is the Mill Valley Market in the heart of town at Throckmorton and Corte Madera avenues. One of the finest markets anywhere, it boasts exclusive gourmet supplies, an outstanding bakery, fine wines and liquors, fresh fruit, vegetables, and meat.

Be sure to visit El Paseo (which means "ornamental passage-way"), a narrow old-world Spanish street between Throckmorton and Sunnyside avenues near the Mill Valley Theater, which contains a cluster of shops, offices, studios, and two restaurants. The buildings are constructed of old adobe bricks imported from Mexico, hand-hewn lumber, railroad ties and spikes from the old mountain railroad, and handmade tiles.

The dream of Mill Valley residents Edna and Henry Foster, El Paseo took eight years to build because of delays caused by World War II. The designer, Gus Costigan, was off fighting in the African and Italian campaigns. Edna's interest in Spanish missions and her idea of a complex where artists and craftsmen could live, work,

*The old train depot in Mill Valley is now a bookstore and cafe.*

and display their wares, led to the final design. The complex features arcades, tile roofs, outside stairways, balconies, patios, and built-in seats.

The narrow, uneven, sunken street of red brick winds under a heavy-beamed roof where ivy grows abundantly. Located near the Throckmorton entrance is a tiny shrine to St. Francis showing the saint surrounded by five white doves made of colored tile and abalone shell.

El Paseo opened with a gay Spanish fiesta in 1948. Today you will find ceramics, tableware, plants and the El Paseo Restaurant which provides an attractive atmosphere for French cuisine. The second restaurant is the Dipsea Cafe.

There are several interesting buildings in Mill Valley. At number One Blithedale Avenue stands the beautiful Mill Valley Outdoor Art Club, designed by famous architect Bernard Maybeck and built in 1904. In 1979, it received the protection of a listing on the

National Register of Historic Places and designation as a California State Historical Landmark. It is also protected under a Mill Valley Historic Overlay Ordinance.

Across the street is the round Catholic Church of Our Lady of Mt. Carmel, built in 1968 to replace the original. The twelve-sided sanctuary of brick and stone holds 900 worshippers. The church also features a 134-foot copper spire and gold leaf cross.

In keeping with the decor of the town is the old European-style architecture of the city hall and firehouse built in 1936 at 26 Corte Madera Avenue. The building is red brick, half-timbers over stucco with a steep-pitched shingle roof, mullioned windows, and a tower topped by a weather vane. The police station and most of the fire department have now moved to larger quarters.

The old railroad depot, built in 1925, stands on the corner of Miller Avenue and Throckmorton (87 Throckmorton). The building was bought by the city in 1954 along with the railroad right-of-way. It is now a bus station and houses the Mill Valley Depot Bookstore and Cafe where you can buy deli-type foods in addition to paperback books, magazines, and newspapers. (The original depot was located where the crosswalk from Sunnyside to Miller is today.) Behind the Depot is a lovely brick plaza with trees.

Of special interest is the award-winning Mill Valley Public Library at 375 Throckmorton which overlooks a picturesque flowing creek in Old Mill Park. The building, completed in 1966, was designed by architect Donn Emmons of Wurster, Bernardi and Emmons. It is built of concrete with exposed aggregate. A steep roof with a wide overhang, covered with flat shingle-like clay tiles, plus four dormer windows, make an attractive street facade.

To the right of the main entrance is a sculpture group of grey and black granite designed by the late Richard O'Hanlon, a Mill Valley resident and professor emeritus of art at the University of California at Berkeley. A bench, also of his design, is on the left; it was given to the library in memory of the writer Nathan Asch by his wife, a Mill Valley resident.

Upon entering the library, a sweeping view through large windows across the width of the building to the deck and redwood trees beyond gives an open feeling and sense of being outside. The deck is suspended ten feet above the ground, becoming part of the park.

The furniture was custom-designed and built by Arthur

Carpenter in collaboration with the architect. Carpenter's shop, Espenet, is near Bolinas. Except for the chairs, the library furniture is fine hand-rubbed walnut with an oil finish.

Downstairs is the History Room, dedicated in June 1977 in honor of Lucretia Hanson Little, official city historian and retired deputy city clerk, who died later that year. The Mill Valley Historical Society provides docents and helps collect historical materials. A collection of books and photographs on California, Marin, and Mill Valley history line the walls.

Old Mill Park below the library on Cascade Drive contains the original site of John Reed's mill, California Historical Landmark Number 207. The remains of the old structure are beside the creek: nine large timbers laid across side beams which supported the floor of the mill. A roof has been added. The park, open from sunrise to sunset, also provides a children's plaground, barbecues, picnic tables, and restrooms.

Old Mill Park is the site of the Mill Valley Fall Arts Festival, held annually in September. The festival features fine arts and crafts of ceramics, glass works, jewelry, leather, fabrics, woodwork, and sculpture. Varied entertainment is provided for the two days of the fair.

Continue up curvy Throckmorton Avenue to Cascade Park at the north end of Cascade Drive. The "cascade" is actually a waterfall dropping thirty feet over a rock channel in a canyon of redwoods and other trees. A small tributary, the East Fork, joins the stream below the falls. The combined stream then flows under Cascade Drive and joins Old Mill Creek. About a hundred yards downstream is the "Three Wells" area, actually three natural pools.

At Cascade Park there are hiking trails (one connects with the Panoramic Highway) and beaches, but no restrooms or picnic areas. The park is open from sunrise to sunset, and no parking is allowed in the area from 11:00 P.M. to 6:00 A.M. Call the Parks and Recreation Department at 383-1370 for more information.

In 1938, Mill Valley bought out a private golf course and opened it to the public. This lovely nine-hole course, the first public course in Marin, is open seven days a week and is located at 280 Buena Vista Avenue. (Turn off Blithedale Avenue at Carmelita, then right on Buena Vista.) It features a pro shop, instructions, club sales, and repairs. The hours are 7:30 A.M. until dark.

# Strawberry Peninsula

On the east side of Highway 101, opposite Mill Valley, is the Strawberry Peninsula. To get there, turn onto Tiburon Boulevard, then make a right turn at the first stoplight onto Frontage Road. The red tile roofs of the Town and Country Village are visible from the freeway. This popular shopping center includes a supermarket, gas station, several restaurants, pharmacy, exclusive clothing shops, and dozens of specialty stores.

To visit the 146-acre Golden Gate Baptist Theological Seminary, continue on Frontage Road to Seminary Drive and turn left. On your right will be Belloc's Lagoon, a salt water marsh which provides an excellent spot for watching migratory birds. There is a parking area to the right and an asphalt path that runs along the edge of the marsh. Hilary Belloc and his wife once owned the adjacent de Silva Island, which is the home for many deer, raccoons, and a variety of birds. In 1980, a great blue heron rookery was built.

Stay to your right on Seminary Drive for half a mile, then turn left on Hodges Drive. Golden Gate Baptist Theological Seminary was organized in 1944 in Berkeley and is one of six seminaries sponsored by the Southern Baptist Convention, which has 15 million members in the United States.

This site on the Strawberry Peninsula was considered for permanent world headquarters for the United Nations before New York City was finally selected. The Southern Baptist Convention bought the property in 1954 and engaged John Carl Warnecke, a prominent San Francisco architect, to design the buildings. Classes began in 1959. Today, there are 500 students here from all over the world.

Visits by the public are encouraged. You may take a scenic drive through the peaceful campus and enjoy views of Richardson Bay and Mt. Tamalpais. As you wind up and around, you can see Belvedere and Sausalito along with San Francisco and the Oakland Bay Bridge. For more information on the Golden Gate Seminary, stop by or call its communications office at 388-8080.

To tour the Strawberry Peninsula, continue on Seminary Drive

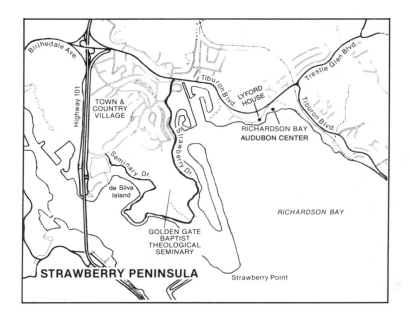

which joins Strawberry Drive in a circle that will bring you out to Tiburon Boulevard, a drive of about two-and-a-half miles. This land once belonged to Hilarita Reed who inherited 1,467 acres from her mother, Ylaria Sanchez Reed de Garcia. She received 446 acres in Strawberry and 1,021 acres at *Punta de Tiburon*. Hilarita married Dr. Benjamin Franklin Lyford in 1872. Four years later, they visited the Centennial Exposition in Philadelphia where they viewed all the latest inventions from the Industrial Revolution to get ideas for the house they were planning. Two years later, they built a three-story Victorian home with a tower at Harbor Cove.

Behind the Lyford mansion, the North Pacific Coast Railroad operated a line along the eastern shore of the Strawberry Peninsula. The trains ran from Sausalito to San Rafael, and the Lyford family was allowed to ride free in exchange for the right-of-way. Dr. Lyford is remembered not only for the development of his wife's property and his "Eagle Diary" of Jersey cows, but for his unique embalming experiments which caused many a lifted eyebrow.

In 1957, the Lyford mansion was barged across the waters of Richardson Bay to the headquarters of the Richardson Bay

Audubon Center and Sanctuary operated by the National Audubon Society. The house was donated by Sam Neider and $25,000 for restoration work was given by Mrs. Donald Dickey in memory of her husband, a well-known ornithologist.

# Tiburon Peninsula

A s you come out of Strawberry, turn right on Tiburon Boulevard, which winds along the shoreline toward the town of Tiburon. At the first traffic light, opposite the Cove Shopping Center, is Greenwood Cove Drive. To visit the Richardson Bay Wildlife Sanctuary, turn right from Tiburon Boulevard and follow Greenwood Cove Drive (which becomes Greenwood Beach Road).

## Richardson Bay Audubon Center and Sanctuary

About half a mile down Greenwood Beach Road are nearly nine hundred acres of rich tidelands saved from development by the efforts of many local conservationists. The tidelands are part of the Richardson Bay Audubon Center and Sanctuary, which provides shelter for flocks of migrating waterfowl. This area is closed to boating from October to March for the protection of the birds.

The grounds of the center are open all year, Wednesday through Sunday, except holidays, 9:00 A.M. to 5:00 P.M. Public programs such as bay shore studies and field trips are conducted on Sundays.

A bookstore called the "Book Nest" is located in a building across from the Lyford House. You can pick up information and trail maps. There is also an education center which has displays on endangered species and outdoor native plants and gardens.

Beyond the education center at 376 Greenwood Beach Road is the Lyford House, painted yellow with white trim. The charming old mansion is situated on land donated by Rosa Rodrigues da Fonte Verrall who had received it as a gift from John Paul Reed, Hilarita's nephew, in 1919. "Rosie" lived with her husband, a printer, in a house adjacent to the mansion for twenty-five years.

Admission is $2 (free for Audubon members); $1.00 for children ages 6-16. No pets, no picnicking. Open 1:00 P.M. to 4:00 P.M.

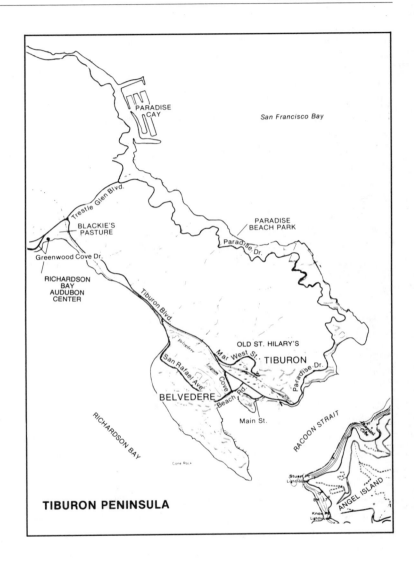

PARADISE
CAY

San Francisco Bay

Trestle Glen Blvd.

BLACKIE'S
PASTURE

PARADISE
BEACH PARK

Paradise Dr.

Greenwood Cove Dr.

RICHARDSON
BAY
AUDUBON
CENTER

Tiburon Blvd.

Belvedere

OLD ST. HILARY'S

Mar West St.  TIBURON

San Rafael Ave.

Lagoon

Cove Rd.

Paradise Dr.

BELVEDERE

Beach Rd.

Main St.

RACOON STRAIT

RICHARDSON BAY

Cone Rock

Stuart
Lighthouse

ANGEL ISLAND

Knox
Lighthouse

**TIBURON PENINSULA**

on Sundays, November through the end of April. (388-2524)

Benches outside the mansion were dedicated to Carol Sealy Livermore in 1960, and to Rosa da Fonte Verall on her eightieth birthday, August 8, 1963. Immediately inside the Lyford House is an elegant, curved African mahogany staircase. Interesting items on display include the sheet music for a schottische, "Flowers of California," dedicated to Hilarita Reed in 1860, horsehair furniture, an old rolltop deak, sealing wax, a portable writing case, a sewing case and a 100-year-old quilt. Furnished rooms include a living room, study, library, bedroom, and child's room with toy furniture and animal cartoons. On display are photographs of birds taken by Dr. Dickey with a box camera from 1910 and 1920.

Dr. Lyford, an embalming surgeon during the Civil War, was one of the first persons to ever use color on corpses. In his 1871 embalming patent Lyford included instructions to "color the lips, cheeks and other parts of the face to life." This was far in advance of the techniques of the time. In 1870, the *San Francisco Evening Bulletin* reported that a woman Lyford embalmed was still lifelike (and unburied) two-and-one-half years later.

You can climb up the nearly-straight eighteen steps to the tower of the Lyford House and look toward San Francisco through and old E. Krauss telescope from Paris. The view all around is lovely.

## Blackie's Pasture and the Richardson Bay Path

As you continue northeast on Greenwood Beach Road to Tiburon Boulevard, you'll notice a large open field that is known as Blackie's Pasture. Blackie was an old sway-back horse who grazed here for a quarter of a century. A white picket fence and a sign that reads "Blackie" mark his grave site. There is also a plaque in one corner of the field.

From Blackie's Pasture, a two-mile blacktop path, used for bicycling, jogging, walking, and skating, runs all the way into Tiburon mostly along what was once the railroad right-of-way. Bicyclists may continue from downtown Tiburon by ferry to Angel Island.

Following the shoreline is the fifty-five-acre Richardson Bay Lineal Park. The McKegney Green sports field, used mainly for soccer, is named in memory of George McKegney, a popular member of the Tiburon Parks and Recreation Commission. It is just a short distance from the pasture where ample free parking is available.

Turn right on Tiburon Boulevard and continue down the peninsula. The road narrows and takes a sharp right turn around Blackie's Pasture. On your left is Trestle Glen Boulevard, where an old wooden railroad trestle once crossed Tiburon Boulevard. Trestle Glen Boulevard leads northeast to Paradise Drive, which winds along the east side of the Tiburon Peninsula facing San Francisco Bay.

## Old St. Hilary's Historic Preserve

About two miles past Blackie's Pasture, watch for a sign on the right which announces a historical landmark. Turn left on Beach Road (stop lights), cross Mar West Street where the street name changes to Esperanza, and drive a mile or so to Old St. Hilary's Church. Here you will have a lovely panoramic view of downtown Tiburon, Belvedere, and San Francisco.

Old St. Hilary's is an example of "Carpenter's Gothic," defined as a simplified interpretation of Gothic Revival architecture by a carpenter using available materials. The Catholic mission church, built of redwood and Douglas fir, held services for residents of the area from 1888 to 1954. In 1959, Old St. Hilary's was acquired by the Belvedere-Tiburon Landmarks Society, which maintains the building and wildflower preserve. It is used for lectures, concerts, ceremonies and is a favorite place for weddings. Inside the church the woodwork is redwood while the ceiling is Douglas fir. Wooden knobs on the walls mark the former Stations of the Cross. There are also round-end pews, chandeliers, replicas of the original oil lamps and an original window donated by Dr. and Mrs. Benjamin Lyford depicting St. Hilary, patron saint of scholars. A Spanish copper cross from Sante Fe is on the back wall.

On exhibit are color photographs of local wildflowers by Ann-Jean Cole with signs in calligraphy by Sylvia Ross. Postcards and books on wildflowers and on the history of the Tiburon area may be purchased.

To preserve the unique wildflowers of the area, in the 1960s three-and-a-half acres were added to the original half-acre lot donated by Dr. and Mrs. Lyford for the church. Two-hundred-and-seventeen plant species have been identified on the site, including the black jewel flower *(Streptanthus niger),* a member of the mustard family found growing only on serpentine rock on the southern end of the Tiburon Peninsula. There are also several endangered flowers: the Tiburon paintbush *(Castilleja neglecta);* the Tiburon buckwheat *(Eriogonum caninum);* and the Marin dwarf flax *(Hesperolinon congestum).*

Some flowers bloom all year long, but most blossom in April

*Old St. Hilary's, Tiburon.*

and May. Spring flowers include biscuit root, blue dicks, gold fields, tidy tips, and California placella. From May to July there are many species of lilies blooming, while summer and fall plants include common buckwheat, tar weed, and Bigelow's sneezeweed.

In the fall, members of the grass families are on display, such as grass of Parnassus and Pacific hairgrass. These grow on the lower portion of the preserve where there are natural springs.

You may climb down the steps from the church to the lower section and walk along the path called the Old Alemany Road. Benches are built into a stone wall. You may also walk the trails over the hill.

The preserve includes the John Thomas Howell Botanical Garden, the Caroline S. Livermore Vista Point, and Dakin Lane, a pedestrian link between streets named in honor of a family of benefactors to the society.

Old St. Hilary's is open from April to October on Wednesdays and Sundays from 1:00 P.M. to 4:00 P.M. Group tours may be arranged all year by calling the Landmarks Society at 435-1853.

## Tiburon

The name "Tiburon" came from the Spanish *Punta de Tiburon* or "shark point." The small town grew up around a railroad complex built at Tiburon Point in 1884 by Peter Donahue, owner of the San Francisco and North Pacific Coast Railroad. Donahue ran a branch line to Tiburon, which he called the San Francisco and San Rafael Railroad, and set up connections with ferryboats which carried passengers to San Francisco in thirty minutes for just fifteen cents (twenty-five cents round trip). A roundhouse, shops, depot, train sheds, wharf, and ferry slip served the trains and ferryboats. At 1920 Paradise Drive is the gray, two-story Peter Donahue building, a section of the old depot. It is now a town historical landmark, and is used by the Belvedere-Tiburon Recreation Department.

In its early days, Tiburon's Main Street was a tough waterfront area of stores, hotels, a post office, and several rowdy taverns from which came stories of shootings and rum-running. Fire swept through these commercial waterfront buildings three times, and each time they were rebuilt.

The progressive Dr. Lyford saw an opportunity for real estate development in Tiburon and subdivided an area which he called "Lyford's Hygeia," after the goddess of health. The southern portion had an impressive stone tower and arch at the entrance. The tower, now without an arch, still stands at 2036 Paradise Drive, preserved through the efforts of the Town of Tiburon's Heritage Commission and donations from many individuals. It is listed on the National Register of Historical Places.

Early industries of the Tiburon/Belvedere area were codfishing, working the oyster beds, stripping and burning old ships for salvage, powder and brick works, boat yards, and dairy ranches.

Passenger trains and ferryboats lasted until 1909 when travelers were rerouted to Sausalito. Until 1934, a small boat, the *Marin*, hauled passengers to Sausalito, where they boarded the larger ferries to San Francisco. Freight shipping created in 1907 by the merger of the Tiburon line with others continued until 1967 on the Northwestern Pacific Railroad, or NWP.

*The train yard in Tiburon in the 1950s.* Photo courtesy of Bob Molton.

Ferry service to San Francisco was resumed in 1962 to both the Ferry Building and Fisherman's Wharf. Phone 546-2815 for schedule and fare information.

As you near downtown Tiburon, the Boardwalk shopping complex is on the right. The shopping center and this portion of Tiburon Boulevard were constructed on landfill in the 1950s. It contains a grocery, variety, clothing stores for women and children, a floral shop, cafe, restaurant, antique shops and arts and crafts.

Tiburon stayed small until after World War II, when the town experienced a great burst of population. After the Boardwalk was built, basic business shifted away from Main Street. The old grocery, butcher shop, garage, and post office disappeared, opening up the area for dress shops, gift stores, art galleries, restaurants and bars.

In 1955, as Tiburon was changing from a railroad to a commuter/tourist town, a campaign was launched by volunteers to repaint faded facades of the buildings on Main Street. On the appointed weekend, September 24-25, men, women, and teenagers painted, bagpipes played, and tables were set up in the street to

*Elephant Rock off Paradise Drive, Tiburon.*

provide the hundred or so volunteers with food, coffee, beer, and wine. The fronts of fifteen buildings were painted and new planter boxes were added.

Today, Main Street is a colorful collection of shops and restaurants, some designed to look like stores in the California gold country a century ago. You can easily spend a whole day browsing through the fascinating shops, eating and drinking on an outdoor deck, or listening to the delightful tunes from hundreds of different-shaped sculptures and bells in the Main Street Music Box.

The Sweden House at 35 Main is especially enjoyed by locals and combines a bakery with breakfast and lunch, or just coffee. Delicious pastries and cakes are baked on the premises, and patrons may eat on the deck in back, which overhangs the water.

Also on Main Street are several excellent restaurants and bars. A "must" for visitors is enjoying a gin fizz on Sam's dock while watching the endless panorama of graceful sailboats gliding by. There is always a refreshing breeze, the smell of the sea, the sounds of the waves lapping against the shore, and the call of the gulls.

Where Main Street turns and becomes Ark Row, you will find the entrance to the Corinthian Yacht Club. Walk left, then right, and you will immediately see a forest of boat masts and white sails with the spectacular skyline of San Francisco in the background. The clubhouse itself is a graceful old white wooden building on the water's edge.

Founded in 1886, the Corinthian sponsors several races, including the Buckner Ocean Race and the Midwinter Regatta. The major event of the year is the "Pageantry of the Blessing of the Pleasure Craft" on San Francisco Bay, held on the opening day of yachting season in the spring.

As Main Street curves around to the right, the "Village Ark Row Shops" begin. This block was added to Main Street in 1957. Some of the shops are in old, remodeled arks in which people used to live. Others are remodeled cottages, and still others are brand-new buildings. Tiburon Vintners is on the corner leading to the arks in an old wooden building which was once a rooming house. At the entrance are two antique wine presses. Inside, notice the tongue-and-groove ceiling and the wooden floor. The Vintners is open daily and offers free tasting. Wines are from the Sonoma Vineyards Windsor Winery, which produces premium California quality wines. They are sold only here and at the winery, though some may be purchased by mail order. Additional wines are bottled under the Rodney Strong label and are sold throughout the United States.

Continuing along Ark Row you can find imported clothes, antiques, flowers, an art gallery, deli, toys, books, crafts and antiques.

If you look up as you walk along here, you will see handsome modern homes on what is Corinthian Island, now linked to become a peninsula. Main Street ends at Beach Road.

On November 19, 1979, the Tiburon Town Council approved a master plan submitted by Southern Pacific Railroad to develop thirty-eight acres of downtown Tiburon that once were railroad yards. Included in this plan was a shoreline park connecting the ferry landing to the Donahue Building and Elephant Rock.

The plan was completed in the 1980s changing forever the sleepy railroad town that was once Tiburon. One-hundred-and-fifty-five condos are now located in buildings three stories high with natural wood shingles and steep red roofs. Most look out over the water with views of San Francisco.

*Mike and Mia Jampolsky gaze at the Belvedere Lagoon and Mt. Tamalpais from the end of Peninsula Road in Belvedere.*

The park is a bright green strip of grass adjacent to the rock wall built along the bay. People can rest on benches and enjoy the view.

Part of the plan included 25,000 square feet of commercial space which was built between the housing units and the road. A lagoon with a jet of water added along with a bridge connecting the shopping areas. The sidewalks are an attractive red brick.

This commercial area contains restaurants, a fitness club, bakery, art gallery, florist, jewelry store, boutique with womens clothes, mens clothes and health foods.

### Belvedere

The Belvedere Island peninsula, linked to the former sandspits by what is now San Rafael Avenue and Beach Road, has some of the most elegant homes in the Bay Area, many with waterfront docks and almost all with spectacular views. To get there, turn south off Tiburon Boulevard onto San Rafael Avenue, Cove Road, or Beach Road. Perhaps the best way to see the island is to follow the lovely, landscaped San Rafael Avenue until it ends at Beach Road.

Belvedere was part of the original *Rancho Corte de Madera del*

*Presidio* Mexican land grant awarded to John Reed, but his heirs had to go to court to prove the claim. The "island" had been taken over by a man named Israel Kashow, a blond-haired giant of a man who stood six feet, three inches tall and weighed 250 pounds. Kashow, who married four times and sired seven children, was described as tough, stubborn, and short-tempered. He once fired a mixed dose of birdshot and salt at uninvited visitors who went swimming in the cove in front of his house. The swimmers sued but did not gain much by their efforts: the judge gave them one dollar.

From 1855 to 1885, Kashow and his family lived on what he called Kashow's Island. His thirty-year residency kept the land from premature development. In 1868, James C. Bolton, the Reed family's attorney, received some land in payment for his successful court case against Kashow; this was eventually sold to Thomas B. Valentine. Valentine organized the original Belvedere Land Company, subdivided the island in 1890, and in 1896, Belvedere's few residents voted thirty-three to twenty-four to incorporate.

The four-story Belvedere Hotel was built on Belvedere Cove, where Kashow's house used to stand. On this same spot today, at 98 Beach Road, is the San Francisco Yacht Club, the oldest yacht club in the state and one of the oldest in the country. The club started originally in San Francisco, becoming active in 1855 and incorporating in 1869. Club members moved to Sausalito at the turn of the century, and then to Belvedere in 1927 to escape the heavy ferry traffic.

The City of Belvedere has worked for the past several years to provide an open view of the San Francisco skyline from Beach Road. One of the structures that had to be moved to accomplish this was the "China Cabin" which was being used as part of a private home. Slated for demolition, the Landmarks Society intervened which resulted in Belvedere deeding the structure to the Society and leasing the cove site where it is now located.

The "China Cabin" was the elegant social hall on the *S.S. China* a Pacific Mail Steamship Company wooden sidewheel steamer. Designed by W.H. Webb, an American naval architect, the China was built in 1866 in New York and came to its homeport, San Francisco, via the Strait of Magellan. It sailed between California and the Orient until 1879.

Today, visitors can tour the saloon plus the former staterooms of the ship's surgeon and chief engineer. All have been beautifully restored. The interior is white and gold with an oak floor trimmed in walnut. There are etched bulbs, cut glass windows, and brass and crystal chandeliers, replicas of old oil burning lights.

The China Cabin is open on Wednesdays and Sundays from 1-4 P.M. There is no admission charge, but donations are welcome. It is also open all year by appointment and is available for private social events. Call the Landmarks Society, 435-1853 or 435-2251.

## Paradise Drive

Paradise Drive winds its way from the town of Tiburon around the peninsula and ends back at Highway 101. As you follow Paradise Drive from town, you will pass large gates on your right with signs identifying the National Oceanic and Atmospheric Administration, National Marine Fisheries Service and the Romberg Tiburon Centers, San Francisco State University.

Ocean-related work has been going on here for about one-hundred years, beginning with a cod fishery and including a Naval Coaling Station, Nautical School, Net Depot, and Oceanographic Center. Today, the Tiburon Laboratory of the National Marine Fisheries Service conducts research on commercial and sport fish, but it is not open to the public.

San Francisco State University took over much of the land in 1978 to establish the Tiburon Center for Environmental Studies. The facilities occupy 13 acres overlooking San Pablo Bay and include a conference center, administration offices, classrooms, laboratories, library, computer room, machine shop and studio living quarters for visiting scientists.

Research being conducted is concerned with the ecosystems of San Francisco Bay, restoring wetlands, the growth of striped bass, oil spills and toxic and other pollutants of the bay. Special projects include cancer research and the evolution of birds in relation to species.

The Bay Conference Center, opened for day use only, is located in the old Naval Officer's Club which was used during World War II and the Korean War. The remodeled facilities include a 150-seat main hall, lounge area with fireplace, two meeting rooms, picnic areas and parking. Call (415) 338-1207.

Paradise Beach County Park, just beyond the Bay Conference Center, is a curvy 3.2 miles from downtown Tiburon. Surplus land

*World War II cartoons decorate the old Naval Officers' Club, now the Bay Conference Center on Paradise Drive.*

from original government property was used to establish this nineteen-acre beachfront park plus the open space area called the Tiburon Uplands Nature Reserve consisting of twenty-four acres of steep hillside.

Paradise Park has a beach and a long fishing pier where people fish for striped bass, steelhead, rockfish, salmon, jack smelt, sea perch, sturgeon and sharks. Picnic facilities and restrooms are available. From April 1 to September 30, the entrance fee for cars and motorcycles is $5 on weekends and holidays, and $3 on weekdays. "Walk-ins" and bicycles are charged $1. During the rest of the year, the fee is $1, with no charge for walk-ins and bicycles.

Before arriving back at the freeway, you will pass Paradise Cay, a water-oriented community with houses built out over the water; Marin Country Day School, a private elementary school; and the newly created Ring Mountain Preserve managed by the Nature Conservancy.

One-hundred-seventeen acres were acquired to establish the preserve in 1981-82, and another 260 acres in 1984. Besides rare plant species, the area is interesting for the mysterious markings on ridge outcroppings made by Native Americans nearly 2,000 years ago. The significance of these petroglyphs is unknown.

Before reaching the Paradise Shopping Center, turn left on El Camino Drive to visit the Terwilliger Nature Education Center located in the Granada School at 50 El Camino Drive, Corte Madera. Elizabeth Terwilliger is beloved by all for the creative way she has taught outdoor education to generations of Marin children.

Groups of both children and adults follow Elizabeth through the woods, along the beaches, and over the mountains of Marin. These field trips have proved so popular over the years that a group of volunteers was organized to assist this very special teacher. The Elizabeth Terwilliger Nature Education Foundation produces records and tapes of her naturalist teachings and a "Tripping with Terwilliger" film series that is seen by six million school children annually throughout the United States.

"Mrs. T." has also written a series of articles for the *Marin Independent Journal* in Marin and a book, *Sights and Sounds of the Seasons*. In 1972, she was voted one of the Bay Area's "Ten Most Distinguished Citizens." She was also honored by the President of the United States, Ronald Reagan, in 1984.

Programs sponsored by the foundation today include school field trips, visiting nature vans, free loan of films, classroom nature kits, center tours and exhibits, family and group walks, summer nature camp, and after school programs. Children especially delight in touching specimens used for Terwilliger Center teaching. All these animals and birds were results of natural casualties.

The Terwilliger Nature Education Center and Gift Shop are open Monday through Friday, 8:30 A.M. to 4:30 P.M.

After leaving the Terwilliger Nature Center, return to Paradise Drive where you will pass the small Paradise Shopping Center before returning to Highway 101.

Another way to see this side of the Tiburon peninsula is by riding the ferryboat from Larkspur to San Francisco. Bring binoculars and a map to help orient yourself. There will be some excellent views of Alcatraz, Paradise Drive, Paradise Park, the National Marine Fisheries buildings, and the east side of Angel Island. It is a beautiful, scenic ride.

# Angel Island State Park

# 5

A ngel Island has a colorful history, from its early ranching days to its use as a site for sophisticated Nike missiles. In between, the island has served as a detention camp for enemy aliens, a quarantine station, an embarkation area for soldiers on their way to war, a discharge point for servicemen returning home, and, like Ellis Island off New York, an immigration center.

The island was discovered by either Sir Francis Drake in 1579, or Don Juan Manuel de Ayala (pronounced I-ya-la) in 1775, depending on with whom you discuss this lively issue. Since Drake's journal was lost, the honor appears to go to Ayala, who sailed through the Golden Gate on the Spanish naval vessel *San Carlos*.

This Spanish lieutenant is credited with naming the island *Isla de los Angeles,* which has been translated and shortened to Angel Island. Ayala's men explored the island between August 13 and September 7, exchanging presents with local Indians of the Coast Miwok tribes whose ancestors had been living there for 2,000 years. Ayala was also the first to survey and chart San Francisco Bay.

Angel Island was awarded as a land grant to Antonio Maria Osio by the Mexican governor, Juan Alvarado, on June 11, 1839. Osio used the land for ranching. He built a small house for his *mayordomo,* erected a dam to create a reservoir to provide water for cattle, built three other houses, and cultivated part of the land. Osio had the bad luck to be on the losing side of America's war with Mexico, however, and the entire island was taken from him

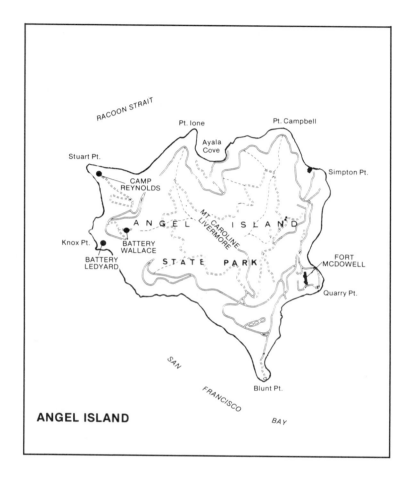

in a decision by the United States Supreme Court in 1859. Osio returned to Mexico and the military moved in. Nothing is left to show evidence of his occupation. There are some scattered remains of Indian burial mounds, but these have been left unmarked and could not be easily-identified.

You can see plenty of evidence of the military installations that were built on Angel Island in the next hundred years. Camp Reynolds (West Garrison) was established in 1863; Fort McDowell (East Garrison) was erected from 1910 to 1912; Point Simpton (North Garrison) was an immigration station from 1910 until a fire forced it to close in 1940. Fort McDowell took over this station, renamed it North Garrison, and set up a camp for enemy aliens detained during the Second World War. An asphalt helicopter landing pad on top of the 781-foot summit was built in 1955, as well as missile control radar facilities. A Nike missile site was installed above Point Blunt at the same time. The site was closed in 1962.

Angel Island is especially beautiful to visit in the spring when wildflowers seem to blossom everywhere. Park rangers recommend April, May, June, September, and October as the best months to visit—the weather is warmest and there is less likely to be fog.

Getting to the island is half the fun. If you don't have a private sailboat or yacht, you can board a Red and White Fleet boat in San Francisco at Pier 41 (call 546-2815 for current fares and schedules). The boats generally run every day during summer months (Memorial Day to Labor Day), and on weekends and holidays the rest of the year. The trip is about a half-hour long, with boats leaving at 10:00 A.M., 12:00 noon, 2:00 P.M., and 3:45 P.M. During winter, the schedule for weekends and holidays is a 10:45 A.M. departure from San Francisco with a return leaving Angel Island at 4:40 PM. Bicycles may be taken aboard.

From Marin, the Angel Island State Park Ferry Company makes the ten-minute run from Tiburon to Angel Island every day during the summer, and on weekends and holidays the rest of the year. A sign on Main Street identifies the pier where the ferries dock. Phone 435-2131 for current fares and schedules. Bicycles may be taken to the island for a charge of 50 cents.

Generally, the ferries run every hour on weekends beginning at 10:00 AM. Between April and Labor Day, they also run on weekdays every two hours.

Private boats may dock in Ayala Cove at the finger piers for $5 per day but must leave by sunset. Boats may also anchor around the island or tie up to the buoys in Ayala Cove and stay for up to five days and nights at $5 per night. This is a favorite rendezvous spot for Bay Area yachtsmen, and on any sunny weekend, summer or winter, there are sure to be boats rafted-up and quiet parties in progress.

On the island there is a lot to explore either on foot or by bicycle. Interpretive programs are offered daily in the summer by a volunteer organization called the Angel Island Association.

This group is open for membership (435-3522).

A twenty-minute video film describing the general culture and natural history of the island is shown on weekends, and there are nature walks on Saturdays led by ranger. No reservations are necessary.

Past the docking area at Ayala Cove, there are picnic and barbecue facilities, a snack bar, restrooms, grassy areas for sun-bathing, and beaches. Swimming is not recommended, however, as there is no lifeguard on duty.

The Park Ranger Station is located in this area, and the Angel Island Association sells brochures and books. First aid is available.

Overnight camping is allowed on the island on nine environmental campsites which supply BBQ's and picnic tables. The camps are set up for backpackers and require one to two-and-one-half miles of hiking. People usually bring their own tents. No dogs are allowed. No wood gathering is allowed, so bring wood or charcoal.

Each camp site holds up to eight people and specific camps may be reserved through MISTIX at 1-800-444-7275. At least 14 days advance notice are required and up to 8 weeks. It is all done through the mail though you must phone for the information. The cost is $6 per night plus $2 for making the reservation.

Angel Island is 740 acres, or 100 acres larger than a square mile. There are twelve miles of hiking trails, and Perimeter Road, five miles long, circumnavigates the island. Some parts of this road are blacktop, while others are dirt and gravel. Following the road makes a fine half-hour bicycle ride or a hike of about two and a half hours.

Ayala Cove was once known as "Hospital Cove" because a quarantine hospital was operated here by the United States Public Health Service. It was established before the turn of the century, and the last quarantine case went through in 1936. During that period, all ships coming into San Francisco had to stop here so that sailors, marines, travelers, and immigrants alike could be inspected for the diseases so rampant at this time.

While the ships were docked at Hospital Cove, they were fumigated. An American ship named the Omaha, which was drydocked here, ran hoses containing sulfur dioxide into the ships to kill rats. If the cargo prevented this type of fumigation, sulfur dioxide pots were put aboard instead. The rodents were kept from escaping onto the island by cup-shaped barriers which were at-

*Passengers arrive at Angel Island on the ferryboat from Tiburon.*

tached to the lines running to the dock.

Built in 1930, the Ranger Station at Ayala Cove was once the bachelor officers' quarters. Outside there is a large metal bell which was used in the fog to warn ships of the danger of rocks.

In the Visitor's Center, located in the Ranger Station, you can view a model of the island in a plastic dome-shaped case. This is a good place to orient yourself and decide what you would like to see on the island. There are also displays on the island's history. Ayala Cove, the displays tell you, was originally named "Rac(c)oon Cove" in 1849 for the British sloop-of-war *Rac(c)oon* which visited here for repairs in 1814. (You cross Rac(c)oon Straits to reach the island from Tiburon.) The area became Hospital Cove in 1900, and Ayala Cove in 1969. There are other displays titled "Quarantine Station," "Island Outpost," and "Island Flora," plus information on the old immigration center, Ft. McDowell, Native American culture and Spanish history.

Also in the Visitor's Center is a Southampton light beacon lens. Manufactured in Paris in 1836, it was but into operation with a gaslight in an early lighthouse. You can see a Lyle gun, in the shape of a small cannon, which was used by lifeboat stations to fire a line aboard distressed ships; and on the wall is a case of mounted butterflies.

Hiking or bicycling around the island counterclockwise on Perimeter Road will enable you to view most of the old military facilities in a chronological order. To reach Perimeter Road, take the road leading south from Park Headquarters for about a quarter of a mile. When you reach Perimeter Road, turn right.

Just west of Ayala Cove is Point Ione; to the south is Point Stuart, site of a lighthouse built in 1915. Farther south are the abandoned buildings of Camp Reynolds, built during the Civil War and named to honor Major General John Fulton Reynolds, who was killed at Gettysburg on July 1, 1863. This base was renamed West Garrison when it became part of Fort McDowell.

Still standing at Camp Reynolds today are an old hospital, a mule barn, a church/schoolhouse, and a row of faded yellow wooden officers' houses built side by side running down the hill. They constitute the largest remaining assemblage of wooden civil war era buildings in the United States.

Near the water's edge is a three-story quartermaster storehouse built in 1908, which was once used to store ammunition. Beyond this is a small beach and the remains of an old dock, now a bird sanctuary. Exotic century plants grow near the water. Strange species of trees and plants can be found all over the island, attesting to its former international population. The purplish *Echium fastuosum* called "The Pride of Madeira," started on the north side and has naturalized itself on the island. The eucalyptus trees were planted for windbreaks in the 1880s.

After exploring Camp Reynolds, hike back uphill to the dirt road that runs off to the right past the white painted chapel. Follow it back to Perimeter Road and stay to your right.

Farther south are Battery Wallace and Battery Ledyard, established around the turn of the century for harbor defense. The artillery installations here, and another at Battery Drew a short distance to the east, were all made obsolete by the airplane. Above the concrete gun emplacements at Battery Ledyard is an overlook with lovely vistas of Marin, the Golden Gate Bridge, San Francisco, and Alcatraz Island.

Point Knox, named for an army engineer who participated in the original island survey, is southwest of Battery Ledyard. It is the site of one of the last of Marin's lighthouses, which began operation in 1886 as a fog signal. A mechanical striker would hit a huge bell and the sound would warn ships away from the island. In 1900

*Correne Testa and Gina Burrafato picnic at Angel Island, 1989.*

the fog station converted into a lighthouse, though its mechanical bell was retained.

Many keepers have watched over the bell, including several women. Juliet Nichols is remembered for pounding the bell manually for over twenty hours and 35 minutes in 1906 when the mechanical striking mechanism failed. She went deaf due to her sense of duty.

The lighthouse was used until 1960 when new facilities were built in Point Blunt. In 1963, the Point Knox lighthouse was deliberately burned because it was considered unsafe. A memorial bell, set in cement, marks the spot where the lighthouse stood but the very steep trail that leads down to it is not recommended by the rangers.

Just beyond this trail is a road leading to Perles Beach, a beautiful, wide, sandy area but not well protected from the wind. The south side of the island tends to be cooler with more fog than the north and east. Swimming is not recommended as there are no lifeguards.

A little farther on is a trail on the left, one of several that lead up to the summit of Mt. Caroline Livermore, named for a Marin conservationist who worked hard to make Angel Island into a park.

It takes about an hour to climb to the top if you take time to observe plants and birds. If you are in a hurry and jog, you can probably make it up in half an hour.

Continuing south and east around the island, you pass a grove of eucalyptus trees, once known as "Alcatraz Garden." Gangs of prisoners from Alcatraz were brought here to cultivate vegetables which were used in the prison kitchen. The practice was discontinued because the security risk was too great.

At the southern end of the island you can get a good view of Alcatraz—the flip side of the view from San Francisco. The buildings on the island seem to blend into the San Francisco skyline. The Bay Bridge is also visible, as are Yerba Buena and Treasure Island.

To your left as you continue around the island is an old rock quarry, and along the shoreline, beaches are hidden among the coves. Then on your left is the fenced Nike missile site. Signs warn of unsafe structures and grounds.

The site was built in 1955 along with many others throughout the country for the protection of the United States. The missiles stored inside could be launched to seek out and destroy enemy airplanes, but they were never fired. All that is visible now is flat blacktop, cracked and choked with weeds. It is occasionally used by the rangers for storage. The area, closed to the public, is surrounded by fences.

The road takes a deep dip here, and cyclists are warned to walk their bikes. This side of the island is covered with French broom, a low shrub resembling the yellow-blossoming Scotch broom that grows on the west side of the island. These plants have become a problem because they are taking over the habitats of native wildflowers and shrubs.

You will arrive shortly at Point Blunt in the southeast tip of the island. No signs identify the area, but you will see the Coast Guard light facility. This area was a popular nineteenth-century dueling ground and the site of an equally popular whorehouse. Captain William Waterman of Fairfield (Solano County) lived in this seven-room house, built by the Pacific Mail Steamship Company. His job with the Steamship Company remains a mystery, although it might have been to inspect the fresh water stored in the hulls of the company's ships. As Waterman was well-respected, Antonio Osio decided to hire him as a foreman for his ranch. This was in the late 1850s when squatters were attempting to establish sheep and cattle on the island. Captain Waterman lived on the island six years and the herds of cattle multiplied under his superior management.

When Osio was forced to give up his land grant, Waterman left, also, and Quarry Point workers moved into his house. They were followed by a discharged soldier named Rafferty, who was followed in turn by the whorehouse. It remained in operation until 1867 when the house finally burned, some four years after the United States took over the island.

A seven-acre Coast Guard station at Point Blunt now maintains the light facility and fog signal made fully automatic in the 1970s. None of the area is open to the public.

Walking north of Point Blunt, you may be startled as you round the corner and see in the distance the "thousand-man barracks," a huge, four-story building with broken windows. This faded yellow building and other structures in the area were part of the original Fort McDowell, or East Garrison. The fort was established around 1900 as a tent camp for soldiers returning from the Spanish-American War. Buildings were put up from 1910 to 1912.

Below on the right is a quiet sheltered cove, a popular anchorage for boats. It is tranquil on this side of the island. The silence, disturbed only by the singing of birds and waves lapping at the shoreline of beautiful, warm Quarry Beach, makes it hard to envision this as the site of a base where 20,000 to 80,000 men passed through yearly in the hectic days of World War II.

You can see the remains of what was a busy military base: the huge barracks; other large buildings that housed a PX, gym, mess hall (these old buildings are now closed to visitors); a baseball diamond overgrown with weeds and wild lilies; and an abandoned tennis court. Concrete barbecues and picnic tables are available here for group picnics.

On your left as you continue is "Officer's Row," a group of concrete houses with red tile roofs built around 1910. The two-story houses are a faded army mustard color. All have a front porch with white columns, plus a small attic room with dormer windows facing out to the water.

As you continue walking north, you pass an administration building, a chapel, and the three-story East Garrison hospital, built in 1910, which held seventy beds. A sign tells you that "Veterans

*Thousand-man barracks, Fort McDowell, East Garrison, Angel Island.*

were treated here for tropical diseases contracted in such places as the Philippines after the Spanish-American War and Panama during canal construction."

Eighty years of memories are here, and in the silence you become aware of the ghosts—the soldiers in pain, or perhaps elated at returning home from war. After World War I, 87,000 men were returned to civilian status here. And in 1945, a sixty-foot-high illuminated "WELCOME HOME - WELL DONE" sign was built on the south slope when the American GI's returned from World War II. East Garrison was closed down a year later.

Future park plans include a food outlet in this area, but currently there is a shortage of water. A nearby museum in Winslow Cove has also been closed for that reason.

From this side of Angel Island you can look across to the East Bay—Richmond, Oakland, Berkeley, and the Berkeley Hills. As you round the end of the island, you can see Belvedere Island, Tiburon, San Pablo Bay, the San Rafael-Richmond Bridge, and on a clear day, the hills of Sonoma and Napa counties.

As you continue following the road, you will arrive at a sign that says "North Garrison." A modern firehouse painted gray stands next to the park maintenance yard. The buildings of old Point Simpton, tucked below the road adjacent to Winslow Cove, are now closed to the public.

Point Simpton began operation in 1910 as an immigration station for Asians and Europeans. Mainly immigrants from the Orient, however, passed through here in search of a better life. During World War I, some German and Italian aliens were held here.

In 1940, fire destroyed the main buildings and the immigration center closed. All operations were moved to San Francisco. During World War II, the area was turned into a detention center for a few prisoners of war (the first Japanese POW was held here) and "enemy aliens"—Germans, Italians, and Japanese who happened to be on ships in the area at the outbreak of the war, or people who, for some other reason, were detained by the United State government. After the war, the area was abandoned.

At the northernmost point of the island is Point Campbell. There are no buildings of interest here, but you can enjoy the view. From here it is a half mile back to Ayala Cove where the ferryboat waits to return you to the mainland.

Nearly 175,000 people come to the island annually, and the rangers have set up a volunteer program to help prepare for these visitors. Scouts and adult volunteers may join the Angel Island Service Projects by calling the Ranger Office at 435-1915.

# Mt. Tamalpais and Muir Woods

# 6

## Alpine Trails, Stately Redwoods

M t. Tamalpais is the principal landmark in Marin, as its velvet green slopes and rigid peaks can be viewed from just about everywhere in the southern and central parts of the county. Although the mountain's highest point is just under 2,600 feet, its rise from the sea is so abrupt that it gives a lofty, majestic appearance.

Many names for the mountain appeared on early maps. In the 1800s it was known as Table Mountain or Table Butte, Bay Mountain, and Tamales. "Tamal may have been the Miwok Indian name for "west" or "coast" while "pajis" meant "hill," according to the *Bodega Miwok Dictionary* by Catherine A. Callaghan (University of California Publications, 1970).

If you are looking from the south, the mountain takes on the appearance of a "sleeping maiden," an image that was transposed into literature over the years: in Neil Compton Wilson's poem, "The Legend of Tamalpais," in 1911; and in another poem, George Caldwell's "The Maid of Tamalpais," in 1919. One early mountain play written by Dan Totheroh and first performed in 1921 was titled "Tamalpa"; it created a romantic myth about an Indian princess whose mother was a famous witch with the power of casting plague spells on other tribes. When the witch learned that Piayutuma, a member of a valley tribe, was to be given the secret of healing by the Great Spirit, she sent her daughter Tamalpa to thwart him. While the maiden succeeded, she fell in love with the young brave. She was eventually poisoned, and her body brought back to a bier

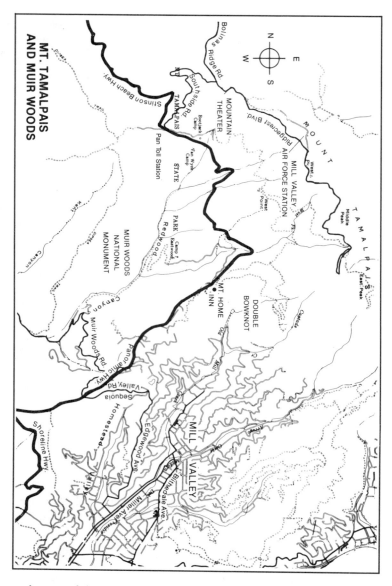

at the top of the mountain. So when you see the sleeping maiden, you are actually viewing the beautiful Tamalpa.

Mt. Tamalpais is so loved by the people of Marin that great efforts have been made over the years to preserve its pristine beauty by establishing parks, a monument, and large areas of watershed. During the 1920s, private development threatened to spread over the entire mountain. Through the efforts of the Tamalpais Conservation Club and others, a bill was passed in the state legislature in 1930 appropriating 892 acres for a park. Now there are 6,000 acres in the State Park and the Golden Gate Recreation Area lands run from the Golden Gate Bridge to the Point Reyes peninsula.

About thirty miles of trails wind through the park boundaries and 200-mile-long trail networks include Muir Woods, the watershed lands, and the Golden Gate National Recreation Area. The mountain provides camping and picnic areas, five clear blue lakes excellent for fishing, and an abundance of wildlife.

Mt. Tamalpais also has an interesting geological formation. Rocks 100 to 150 million years old have been found consisting of serpentine, chert, graywacke (sandstone), shale, greenstone, quartz-tourmaline, and limestone. This is called the Franciscan Formation and matches the geology of other regions of the California coast ranges except that the ridges of Mt. Tamalpais tend to run in a northwest-southeast direction. The rocks and minerals are found in a scrambled or jumbled condition due to the grinding against one another of the North American plate and the Pacific plate along the San Andreas Fault.

It is the magic of the mountain, however, that attracts people who love to hike, camp, or picnic. Virgin redwood forests grow in the lower regions of the fog zone while higher up, hikers may enjoy the sun shining above the fog in the chaparral plant community. Always there are spectacular views of the endless blue sea.

### The Crookedest Railroad in the World

The first road up the mountain, called the Eldridge Grade, was built in 1884. Visitors could ride a stagecoach eleven miles from the Rafael Hotel to the summit. Then, in 1896, the phenomenal Mill Valley and Tamalpais Scenic Railway began hauling passengers up to the top of the mountain from downtown Mill Valley. The "Crookedest Railroad in the World" was 8.19 miles long, had 281 curves, and featured the famous Double Bowknot, a track that paralleled itself five times as it gained elevation.

The Tavern of Tamalpais was built 220 feet below the summit at a reported height of 2,436 feet. It was a first-class hotel with

*The Tavern of Tamalpais and a gravity car on the Mt. Tamalpais and Muir Woods Railway around 1910. Dance Hall is on the left.* Photo courtesy of Nancy Skinner.

rooms, meals, liquid refreshments, and a wide veranda with a 150-degree view of the ocean, Marin, the bay, and San Francisco. Advertisements at the time declared that patrons of the Tavern could view "eighty cities and towns and twenty California counties."

The cars that took people up the mountain were actually backed up the tracks and eased back down by steam locomotives attached to the downhill side for safety. These Shay and Heisler engines were painted a deep maroon with black trim and were kept clean and highly polished.

A line was added to the railroad in 1907 which took passengers by gravity cars into Muir Woods, and the name was changed to the Mt. Tamalpais and Muir Woods Railway. William Kent, an early pioneer and congressman from Marin, had purchased that property, then know as Redwood Canyon, which was covered with giant virgin coast redwood trees. The problem was that it could be reached only by a narrow stagecoach road. Kent promised to build a hotel if the railroad would extend a new spur into the area. He kept his promise and spent $150,000 to construct the Muir Woods Inn.

The gravity cars used on the new spur speeded passengers ten to twelve miles per hour around the seemingly endless curves down the mountain and through the woods. Invented by the railroad's master mechanic, Bill Thomas, each car held thirty passengers and would coast silently down from the 1,800-foot double bowknot for approximately six-and-a-half miles.

The number of passengers using the Mt. Tamalpais and Muir Woods Railway topped 102,000 in 1915. The trains were also used to haul people up to the mountaintop for Easter sunrise services and to attend the mountain plays. Visitors from San Francisco could enjoy a full day's outing by catching a ferryboat from the Ferry Building to Sausalito, taking a train to Mill Valley, then heading up the mountain on the Mt. Tamalpais Railway. Lunch at the top could consist of a tasty picnic or an elegant meal purchased at the Tavern of Tamalpais.

In the afternoon the adventurous visitors might take an open-air gravity car down into Muir Woods, a veritable roller coaster ride with the cars flying along the tracks, around curves, and through tall redwood groves. A peaceful walk among the trees, a quiet drink at the inn, then a return trip by train and ferry to San Francisco completed the day.

Fires on the mountain in 1913, 1923 (when the tavern burned for the second time), and 1929 brought disaster to the railroad. Showing great heroics, crews of the railroad raced raging fires downhill through black smoke and waves of intense heat, managing to save all lives, though paint on the train cars blistered.

The Great Depression and construction of a scenic road to the top of the mountain for automobiles spelled the final end of the Mt. Tamalpais and Muir Woods Railway. It was abandoned in the summer of 1930 but remained a fond memory in the hearts of the thousands of adventurers who rode her rails.

# Muir Woods

Redwood Canyon, which William Kent purchased in 1905 for $45,000, was threatened by the North Coast Water Company, which wanted to cut the trees and flood the area for a reservoir. To block this move, Kent tried to give the land to both the county and state but was turned down. Condem-

nation proceedings were moving along rapidly and the situation was desperate. The trees would soon be cut, a dam built with the profits of the lumber, and the canyon flooded. As the area was too small to qualify for a federal park, that, too, was a dead end.

Then someone remembered a little known law that stated if a parcel of land was extremely valuable, it could be given to the United States as a monument. It was under this statute that Kent's Redwood Canyon was presented to the government. The 295-acre gift was accepted by President Theodore Roosevelt on January 9, 1908 as the Muir Woods Monument, thus ensuring protection for the redwood forest.

When the deed was transferred, Kent wrote to the Secretary of the Interior:

> *"This property is well worthy of being considered a monument, and has surpassing scenic interest.*
>
> *The tract, containing 295 acres, is all heavily wooded with virgin timber, chiefly with redwood and Douglas fir.*
>
> *In the opinion of experts it is a wilderness park such as is accessible to no other great city in the world and should be preserved forever for public use and enjoyment.*
>
> *After having traveled over a large part of the open country in the United States, I consider this tract with its beautiful trees, ferns, wild flowers and shrubs, as the most attractive.*
>
> *In tendering it I request it be known as Muir Woods in honor of John Muir."*

Kent then went on to offer financial help for maintenance and policing of the woods for the next ten years.

John Muir, upon learning that the gift was to be named in his honor, stated:

> *"This is the best tree-lover's monument that could be found in all of the forests of the world. You have done me great honor and I am proud of it. . . . Saving these woods from the axe and saw, from the money changers and water changers [dam builders] is in many ways the most notable service to God and man I have heard of since my forest wandering began."*

◄ *John Muir (with the beard), and the Newton Family at their cabin in Muir Woods around 1910.* Photo courtesy of Nancy Skinner.

*Candy Ireton examines the rings of a redwood tree to learn its age.*

Marinites take years to explore their beloved "Mt. Tam," but if your time is limited, try at least to visit Muir Woods, for it is truly one of the wonders of the world. Each year over a million tourists from all over the world visit this natural wonder. In 1988, the number rose to 1,600,000 visitors.

Man feels very small, indeed, contemplating these soaring giant redwood trees which were living when Columbus discovered our continent in 1492, and when Sir Francis Drake landed on the shores of Marin in 1579. One can touch the redwood trunks and feel a kinship with generations past, and a link to the future. These trees can live 1,000 years and could still be alive when our children's grandchildren are born.

The species of redwood found in the Muir Woods National Monument is *Sequoia sempervirens* or coast redwood, cousin to the *Sequoiadendron giganteum* which grow in the Sierra Nevada Mountains and may live 2,200 years. A University of California (Berkeley) study of 400 samples drilled in 1979 revealed that the trees in Muir

Woods are from 500 to 800 years old. Rangers state there are other trees in the park that are 800 to 1,000 years old.

The redwoods are as tall as 236 feet. Ironically, one Douglas fir in the park, dedicated to the memory of William Kent, is even higher—an incredible 253 feet. The diameters of the coast redwoods have been recorded over 16 feet; the largest here is 13 feet.

Six miles of trails go through Muir Woods. One path, paved with asphalt and eight-tenths of a mile long, is accessible to the handicapped.

You can take an easy walk along Redwood Creek, past the Bohemian Grove and the Cathedral Grove, or you can be more ambitious and go on up the slopes of the mountain. In addition to the redwood and Douglas fir, you will see California bay, tan oak, live oak, madrone, buck eye, and California nutmeg trees. Wildflowers, ferns, and mushrooms grow in the shaded glades; and you might see black-tail deer, raccoons, chipmunks, woodpeckers, and a variety of birds: sparrows, towhees, hummingbirds, and warblers. But most important will be the awe-inspiring beauty of the tall trees themselves. People tend to whisper in Muir Woods as though they are seeing and touching the very mystery of life.

To get to Muir Woods, leave Highway 101 at the Stinson Beach exit. Go half a mile to a stoplight and turn left on Highway 1, which is also Shoreline Highway. Continue two and a half miles to the junction of the Panoramic Highway, turn right, drive seven-tenths of a mile, then turn left on the Muir Woods road.

The monument is open daily from 8:00 A.M. to sunset; the sandwich shop closes at 5:30 P.M. and the gift area at dusk (earlier in the winter). At this shop visitors can buy redwood souvenirs such as clocks, planters, nut dishes, cable cars, and live redwood burls—gnarled knots cut from the side of the trees which, when put in water, sprout lacy, green redwood branches. Large burls can be polished to a rich dark red color and used for furniture such as tabletops. Slides, books, and film are also available.

Admission to the monument is free. No dogs are allowed. Parking areas and restrooms are located outside the entrance (and may be moved even farther beyond the area of the trees to reduce congestion). For more information call the Ranger Station at 388-2959.

# Mt. Tamalpais State Park

To visit the rest of the mountain, return to Panoramic Highway and turn north—or left. On the way up the mountain, the road passes Camp Alice Eastwood Road and then the Boot Jack Picnic Area, which has tables, stoves, drinking water, and restrooms.

State park headquarters is at the Pan Toll Ranger Station, about four miles from the Muir Woods Road-Panoramic Highway intersection. Here you may obtain a brochure with a map of the hiking trails plus information about camping along the Coast Trail and at Pan Toll. A parking toll of $3 at East Peak, Bootjack and Pan Toll was levied in 1989.

The Alice Eastwood Group Camp is open year round and handles up to seventy-five people. Accommodations include two camp sites: Camp A handles 50 people and costs $75 for adults and $37.50 for children; Camp B handles 25 people and costs $37.50 for adults and $18.75 for children. Each site furnishes tables, drinking water, and pit toilets. Because of fire hazards, only self-contained gas-burning stoves may be used in this camp. Make reservations by calling MISTIX 1-800-444-7275. Firewood may be purchased for $3.00 at Pan Toll. No trailers or motor homes are allowed.

Other maps may be purchased that show the trails in more detail. The Erickson Trail Map ($3.75), notes the picnic areas at Laurel Dell, Potrero Meadows, and Rifle Camp. A newer map becoming very popular with hikers is Jerry Olmsted's "A Rambler's Guide to the Trails of Mt. Tamalpais and the Marin Headlands" which sells for $6.

Hikers can stop at the West Point Inn and enjoy coffee, tea, or lemonade on its wide veranda. Built in 1904, the inn is located on the old stage road that connected with Stinson Beach and Bolinas. That road is now used as a fireroad and by hikers. The inn was also a stop on the old mountain railroad for passengers on their way to the summit or to the connecting stage to Willow Camp.

No dogs are allowed on the state park trails or fire roads. For more information phone the Mt. Tamalpais State Park Headquarters at 388-2070.

*The 5000-seat Mountain Theater on top of Mt. Tamalpais.*

## The Mountain Theater

To reach the Mountain Theater, turn right on Pan Toll Road across from park headquarters. This road is open the same hours as the park, generally half-an-hour before sunrise to half-an-hour after sunset.

Up the road one and one-half miles you will reach Ridgecrest Boulevard and the popular picnic area, Rock Spring Meadow. Turn right on Ridgecrest and you will immediately arrive at the Mountain Theater.

This 5,000-seat amphitheater is worth taking the time to explore. Here, 2,000 feet above sea level, are incredible views of Richardson and San Francisco Bays, Angel Island, Alcatraz Island, the Oakland Bay Bridge, the Berkeley Hills, and Mt. Diablo beyond.

This entire area was donated by William Kent in 1915 and named for Sidney B. Cushing, president of the Mt. Tamalpais and Muir Woods Railway. In the 1930s, the Civilian Conservation Corps built the seats out of serpentine hauled down from the West Peak. Since 1913, visitors have enjoyed the annual Mountain Play and other dramatic productions, religious services, concerts, weddings, and picnics in the theater.

## Mill Valley Air Force Station (Closed)

A mile beyond the theater is the former Mill Valley Air Force Station which at one time operated the huge white radar domes. They look somewhat like a pair of large golf balls sitting on top of the summit. The radar equipment is now under the jurisdiction of the Federal Aviation Agency.

Site facilities on top of the mountain used to include a dining room, base exchange, motor pool, housing, and recreational facilities—even a tennis court, swimming pool, and bowling alley.

Since the facility closed in 1983 and was taken over by the Golden Gate National Recreation Area, some of the buildings have been torn down by volunteers.

## East Peak

Continue one and eight-tenths miles to the East Peak where the Tavern of Tamalpais used to stand. The road passes through thick manzanita and becomes a one-way loop at the end. Restrooms are available near the parking lot.

You can hike up to a fire lookout at the top of the mountain to an altitude of 2,571 feet by way of a short but steep, rocky trail. On a clear day you can see Mt. St. Helena to the north, the Sierra Nevada in the east, and Mt. Hamilton to the south. Mt. Diablo is also to the east behind the Berkeley Hills. Below you may notice people practicing mountain climbing on the rock outcrops.

For unsurpassed views of the Pacific Ocean, the bay, San Francisco, and the East Bay, follow the asphalt Verna Dunshee Memorial Trail, dedicated in June 1973. Looking south from Sunrise Point, you can gaze down onto the area of the Double Bow Knot and see the enormous slide region on which the railroad had a stop called the Mesa Station.

As you follow the trail around the mountain, you can identify the towns in Marin (binoculars will help here)—first the picturesque towns of Sausalito, Tiburon, and Belvedere, with houses built on the hills and sailboat masts ringing the shoreline. Closer to the mountain base are Mill Valley and Corte Madera, then Greenbrae with its Boardwalk stretching out into the tidelands of the bay; adjacent to Greenbrae is the Larkspur Ferry Terminal and a huge new shopping center. To the northeast is the sprawling city of San Rafael. As you continue around, you may glimpse Kent-

*No. 430. Porch at Tavern of Tamalpais, on Summit of Mt. Tamalpais,*

*Porch on Tavern of Tamalpais on summit of Mt. Tamalpais around the turn of the 20th century.* Photo courtesy of Nancy Skinner.

field, Ross, San Anselmo, Fairfax, and the rural countryside to the west. These towns would run into each other but for the ridges of open space separating one from another.

To the northeast you can also view Phoenix Lake; north of that are Lagunitas and Bon Tempe lakes, plus a small slice of the upper end of Lake Alpine. Mt. Barnabee, Mt. Vision, and Black Mountain are in the distance to the west.

A refurbished visitors center opened in May 1988 and is operated by a volunteer group called "The Mount Tamalpais Interpretive Association." Members also lead hikes.

Hikers can choose from many varied and incredibly beautiful trails from Pan Toll Ranger Station, Rock Spring, Mountain Home, Phoenix Lake, or the Lake Lagunitas picnic area using the Olmsted map.

One of the most delightful loops on the mountain begins from Rock Spring. From the parking lot, hike on the Cataract Trail around the knoll on the left. A trail, the Simmons and re-routed Bernstein, takes off to the right. Bear left past the water tank and concrete trough and follow Cataract Creek down through some of the most captivating forest and meadow areas on the mountain. In about a mile-and-a-quarter you will come to the Laurel

Dell, an attractive picnic area under fir and laurel trees. You can either stay here for lunch or retrace your steps back up the Cataract Trail to the Mickey O'Brien Trail, renamed in 1948 for one of the earlier old-timers on the mountain. The Mickey O'Brien Trail is about three-quarters of a mile long and climbs slowly along the south side of Barth's Creek through large stands of fir and bay. At Barth's Retreat, you can wander around the little meadow or sit under the trees. Barth's Retreat was named after Emil Barth, a devoted hiker on the mountain from 1886 to his death in 1927.

After a sojourn here, retrace your steps back across the little bridge and turn left immediately onto the Simmons Trail. The trail climbs up the ridge through fine stands of Sergeant cypress and other plants of the chaparral plant community. At the top, take some time to look around to the north and west at the ridges of hills repeating themselves ad infinitum in the distance. Continue hiking down through the chaparral and into the fir forest. Cross Ziesche Creek, follow the creek down awhile, and return to the parking lot. The entire loop is three miles long with 700 feet of elevation gain.

If you are hungry after a day on the mountain, stop at the Moun-

*Bikers pause near the top of Mt. Tamalpais.*

*Diners enjoy the view from the Mountain Home Inn on Mt. Tamalpais.*

tain Home Inn as you drive back down. Founded in 1912, the inn is located at 810 Panoramic Highway near the Alice Eastwood Camp. It has been totally remodeled and now offers outdoor dining plus rooms to rent.

From here you can return down the mountain through Mill Valley by taking the Sequoia Valley Road opposite the road into Muir Woods. Just follow the yellow line as Sequoia becomes Edgewood which becomes Molino. When Molino ends, turn left on Montford, then right on Miller Avenue which will bring you back to Highway 101. The distance is three-and-a-half miles from the Pan Toll Station to Miller Avenue.

Or you can continue up over the mountain to Bolinas and Stinson Beach. The distance from the Ridgecrest- Pan Toll Intersection to Highway 1 opposite the entrance road to Bolinas is four miles. This winding narrow road is a slow but lovely drive through wild mountain country with the reward of the beautiful West Marin beaches at the end.

# Ross Valley and the San Quentin Peninsula  7

## Quiet Marin Towns

One hundred years ago, the beautiful Ross Valley was a favorite location for country homes and mansions built by wealthy San Francisco commuters. In the early 1800s, large tracts of timber had covered the valley, but these were soon logged-off and replaced by houses, dairy ranches, gardens, and orchards.

Life moved at a gentler pace, then. Visitors staying in elegant hotels swam and bathed in the Corte Madera Slough which wound all the way up the valley. They played tennis, rode horses, danced, and bowled. Fourth of July parades were an ever-popular entertainment. Fine carriages could be seen each evening on all the roads and clustered around railroad stations, waiting to pick up commuters from San Francisco. The Ross Valley women occupied themselves with cultural and charitable activities; the men joined fashionable private hunting clubs and went out to shoot the plentiful game: deer, fox, raccoon, mountain lion, dove, quail, and pheasant.

Today, the Ross Valley, which runs northwest from the town of Corte Madera to Fairfax, remains a fine residential area with several unique small towns and lovely parks. It is still a quiet area, with narrow roads and a lifestyle as peaceful as can be in this late twentieth century.

Generally, the area is divided into Lower Ross Valley and Upper Ross Valley. In the lower valley are the twin towns of Corte Madera and Larkspur (which share some public services), the San Quentin peninsula, Greenbrae, Kentfield, and the

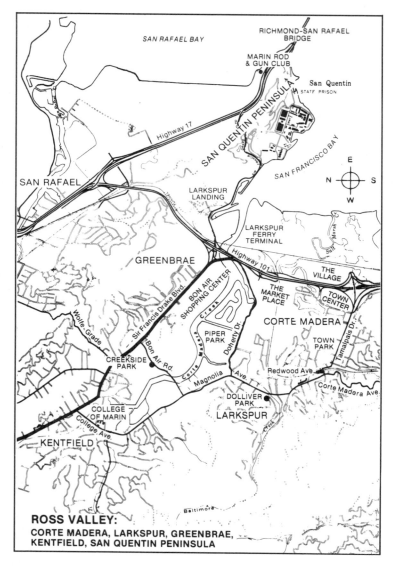

**ROSS VALLEY:**
**CORTE MADERA, LARKSPUR, GREENBRAE,**
**KENTFIELD, SAN QUENTIN PENINSULA**

subdivision of Kent Woodlands. Upper Ross Valley includes the towns of Ross, San Anselmo, and Fairfax, and some unincorporated residential areas such as Sleepy Hollow (adjacent to San Anselmo), Oak Manor (Fairfax), and the area west of Fairfax to White's Hill.

From 1875 to 1941 trains ran through the entire valley bringing commuters from the northwest side of Fairfax (known as Manor) to San Anselmo (then called The Junction), through Ross, Kentfield, Larkspur, and Corte Madera to Sausalito, and on to San Francisco by ferryboat. The trip took less time than it does today by automobile on Highway 101 during commute hours.

# Corte Madera

Corte Madera, named for John Reed's Mexican land grant the *Corte de Madera del'Presidio,* actually adjoined the fringes of that territory to the northwest. When Mexico gave California to the United States after the Mexican War in 1848, the area was called *Reed Sobrantes,* meaning "Reed leftovers." Squatters and homesteaders resided on the land until 1885 when Hilarita Reed, John's daughter, was able to reestablish ownership after a legal battle in Washington, D.C. It was then sold to speculators from San Francisco who made settlements with the homesteaders.

Corte Madera's most famous resident was a flamboyant easterner by the name of Frank Morrison Pixley. Educated into the law profession at Utica College in New York, Pixley rode west in 1848 at the age of twenty-four. After a fruitless year of prospecting gold on the Yuba River, he moved to San Francisco and began a law practice.

In 1853, Pixley married Amelia Van Reynegom, whose family lived on an estate named Owl's Wood, in what was the Chevy Chase area of what is now Corte Madera. John L. Van Reynegom, Amelia's father, who was a sea captain from Philadelphia, had settled on 160 acres of land where he planted an orchard and a vineyard, built a reservoir, and raised cattle. In 1860 and 1862, he applied unsuccessfully for a homestead. After Van Reynegom's death, Pixley bought Owl's Wood from the Reed heirs for $2,000 in gold, then put the entire property in his wife's name. By 1885, Pixley had enlarged the estate to 191 acres.

During the years that the family divided their time between San Francisco and Corte Madera, Frank Pixley held many political offices including state attorney general and state assemblyman. In 1877, at the age of fifty-three, Pixley founded a newspaper called the *San Francisco Argonaut,* which continued to be published until 1958. Famous writers such as Gertrude Atherton, Mark Twain, John Stoddard, and Ambrose Bierce contributed to this very popular newspaper.

After Pixley's death in 1895, a portion of the Corte Madera land was subdivided, and a town grew up around the old railroad depot (in the area that is now the Village Square and Menke Park). Adjacent Larkspur incorporated in 1908 and annexed the portion of Owl's Wood where Pixley's original home stood—much to the outrage of Corte Madera citizens, who did not get around to incorporating until 1916.

Today, the town of Corte Madera extends from San Francisco Bay on the east side of Highway 101 to the Larkspur city limits on the west. Directly off the freeway to the west is the Town Center, built in 1952 on land that once belonged to the Meadowsweet Dairy. It contains several large chain stores and a total of around 60 shops, restaurants and services.

In 1986, the shopping center was renovated and expanded to look like a Mediterranean village square. Included in the new design were a series of open-air courtyards, fountains, plazas and covered walkways. The major stores include J.C. Penney, Marshall's, Safeway and Thrifty.

One of the county's outstanding restaurants is located behind Penny's. Il Fornaio Cucina Italiana was opened by Larry Mindel in 1988. (Mindel also started MacArthur Park, Ciao, Prego and Harry's Bar in San Francisco.) The decor of the restaurant is strictly Italian with polished marble floors and a menu featuring fresh pasta dishes, delicious pizzas and wonderful rissato. Regional Italian wines are a specialty. Mindel also sells fresh bakery goods in the restaurant conveniently supplied by a bakery chain he purchased in 1987.

The Discovery Museum for children is also located at 428 Corte Madera Town Center. The theory behind this institution is that children learn through play. Exhibits relating to architecture, a stage with costumes, a fishing boat complete with crab nets and an underwater tunnel all teach by direct involvement.

The Discovery Museum will move into seven buildings at East Fort Baker around 1991. Phone 924-4722 for current hours and admission charge. Children must be accompanied by an adult.

A smaller shopping center located one block west of Highway

101 contains one of the top bookstores in Marin. Take the Lucky/Doherty exit off Highway 101, go straight on Fifer one block, then turn left on Tamal Vista. Just past the Department of Motor Vehicles on the left is "The Market" which contains shops renting videos, offering interior designs and selling clothes plus a couple of restaurants.

"Book Passage" at 51 Tamal Vista Blvd. is owned by Elaine Petrocelli who claims her store contains the largest travel book section of any bookstore in the United States. They also sell everything from children's books to fine art volumes. Elaine sponsors many authors events, writing classes and seminars making her bookstore especially popular with authors.

Across the freeway from Town Center at 1554 Redwood Highway is a high-fashion shopping mall, The Village. (Tamalpais/Paradise Drive freeway exit)

Anchored by Macy's and Nordstrom's, The Village contains around 95 specialty and fashion shops. Popular ones include Any Mountain for outdoor clothing and Crate and Barrel for home furnishings. For information, phone The Village at 924-8557.

Corte Madera retains a small town flavor, and residents are especially proud of their annual Fourth of July celebrations. The whole town turns out for a spirited parade, with fire trucks ringing their bells, city officials riding in convertibles and waving to the crowd, school bands playing, clowns cavorting, and kids riding bikes decorated in red, white, and blue. An arts and crafts festival and picnic are held in the Town Park.

Take the Corte Madera/Larkspur exit off Highway 101 west onto Tamalpais Drive to arrive at the old Village Square, seven-tenths of a mile from the turnoff. When you have gone half a mile, you will pass the 22.7-acre Town Park on your right, purchased in 1939 and built on an area of land fill; the Recreation Center; the Public Safety Building which contains the police and fire departments; the post office, just behind the Public Safety Building on Pixley; and, beyond the parking lot, the Town Hall at 300 Tamalpais Drive.

Tamalpais Drive turns right and arrives almost immediately at the Village Square and a bus shelter near the site of the old train station.

Business in this area today includes Mike Ulrich's excellent beauty shop, Amazing Hair Company; the Village Paint Shoppe (on Tamalpais Dr. and Sierra St.); the Corte Madera Hardware;

a launderette; Benissimo Italian Pizza; the Madera Station Deli;
Video Varieties; and Golden Gate Coins owned by Fred Velten.

Above the bus stop is the lovely landscaped Menke Park on
the corner of Montecito Drive and Redwood Avenue. There are
benches and an old brick wall. Tamalpais Drive becomes Redwood
Avenue at this point, which then intersects Corte Madera Avenue,
and, in a northerly direction (to your right), becomes Magnolia
Avenue at the Larkspur city limits.

Above the park on Corte Madera Avenue are some interesting
shops.

# Larkspur

Around 1869, William Murray and Patrick King purchased
1,233 acres in the area of Kentfield and Larkspur from
the Ross family. The partners divided the property in half,
with Murray taking the northern area near Kentfield. King's portion included what is now downtown Larkspur. He built a home
at 105 King Street and established a cattle and dairy operation.

The town of Larkspur was actually developed by a man named
C. W. Wright, who bought the King Ranch in 1887 for $21,000.
He had the land subdivided into lots large enough for a house,
with space for some livestock, and he built five Victorian
cottages—enough to qualify the "town" for a railroad station. The
town was named after a blue flower his English wife misidentified
as larkspur instead of lupine.

After the 1906 earthquake and fire, survivors from San Francisco poured into Larkspur, and many stayed permanently. These
new residents had an understandable interest in establishing a fire
department, and one was organized in 1909. To raise money for
fire-fighting equipment, they held fund-raising dances at the railroad
station park. The dances proved so successful that they were
moved to a fancy new location at 476 Cane Street and held on
a regular basis. Situated next to a bubbling creek was a half-acre
of hardwood dance floors surrounded by rose-covered trellises.

These famous Rose Bowl dances drew three to four thousand
people weekly from all over the Bay Area from 1913 until 1963.
Glowing Chinese lanterns and strings of colored lights made it the
ideal spot for romance. Both engagements and anniversaries of

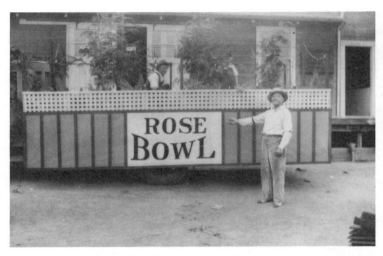

*Cap Larsen at the Rose Bowl in Larkspur, 1930.* Coutesty of Betty Krause.

couples who had met at the dances were announced by "Cap" Larsen, secretary of the Larkspur Volunteer Fireman's Association. The highlight of the evening was the famous Rose Bowl "firefall," twenty seconds of falling white sparks cascading down from forty feet in the sky. It was masterminded by Willie Frizzi, who was known as a "one-man electrical company."

To get to downtown Larkspur, continue north from Corte Madera on Corte Madera Avenue. This becomes Magnolia Avenue at the Larkspur city limits. (You may also drive south on Magnolia Avenue, off Sir Francis Drake Boulevard via College Avenue in Kentfield, or southwest on Bon Air Road through Greenbrae.)

If you have time to really explore the town, pick up a copy of *Larkspur, Past and Present,* published by the Larkspur Heritage Committee. This paperback publication (updated in 1989) will guide you on eight walking tours which cover everything from Victorian houses to an old railroad trestle and brickyard. The book is available at most local bookstores, including Artist's Proof at 460 Magnolia.

For a brief tour of Larkspur, begin at the Lark Creek Inn, 234 Magnolia. This restaurant is located in the old Murphy house built in 1888. The house was thought to be haunted during the 1920s and 1930s, and was occupied by a vet plus several hobos who lived in the bottom part during the Depression. In 1938, it was converted into a gas station, service garage, and automobile sales room. Then, in 1971, the property was remodeled into the restaurant and shops. It is now owned by realtor Sue Schaefer.

Across Magnolia Avenue from the Lark Creek Inn is Madrone Avenue which runs west into Baltimore Canyon, parallel to Larkspur Creek. This creek, also known as Arroyo Holon, was the boundary of the *Corte de Madera del Presidio* Mexican land grant.

Dolliver Park is located on both sides of Madrone, beginning at Magnolia. Ellen Dolliver Jewell, a member of the pioneer San Francisco Dolliver family, gave the north portion of the park to the city of Larkspur in 1923, noting on a plaque that this was "the first redwood grove on the Redwood Highway." You will see redwood trees growing right out of the street.

The property to the south was given by Mr. and Mrs. C. S. Burtchaell (he was the grandson of Thomas Dolliver who owned a leather goods manufacturing company in San Francisco) to honor his grandmother, Ann C. Dolliver. The park includes a children's playground with new equipment installed at the end of 1988.

At 58 Madrone Avenue is the original Dolliver house, a Victorian-style summer home built in 1888. This was the first house constructed in the new Larkspur township laid out by C. W. Wright. It is listed on the National Register of Historic Places, but is still used as a private residence and is not open to the public.

Madrone Avenue ends about a mile from Magnolia. A trail begins here and follows Larkspur Creek to the old blue-rock quarry and through a dense redwood forest to Dawn Falls. Here, a mile from Madrone, two natural springs join to form the source of Larkspur Creek.

Coming back to the business part, continue on Magnolia Avenue through downtown Larkspur, an interesting place to explore since many of the original buildings have been preserved and now house unique shops.

At 400 Magnolia you will see the Larkspur City Hall, which was constructed in 1913. It now includes the fire department as well as the library. The building was designed by San Francisco architect Charles O. Claussen in what is known as a Mission Revival style with influences of Italian villa. The Larkspur Heritage Committee has historical photos on display here.

An unusual shop, Artist's Proof at 460 Magnolia, combines a

*A parade in Larkspur in 1910. Frizzi Saloon on the left, Larkspur Hotel on the right.* Courtesy of Betty Krause.

bookstore owned and operated by Maryjane Dunstan with an upstairs room containing out of print books. This section is operated by Robert Oliver. The bookstore has strong selections in environment energy, art, health, and the study of "noetics," the science of intellect or higher consciousness. There is also a humanistic psychology and Jungian section. A fall and spring series of literary luncheons sponsored by the bookstore are held at Fabrizio Restaurant, 455 Magnolia.

In the middle of town, at 507 Magnolia, is the Blue Rock Inn. Built in 1895, it was designed in the Queen Anne style and included a short tower. This inn was then known as the Hotel Larkspur and was billed as "A First Class Family Resort." The building survived the 1906 earthquake, but residents of the hotel were startled when bricks from the chimney fell onto the roof and hotel furniture rolled around uncontrollably. They rushed outside for safety only to learn that a neighbor living on Ward St. just across the way, August Frizzi, had died of a sudden heart attack during the quake. Frizzi had been known to train boxers in the basement of his yellow house.

In 1910, the hotel was sold to Elizabeth and Serefino Marilli. The

*Larkspur men prepare for Ft. Lewis Washington and World War I, September 19, 1917. (L to R) Messrs. Polley, Mert Bain, Walter Frizzi, Henry Foster, Barns, and Rose. In the background on the left is Serefino Marilli, owner of the Blue Rock Inn.* Courtesy of Betty Krause.

new owners remodeled immediately, and on the first story they put a facing of blue basalt rock which had been quarried on a hill above Paradise Drive. Blue rock pillars were added, and the name of the hotel changed to reflect the new look. Around 12 years later, the Marilli's took in a partner, William Stringa, who had arrived in town as an umbrella salesman.

A historic plaque may be seen farther north in the Larkspur Plaza Shopping Center on Magnolia and Doherty Drive. It states that on or near this Larkspur site were discovered ancient shell mounds and burial grounds of the Miwok Indians. The plaque also makes note of a sawmill landing, a wharf on the salt water which was used by Mexican soldiers in 1816, and a government sawmill which operated here from 1847 to 1850. It goes on to state that the first house in town, built by Jonathan Bickerstaff, was erected near this spot and that the North Pacific Coast Railroad began service in this area in 1875.

The old train station, now being used as the Fixit Shop, is located just south of here. As you look at the plaque, the two buildings off the train station are directly to your left down the old railroad right-of-way which is now a bicycle path.

The buildings are a light beige stucco with falling tile roofs and boarded-up wooden double doors. The smaller building on the left labeled LARKSPUR was the waiting room while the larger one is where tickets were sold. The original Northwestern Pacific Railroad logos remain on each end of the building on the right. The warehouse beyond was once the location of the station masters house.

## Piper Park

As you leave the downtown area, stop at Piper Park to view the old arks along Larkspur Boardwalk One and Two. Before World War II, there were three boardwalks that went all the way up to the Bon Air Bridge. Driving north on Magnolia, turn east (or right) on Doherty Drive. The park is about three blocks away, behind the police station. Pioneer families from the area say that Mr. Doherty lived on the hill above here and was considered the boss of the town.

Piper Park is a 22-acre park is on landfill surrounded by the Corte Madera Creek. It has two softball diamonds, a soccer field, cricket field, four tennis courts, volleyball court, and horseshoe pitching area. There is also a fishing dock and 24 picnic tables with six barbecues. 250 people can use this area at one time. Phone the Larkspur Recreation Dept. at 927-5031 for reservations. Some small fees apply.

To view the old arks, go to the gravel road to the west of the baseball diamond and behind the Henry C. Hall Elementary School, 200 Doherty Drive. There have been arks along the Corte Madera Creek since 1906. At first, they were vacation homes but later were lived in all year around. Today, the private residences here are a combination of very old arks and newly constructed homes.

## Marin Community Fields

Also on Doherty Drive adjacent to Redwood High School, are the Marin Community Fields which opened in September 1987. The facilities include 17 acres of public playing fields providing for softball, baseball, rugby, soccer and a beep ball field for the blind.

This project was a vision of Bob Troppman's in the late 1950s. It was brought to reality by Don Wihlborg through his design of the fields. Fred Kritzberg, for whom the amphitheater was named, was the consulting engineer and a great benefactor for the fields.

The driving volunteer force in this project included the Community Fields Association, Henry Moody, Shirley Walker, Bob

*Marin Community Fields, Larkspur, with Mt. Tamalpais in the background.*

Troppman, and Dolly Nave from San Rafael who acted as project coordinator. Major donations from business people included Tom Cagwin and David Dorward of Cagwin and Dorward Landscape Contractors; Dan Boyd of Able Fence Co; Alfred Dalecio of Bresnan and Dalecio Construction; The Ghilotti Brothers Contractors (Mario, Dino, Mike, Dick, plus Nick Rado, Jerry Pagna, Frank Palagi and Jerry Elenberger); Maggiora and Ghilotti Contractors (H.J. Babe Ghilotti and his four sons, Greg, Jim, Gary and Glen, plus Ted Lehman); Jim Mahoney of Mahoney Steel; Bruce Mac Phail of McPhail's Inc.; Rich Epidendo of Rich Ready Mix; San Marin/Golden State Lumber (Al and Rich Bonfiglio, Glen Nobin); Bill Dutra and Marv Larsen of San Rafael Rock Quarry; Shamrock Materials (Lee and Eugene Ceccotti, Max Cherini); Tom Bradall of V. Dolan Trucking and Woody Van Lackum of Woodmasters.

The Community Fields Assn. solicited a grant of $300,000 from the Buck Trust in 1984. A three-to-one match was required after the initial $50,000 for the study. $600,000 was raised in cash from the community and over $900,000 was raised in donated labor, materials and equipment.

In the fall of 1985, the grading and hydroseeding for erosion control was completed in just three weekends with the help of eighteen pieces of equipment and labor provided by the Northern California Contractors Association. Seven months later, a sand turf plus irrigation and drainage lines were installed. Hydroseeding was done again for the playing surface of the fields. A thousand-seat amphitheater was built in the spring of 1986.

Plans have now been drawn up for a building to be converted into handicap restrooms. There will be space for a maintenance worker and his supplies, a room for CPR classes and a meeting room for coaches and users of the fields.

A representative from each "user group" is required to join the Community Fields User Group Committee. This committee has provided a guideline for rules and made each member responsible for clean-up. All fees are used for the maintenance of the fields.

A survey of the first years activities showed that the fields had been used by 35 groups representing about 13,000 participants and spectators. The Redwood High School graduation was held in the amphitheatre.

The fields may be rented by the hour. Call Lyn Moody for permits at 924-2306.

### North Larkspur

As you continue northwest on Magnolia Avenue, you will pass the old Escalle Vineyards at 771 Magnolia. The area began as a brickyard operated by Claude Callot, a Frenchman, who sent the bricks to San Francisco by barge down the Corte Madera Creek.

Callot's friends, Jean Escalle and his brother Pierre came from France to help with the brick making. They added some vineyards to the property and began producing an excellent table claret. When Callot died, Jean Escalle married his Irish widow, Ellen. He bought forty more acres and planted Riesling and Zinfandel grapes. Jean and Ellen then opened the Limerick Inn, which served good food and wine in an outdoor setting. A train stopped at the Escalle Station so patrons could eat, drink, and play bocci ball, a game somewhat like bowling. Additional entertainment was provided by a live band. A special celebration, the Vintage Festival, was held in the fall, and another on Bastille Day.

The old red brick wall of the Limerick Inn can be seen from Magnolia Avenue, although the property is now closed to the public. Above and to the back is the original winery with the name "Jean Escalle" proudly displayed across the front.

Just north of Escalle's is Bon Air Road, which runs northeast to Sir Francis Drake Boulevard past Marin General Hospital. The hospital grounds were once the site of the elegant Bon Air Hotel, which could brag of the county's first swimming pool, a bowling alley, and a dance pavilion. Stately palm trees still stand in front.

Across from the hospital is the twenty-six-acre Creekside Park behind Marin Catholic High School. The marsh beside the Corte Madera Creek was purchased by the County of Marin in 1975 as a service area. It includes portions of Larkspur, Greenbrae, and Kentfield along Sir Francis Drake Boulevard. A $750,000 bond issue was passed for the purpose of restoring the marsh, which the Army Corp of Engineers had used as a dumping grounds for spoils when they dredged the adjacent portion of Corte Madera Creek.

The restoration of this salt marsh represents a unique environmental achievement and has received national recognition. Trees and shrubs native to Marin were planted, along with a multitude of wildflowers which bloom here in the spring. A few benches, picnic tables, and winding pathways have been placed on dry land. From any point, there is a magnificent view of Mt. Tamalpais. In 1989, the area was refurbished with the planting of additional trees and plants.

The Corte Madera Creek winds out toward the bay, and where it passes under Bon Air Road there is a small bridge. The Bon Air bridge was once a drawbridge that was raised to let barges through. Located nearby was Hill's Boat House where people from the hotel and from other parts of the county came to swim in "warm salt creek water baths."

At 1201 South Eliseo Drive, just south of the bridge, is tiny Hamilton Park. Clarabelle Hamilton, a resident of nearby Tamalpais Retirement Center, donated this lot in 1975 to provide lasting access to Corte Madera Creek. In an area of doctors' offices, medical clinics, and convalescent homes, this park's lovely blooming flowers and green grass offer a spot of tranquility. A curving path forms a circle from South Eliseo to a spot overlooking Corte Madera Creek, where on most days, a family of mallards can be seen swimming below. Facilities include benches and picnic tables.

Another small park, also overlooking the Corte Madera Creek, is the Bon Air Landing Park at 557 South Eliseo. It contains two benches and one picnic table plus a pier running into the creek.

North Larkspur, along Magnolia Avenue near the Kentfield border, has more shops and restaurants.

# Greenbrae

The City of Larkspur has annexed property on the north side of the Corte Madera Creek, known as Greenbrae. Once an old dairy ranch consisting of 8,840 acres, Greenbrae today contains many apartments, a subdivision of expensive private homes, and the Bon Air Shopping Center, adjacent to Sir Francis Drake Boulevard which was remodeled in 1984. In this shopping center is Petrini's, a supermarket with a deli and a large butcher department providing old-fashioned service. You can have meat cut to order or choose a fish to be cleaned and dressed.

There are 46 stores in the Bon Air Shopping Center including a coffee shop called the Coffee Mill which sells coffee and chocolates. Other interesting businesses here include the Swiss Kitchen, Lothar's Flowers Etc., La Pastaria (fresh-made pasta), Catania Sound and a gift store named Inge's Treasures.

# The San Quentin Peninsula

This peninsula on the east side of the county juts out into the waters of San Francisco and San Rafael bays. It was named for the courageous Indian warrior Quintin, who

*Inside the Larkspur ferry terminal.*

was a follower of the Indian chief, Marin. The spelling of the name was changed to "Quentin," and he mysteriously became a saint.

In 1968 and 1972, Larkspur annexed property in this area, once part of a Mexican land grant called *Rancho Punta de Quintin,* which had been awarded to John (Juan) B. R. Cooper in 1840. The land grant stretched from Point San Quentin into the Ross Valley.

## The Larkspur Ferry Terminal and Larkspur Landing

The Larkspur Ferry Terminal is located on East Sir Francis Drake Boulevard on twenty-five acres at the mouth of the Corte Madera Creek. It is a white, equilateral triangle-shaped steel frame looking somewhat like it was built out of gigantic Tinker Toys. Designed by San Francisco architect Jacques de Brer, this landmark is visible from both Highway 101 and the water. Its ultramodern triangular design presents a light, airy feeling which is what the Golden Gate Bridge directors wanted, as opposed to a heavy, massive building blocking the view of the bay.

The design was controversial when the structure was built, however, for it failed to include adequate shelter for waiting passengers. Winter rain, cold winds, and fog blew leaving patrons wet and cold. To solve the problem, the District installed plastic weather protection within the space frame. A section for air at the bottom was left open, and heaters were placed inside.

The Larkspur Ferry Terminal handles 3,500 passengers a day. It provides a large parking lot and feeder buses for passengers from all over the county both mornings and evenings. Phone 453-2100 from Northern Marin, and 332-6600 from Southern Marin and San Francisco for bus and ferry schedules plus current fares.

To get to the ferry terminal from Highway 101, take the East Sir Francis Drake Boulevard exit.

Golden Gate Bridge staff, state transportation planners and the "101 Corridor Action Committee" have conducted studies for possible construction of a seventeen-mile passenger rail or bus link between Novato and the ferry terminal, along the old Northwestern Pacific Railroad right-of-way next to the freeway. The right-of-way should be purchased in the near future.

Ferry service between Larkspur and San Francisco began in 1976 with gas-turbine ferries built for the District by Campbell Industries in San Diego. These boats were later modified by installing diesel engines because of skyrocketing fuel costs. Each carries 725 passengers in great luxury with large, comfortable chairs and tables. Coffee and rolls are sold in the morning, and cocktails on the evening run. Cellular telephones are a recent addition.

From the parking lot at the ferry terminal, looking south, you can see another ark community called the Greenbrae Boardwalk; beyond is the ninety-five acre Corte Madera Marsh Ecological Reserve. This marsh is rich in feed for shorebirds and you might see an elegant Great Egret with long white plumes stalking the shallow waters.

Across from the ferry terminal is Larkspur Landing, an extensive development of offices, apartments, shops, and restaurants, which opened in 1978. This complex was built on the site of the old Hutchinson Quarry, a landmark from 1924. Huge rocks from this quarry were once shippped all over the Bay Area for a variety of projects, including the Bay Bridge ballast, railroad beds, and dikes in the Sacramento delta.

The gray and tan wooden buildings at Larkspur Landing have

a nautical, weathered look. They were designed to resemble old New England, but a touch of California was added with colorful awnings and decks built onto restaurants with a view of the water.

Larkspur Landing has around forty-five shops and restaurants, including "A Clean Well-Lighted Place for Books," a favorite shop which lives up to its name. It stays open at night until 11:00 P.M. (Friday and Saturdays until midnight) so restaurant goers can browse after dinner. Other unusual shops include Games and Things, a unique selection of children's and adult games; L'Ark, with animal-related gifts; Rubber Ducky's Bath Emporium; plus an excellent selection of clothing stores. There is a variety of services at Larkspur Landing, including the Ragged Sailor Frame Shop which advertises professional picture framing at do-it-yourself prices. You can get your hair cut, arrange for a trip around the world, attend four different movie theaters, or try one of the wide variety of restaurants.

## Remillard Brickyard

East of Larkspur Landing is the Remillard Brickyard, a State Historical Landmark. From 1891 to 1915, it supplied 500,000 bricks annually to the Bay Area. Bricks from this yard were used to help rebuild San Francisco after the 1906 earthquake and fire. Today the building has been renovated into office space and contains a French restaurant which opened in October 1989.

Some historians believe that the English explorer, Sir Francis Drake, landed near this spot and stayed for a month while he explored the inland area and repaired the *Golden Hinde*.

Across Sir Francis Drake Blvd. is Remillard Park consisting of a jogging path, benches, picnic tables and a large pond. Hikers and picnickers can enjoy watching the ferry boats maneuver in and out of the terminal and wind surfers with their colorful sails skim across the top of the water.

## San Quentin Prison

East Sir Francis Drake Boulevard follows the bay around the San Quentin peninsula, and as you round a bend, the mood changes abruptly. Suddenly, there are high chain-link fences topped with strands of barbed wire and a black and white sign announces "Department of Correction, California State Prison, San Quentin."

You will pass a back gate with a guard and see a single watchtower atop a hill to your right. Around the next curve, the whole prison spreads out before you. Many of the buildings have been painted a fresh-looking cream color with red and green trim. Small wooden houses are clustered below the fence adjacent to the road.

The main entrance to San Quentin Prison is the last exit before reaching the Richmond-San Rafael Bridge. Turn right and drive down Main Street. The bay is on your left, beyond a row of towering eucalyptus trees. It takes only a couple of minutes to pass through the village of San Quentin, which consists of a few houses, a post office, and the yellow "House"—a resting place for families visiting the prison. At the end of Main Street is the entrance to the infamous prison, scene of riots, murders, prison breaks, and over four hundred state executions.

The first prison was an old brig called the *Waban*, known as the "hell ship," which was anchored off Angel Island, then towed to San Quentin with both men and women prisoners aboard. The state had purchased twenty acres from Benjamin Buckelew for a prison which opened in 1854. During the early years, the prisoners were used to build roads and houses in the county. Conditions inside the prison were described as grim, with prisoners lacking blankets and being forced to sleep in their striped convict suits.

On July 22, 1862, 400 convicts escaped, taking Warden John Challis as hostage. This was reportedly the fifth escape in five weeks. Sheriff Valentino Doub gathered a small posse and rode over the trail (on what is now D Street in San Rafael) to Ross Landing (now Kentfield). As the sheriff came down over the ridge, he saw a gun battle going on between the citizens of Corte Madera and some of the convicts who were trying to escape across Corte Madera Creek. In the confusion the warden escaped. Accounts vary as to what happened in the battle that followed, but it is known that a large number of the convicts were recaptured. Some were injured, a few were killed.

Thirty-five acres of additional land for the prison were purchased in 1864 and two more cellblocks were built. The *1880 History of Marin* describes one of these buildings as two stories high, forty by twenty feet, and built of poor-quality brick. "In the basement is the dungeon of the prison which contains fourteen cells, seven on each side of the passageway, each cell eleven-and-a-half by six feet, and nine feet high; near the entrance to the dungeon stands the whipping post."

Between 1912 and 1922, there were around 1,500 prisoners at San Quentin. The number of prisoners jumped to 5,000 after World War I, with 700 paid guards and other personnel. In 1933, the female prisoners were moved to Tehachapi, and by 1934, the number of male prisoners had increased to 6,400. Escape attempts continued.

Probably no escape has caught the attention and fancy of the public as much as the "Rub-a-Dub-Dub" caper, which occurred on August 9, 1979. Three men escaped in a 14-foot blue kayak on which they had painted "Rub-a-Dub-Dub—Marin Yacht Club." The kayak, built in the prison shop, was launched near an unmanned watchtower and soon began taking on water. It was spotted by an unsuspecting guard who offered to call for help. The escapees waved and thanked him politely but refused the offer. Two of the men, William McGirk and John Waller, were recaptured within a year but two different juries, after hearing conflicting stories from guards, refused to convict them of escape. The third, Forrest Tucker, was not captured until 1983 when he was found living in West Palm Beach, Florida married to a wealthy socialite. He is now back at San Quentin.

Some attempts at reform have been made within the prison. Since 1975, prisoners have been allowed to marry and may apply for overnight conjugal visits with their wives. Classes have been set up so that convicts can work toward earning a high school diploma or developing special skills. Sports are popular and the San Quentin Pirates baseball team plays a regular scheduled season against local teams. The inmates also produce a lively newspaper called the *San Quentin News* with coverage of prison events plus state and federal court decisions affecting prisoners.

Still, racial and other violence continues at the prison. In 1972, then-governor Ronald Reagan announced that San Quentin Prison would be phased out in five years, but nothing came of his plan and the antiquated prison labors on.

No tours of the prison are allowed, but there is a gift shop just outside the gates. The San Quentin Handicraft Shop carries items made by prisoners such as leather purses, billfolds, and belts, candles, carved wooden cable cars and covered wagons, jewelry, jewelry boxes, decorated T-shirts, paintings, and copper pictures. No checks or credit cards are accepted. According to a prison spokesman, it is sometimes difficult finding a suitable person to run this shop so it is not always open. Phone 454-1460, extension

2397 for current hours.

### Richmond-San Rafael Bridge

East Sir Francis Drake Boulevard ends at the Richmond-San Rafael Bridge, where you can take Highway 580 back to Highway 101, or cross the bridge to Richmond in the East Bay.

The two-deck, four-mile bridge (with three quarter-mile bridge approaches) was opened in 1956 after three years of construction. The bridge lacks the open viewing built into the Golden Gate Bridge, and no bicycles or pedestrians are allowed.

### The Marin Rod and Gun Club

The Marin Rod and Gun Club is located on fifty-five acres of uplands and tidelands on San Pablo Bay at Point San Quentin, adjacent to the Richmond-San Rafael Bridge. Organized in 1926 with 35 men, the club now has grown to 2,800 active sportsmen who enjoy fishing for recreation. They are also concerned with the preservation and propagation of fish and wildlife. Over the years, members claim to have fought successfully against commercial net fishing in inland waters and against the commercial fishing of striped bass and abalone. Facilities, which are not open to the public, include a half-mile-long fishing pier built by the C&H Sugar Company in 1924 for loading Marin County water into tankers. This water was taken to the C&H Sugar Refinery at Crockett near the Carquinez Strait.

The Marin Rod and Gun Club also has a small boat ramp and several acres of picnic grounds.

# Kentfield

The community of Kentfield is named after the pioneer family who purchased land in the area in 1871. Adaline and Albert Kent, along with their seven-year-old son, William, left Chicago where Albert owned a large meat-packing plant, cattle, and land. The family moved west looking for a better climate for Albert's health. They eventually found an ideal spot in an area then known as Ross Landing, a busy shipping point on the Corte Madera Creek where flat-bottomed schooners and other vessels, ranging from ten to fifty tons, loaded cordwood,

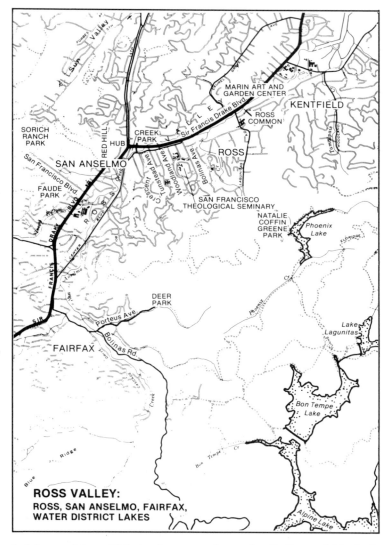

**ROSS VALLEY:**
ROSS, SAN ANSELMO, FAIRFAX,
WATER DISTRICT LAKES

bricks, and hay. This is the area where the College of Marin is now located, approximately two miles west of Highway 101 on Sir Francis Drake Boulevard.

The Kents bought land from the Murray and Ross families and built a house which is still standing. William was sent east for a college education at Yale. There he met Elizabeth Thacher, the daughter of a Latin professor, and married her in 1890. The young couple first lived in Chicago but moved to California in 1906. In 1915, William remodeled the Kent estate to accommodate his seven children.

The Kents became active in Marin affairs, especially conservation causes. In 1909, shortly after donating the Muir Woods Monument to the United States, William and his mother Adaline built the Tamalpais Centre for recreation (where the College of Marin gym stands today). Adaline was concerned that the young people of her day have constructive recreational outlets.

The Tamalpais Centre was a huge mission-style building with arches and tile roof, situated on twenty-nine acres running from Corte Madera Creek to the present College Avenue. The building was so large, in fact, that it was referred to as the Kentfield Stadium, and a small street running along its side was named Stadium Way. It contained a gym, a hardwood dance floor, a kitchen, and a stage with four changes of scenery. Also at the Centre were a racetrack and sports fields. Band concerts provided lively entertainment on Sundays. Dances, plays, luncheons, and Sierra Club meetings were held regularly. A special event was the annual May Day, which continued into the 1930s.

In 1910, William Kent announced his decision to run for Congress on a progressive platform. He was elected to represent California's First District in the Sixty-Second Congress and reelected for two more terms, serving until 1917. He is remembered for authoring legislation to create the National Parks Service, which became effective in 1916. Back in Marin, Kent continued to do major work for conservation. He dreamed of a park on Mt. Tamalpais and donated land to help make this a reality.

While her husband pursued his political career, Elizabeth Thacher Kent became involved in the women's suffrage movement. She picketed the White House in 1917 and, when given a choice of going to jail or paying a fine, she said she preferred jail. (William chose to pay her fine.)

Elizabeth was an inspiration to a Kent woman of a later generation, Martye Kent, daughter of William's son, Thomas, and his wife Anne. Martye made history in April 1969 when she led a fight against the Army Corps of Engineers who had decided to cement Tamalpais Creek, which lies at the entrance to Kent Woodlands, an exclusive subdivision developed by the Kent family.

The project was undertaken in conjunction with the Corps' controversial Corte Madera Creek project, which was designed to prevent flooding by cementing some portions of the creek bank. Tamalpais Creek had not been scheduled for cementing in the proposed plan, nor was public notice adequately provided.

The Corps' action was strongly protested, and forty-three Marin residents and College of Marin students were arrested in a confrontation over tree cutting, but the battle was eventually lost. Martye and the community were forced to watch Tamalpais Creek become a ditch of rippled cement lined by a green plastic-covered cyclone fence.

There were long-term effects. The fight at Tamalpais Creek awakened the aesthetic and political consciousness of the Ross Valley and possibly the nation. An important federally-financed study was conducted and resulted in a published book about nine alternative methods of flood control.

In December 1969, a large crowd gathered to plant a sapling maple tree and to dedicate a plaque fastened to a dead tree stump beside the creek. The inscription read:

> *This tree is dedicated to the*
> *Memory of the natural*
> *Tree-lined Corte Madera Creek*
> *And its tributary, Tamalpais Creek,*
> *destroyed in 1969*
> *By the United States Army*
> *Corps of Engineers.*

Members of the Kent family were often in the news, as they continued their tradition of interest in politics and conservation. Until his death in May 1980, Roger Kent, son of William and Elizabeth was a power in California politics. His brother Sherman had a successful career in U.S. intelligence. Anne Kent (Mrs. Thomas Kent) was a driving force in the effort to preserve Marin County history. A reference room in the Marin County Library was named in her honor after her death in July 1981. It is called the Anne Kent California Room and contains books on California, volumes by California authors, documents, photographs and maps. It also houses the oral history tapes and transcripts of 250 pioneer Marin County families.

Today, the community of Kentfield remains unincorporated, an

*College of Marin, Kentfield.*

area of formal, elegant homes enlivened by a college in its midst.

## The College of Marin

The College of Marin, which is the heart of Kentfield, began in 1926 as a two-year junior college with eighty-five students. Marinites involved in its formation were Thomas Minto and his real estate/insurance partner, Thomas Kent. To establish the college site, they worked without a commission on the sale of property known as the Butler estate. Ernest E. Wood, principal of the Tamalpais High School, used the high school district to receive money raised by public subscription to buy the property. When a college district was formed with official sanctions from Sacramento, the land was turned over from the high school district.

In support of the new school, the Tamalpais Centre and most of the acreage surrounding it were given in 1927 to the Marin Junior College District with the stipulation that the land would forever be used for educational and recreational purposes.

The college used the Tamalpais Centre as an assembly hall. Years later the building was condemned by the local fire department as a hazard and burned in firemen's exercises. The new modern gym was built on the property around 1964.

Today, College of Marin has a seventy-seven-acre campus with more than 10,000 credit students studying in more than 30 vocational and occupational subjects. Another 10,000 attend adult, non-credit courses including active older students who in 1974 opened a senior citizen school known as "Emeritus College." College of Marin also sponsors community classes, programs, and an excellent lecture series. Drama productions are outstanding with such stars emerging as actors Robin Williams, David Dukes and Kathleen Quinlan.

The campus is open from 8:30 A.M. to 10:00 P.M., Monday through Friday. Groups may tour the grounds by making arrangements; call the President's office at 485-9500.

*Carriages gather at the Ross train station to wait for men commuting home from San Francisco, 1895.*

# Ross

The quiet, small town of Ross, just beyond Kentfield, is a place of lovely homes and exclusive estates hidden off shady, tree-lined streets. This area was part of *Rancho Punta de Quintin Canada de San Anselmo* (Quintin Point, Valley of Saint Anselm), an 8,877 acre Mexican land grant awarded to Juan B. R. Cooper in 1940. After extensive logging, Cooper sold to Benjamin Buckelew. In 1857, Buckelew sold the land for $50,000 to James Ross, for whom the town is named.

According to the *1880 History of Marin,* Ross was born in 1812 in Petty, near Inverness, Scotland. At age seventeen, he left for Tasmania (formerly Van Diemen's Land), an island to the south of Australia, where he met and married Anne S. Grayling in 1839. The couple lived in New South Wales, Australia. In 1849, James Ross joined the rush to California leaving the family in Australia until he was established in 1852. Instead of mining for gold, James opened a wholesale wine business in San Francisco, where he worked until 1857 when he bought Buckelew's land in Marin. Ross rebuilt the Buckelew seven-bedroom home near the present town hall and moved there with his wife and three children. The estate included orchards, gardens, and a windmill.

After his death, Ross's wife Anne sold off much of the land. She also deeded one and four-tenths acres to the town for a North Pacific Coast Railroad station, now the site of the Ross Post Office and a beautifully landscaped park on the north side. Residents have placed a white stone bench here dedicated to Ross civic leader Benjamin Harrison Dibblee, 1876-1945.

Mrs. Ross also donated another site near the railroad tracks for the valley's first church. This area is now a tiny park at the southwest corner of Sir Francis Drake Boulevard and Lagunitas Road, across the street from the town hall. A plaque reads "On this spot stood San Anselmo Chapel, Protestant Episcopal, the first place of worship in the Ross Valley, built in 1881 on ground given by Mrs. A.S. Ross." As the Episcopalian congregation grew, the tiny chapel became too small and was torn down.

Anne Ross sold the family home and twenty-three acres in 1885, but the lovely old house burned in 1897. She lived in a small home across from the Ross train station until her death in 1901.

Ross incorporated in 1908, and, at the first meeting of the town council, moved to protect the trees in the area by making it illegal to cut them without permission. Soon the streets were paved, streetlights installed, concrete bridges built over the creek, and a firehouse constructed. Land for the Ross Commons was sold to the town by Ross's daughter, Annie Ross Worn, in 1911. In 1927, a town hall and new firehouse were built on Sir Francis Drake Boulevard and remain in use today.

Ross is the home of a fine private college-preparatory day school (grades nine through twelve) called The Branson School which is located on Fernhill Avenue on the old Albert Dibblee estate.

Dibblee owned seventy-eight acres of orchards, gardens, and rolling grounds plus a mansion called Fernhill. It was one of several huge estates established in this area in the late nineteenth century.

The school, at first coeducational and called the Little Gray School, was founded in San Rafael by a group of parents in 1916. In 1920, Miss Katharine Fleming Branson came from the East Coast to become its first headmistress, and the trustees renamed the school in her honor. Two years later, the school moved to the present Ross campus. In 1972, the trustees founded Mount Tamalpais School for boys on the same campus. In 1985, the school was renamed The Branson School.

Another prominent institution in Ross, also on the site of an old estate, is the Marin Art and Garden Center, located on Sir Francis Drake Boulevard. It is surrounded by an unusual red brick serpentine wall built in memory of Caroline Livermore, the original founder. The Center contains facilities for a variety of nonprofit groups that run a children's playground, display art and crafts, sell antiques, present flower shows, sponsor theatrical productions, operate a restaurant, present summer fashion shows, and maintains a unique library.

The Center was founded in 1945 with the purchase of ten acres from A. J. Kittle, a member of the first Ross Town Council. Kittle had decided to sell his land, part of an estate once owned by Annie Ross Worn and her husband George. The Worns' house, known as Sunnyside, was remodeled by the Kittles but partially burned in 1931 and was eventually destroyed.

Caroline Livermore, the president of the Marin Conservation League, wanted to save the lovely gardens, which contained a magnificent old magnolia tree and a giant sequoia. She organized a nonprofit group to buy the land and develop the Center's activities.

Among the founder groups were the Marin Conservation League, The Garden Society of Marin, the Marin Garden Club, Marin Society of Artists, Ross Valley Players (which celebrated its sixtieth anniversary in 1990), and the Marin Music Chest.

Affiliate groups who make this such an important center for cultural activities now include the Decorations Guild; Northgate Group, which sponsors outdoor luncheons, table displays, and fashion shows; Laurel House Antiques, a consignment shop open

*The Jose Moya del Pino Library in the Octagon House in the Marin Art and Garden Center, Ross.*

11:00 A.M. to 4:00 P.M. Tuesday-Friday and Mondays for consignments from 10:00 A.M. to 2:00 P.M. (454-8472); Pixie Parents, a preschool co-op parents' club, which built and maintains a unique playground; Center Pathfinders, who operate the Center's restaurant with volunteers and donate the profits to the Center; and the Jose Moya del Pino Library in the Octagon House, which contains reference volumes on art and gardens.

From 1950 to 1971, the Marin County Fair was held at the Center and is remembered for the lovely gardens (many of Japanese design), flowers, and displays of original art. This fair is now held at the Marin County Civic Center in San Rafael.

You may visit the Marin Art and Garden Center on Sir Francis Drake Boulevard and Laurel Grove from 9:00 A.M. to 4:00 P.M. For information on rentals or the Pixie Playground call 454-5597. In the Center office you can see an old photo of the Kittle estate.

The Ross Garden Restaurant serves lunch from 11:30 A.M. to 2:00 P.M., Tuesday-Friday (456-7870). The Frances Young Gallery operated by the Marin Society of Artists is open from 11:00 A.M. to 4:00 P.M., Monday-Thursday and 12:00 P.M. to 4:00 P.M. on Saturday and Sunday (454-9561). The Gallery contains art for sale, a rental gallery (the only one in Marin), and displays of sculpture and crafts including jewelry, woven textiles, ceramics, furniture, cut glass, and clothes.

The Barn, a theater used by the Ross Valley Players, has a seating capacity of 300. There are usually five or six shows, including one musical, produced here yearly. Phone 456-9555 for a recording of current productions.

Luncheons and summer fashion shows held outdoors in the Northgate area can serve up to 500 people. This section of the Art and Garden Center is often used for weddings, as is the Livermore Room.

Across from the Art and Garden Center at Lagunitas Road is the Ross firehouse. In front of it is a large statue of a bear cast in compressed marble dust, designed by the late famous sculptor, Benjamino Bufano. The bear was donated by Jerome and Peggy Flax in 1971.

Cross the bridge on Lagunitas Road and turn left to reach the six-acre Ross Commons Town Park, which is in the center of Ross. The area is used mostly for sports by children attending the adjacent Ross Grammar School. In the summer of 1989, a one-hundred-year-old school house, donated by Richard and Clara Hoertkorn, was relocated to a corner of the Ross Commons. It will be restored by the Ross Historical Society and eventually opened as a museum.

On Ross Commons and Poplar Avenue just beyond, there are shops—exclusive clothing stores, a butcher shop, grocery and small restaurant.

About a mile from the center of Ross is the lovely Natalie Coffin Greene Park, twenty-five acres beside a winding creek. There are picnic tables, an open stone house with a fireplace, and privies. The facilities were originally constructed in the 1930s by C.C.C. labor when the property was owned by the water district.

The land was purchased in 1967 with a donation of $15,000 to the town of Ross from A. Crawford Greene in memory of his wife. To get there, drive west on Lagunitas Road. The park is open from sunrise to sunset. No parking is allowed around the gate at anytime, and no motorcycles, buses, or trailers may enter the park. Pets must be on a leash.

Beyond the park, about a five-minute walk, is Phoenix Lake. This reservoir belongs to the Marin Municipal Water District. All the lakes are stocked by the California Department of Fish and Game.

As you hike up the road, on the right you will pass an old stone kiln built in the shape of a beehive. A little farther on the left is a new (1986) spillway. This long, narrow cement water-run looks like a huge children's water slide in an amusement park. At the bottom the water cascades over some jagged rocks before flowing into a creek.

The lake is open for fishing from sunrise to sunset; a valid California fishing license is required. Facilities here include benches and privies. A trail surrounding the lake is popular with cyclists, hikers and joggers. It takes forty-five minutes to an hour to walk around.

# San Anselmo

After winding through Ross on tree-shaded, two-lane Sir Francis Drake Boulevard, you will come to the town of San Anselmo. Here the street becomes a four-lane divided boulevard for the short distance to the "Hub," an intersection of five streets with a total of twenty-one lanes of traffic. At this point, Sir Francis Drake Boulevard makes an abrupt left turn and continues northwest to Fairfax. Red Hill Avenue (also called the "Miracle Mile") goes to the east and into San Rafael.

San Anselmo was originally two land grants. The *Rancho Punta de Quintin,* mentioned in connection with the San Quentin peninsula and the town of Ross, ran approximately to the top of Red Hill in San Anselmo; and the *Canada de Herrera* (Valley of the Blacksmith), awarded to Domingo Sais, was in the northern section.

The grandparents of Sais migrated from Mexico to Monterey, California, around 1772. Don Domingo, born in 1805, was a soldier at the Presidio in Yerba Buena (San Francisco) and a member of the militia from 1826 to 1837. From 1837 to 1839 he was an elector and civil authority called a "Regidor." In 1839, he received two leagues of land in Marin County in return for military and public services. This Mexican land grant included 6,658.35 acres of land where north San Anselmo, Fairfax, and part of San Geronimo Valley are located today.

Sais's first house was made of tule rushes and was located in the San Anselmo area known as Landsdale. A finer house of adobe, called La Pavidion, was later built on the south side of Sir Francis Drake Boulevard, Here, Sais and his wife, the former Manuella

Augustina Miranda, raised seven children. Sais died in 1853, In 1868, a survey was made of the property and the ranch was broken up, with some portions going to the heirs and other parts sold.

In 1881, George and Annie Worn, son-in-law and daughter of Anne and James Ross, subdivided a portion of their *Rancho Punta de Quintin* in the area of San Anselmo they called Sunnyside. Several big portions were sold off, but mortgage problems forced them to sell the land at public auction in 1886. The sale of "villa sites" continued under new ownership.

The railroad arrived in 1875 and officials renamed the growing town "The Junction," as this was the point where the train tracks split for West Marin and continued north to Cazadero in Sonoma County, with a branch line running southeast to San Rafael. The name lasted until 1883 when the original name of San Anselmo was reinstated.

Commute service to San Francisco improved in 1903 when the old narrow-gauge railroad was double-tracked and a new electric railroad was built using an electric third rail for power. It now took only fifty-five minutes, via train and ferry, from San Anselmo to the Ferry Building in San Francisco.

Many visitors came to the area, arriving by train to picnic and camp along San Anselmo Creek. Summer homes began to be built, and then a large number of vacationers moved to San Anselmo permanently after the 1906 earth-quake and fire in San Francisco.

San Anselmo incorporated in 1907, a volunteer fire department was organized, and a city hall was built in 1911 on land donated by James Tunstead, the former county sheriff. The downtown area that grew up around the city hall, one block west of San Anselmo Avenue, is the heart of San Anselmo today. Access streets include Bolinas Avenue, Ross Avenue, and Tunstead Avenue.

In front of the remodeled city hall is a handsome cast-iron deer that once stood in the gardens of the large Dondero estate in the North Beach section of San Francisco. After the 1906 earthquake and fire, the deer was all that remained of the Dondero home. The family moved to San Anselmo in 1914 and brought this graceful animal to decorate the front of their new home. When the house was sold in 1963, Daisy Dondero donated the deer to the town of San Anselmo.

The police and fire departments and post office are all located on San Anselmo Avenue. The library is next to the police depart-

*Children picnic in front of the San Anselmo City Hall.*

ment but fronts on Tunstead Avenue. San Anselmo's Historical Museum, open Tuesday morning and Saturday afternoon, is located in the back of this building and uses the same address as the library, 110 Tunstead Ave. Visitors may check out the "Self-Guided Tour of Downtown San Anselmo," prepared for the San Anselmo Historical Commission by David Leuck and Claire Villa in 1978. (258-4666)

San Anselmo has many delightful shops, offering such things as original handcrafted jewelry, pottery, Indian crafts, and miniature furniture for dollhouses.

Of special interest is the Paper Pile at 20 Woodland Avenue, just off San Anselmo Avenue. Ada Fitzsimmons collects paper, including old maps, postcards, special issue magazines and newspapers, famous and infamous memorabilia of celebrities, old ads, and a hundred more categories. She sells these by mail to collectors from all over the world, and also helps writers with research projects. The Paper Pile is the only such shop in Marin and open by appointment. (454-5552)

An unusual shopping mall is the Courtyard which contains specialty shops, clothing for children, gardens designs, antiques and an Italian restaurant.

"Love 30" is a delightful tennis shop owned by Sally Robbins and Thomas Bowman. Whether you need a new graphite racket, balls, shoes or clothes, you can find it at 631 San Anselmo Avenue.

Throughout the town there is a wide variety of antique shops; in fact, San Anselmo is known as the "Antique Capital of Northern California." Beginning at the Hub are the Pavillion Antiques, a collection of 45 dealers at 610 Sir Francis Drake. Moving southeast on Sir Francis Drake Boulevard is an antique store at 332, the Tamalpais Theater and the Collective Antiques containing 45 shops.

More single stores follow selling antiques, gifts, flowers, fine arts, oriental rugs and the popular dress shop, Ten Bank Street Boutique which is owned and operated by Sydney Halladay at 226 Sir Francis Drake Blvd. This is followed by a travel operator, Ted's (bar and restaurant), another antique store, Italian restaurant and Hunter's Depot with 34 more antique shops. The business section ends with the Merryvale House and Garden and Winkler's Restaurant at 198. Additional antique stores are found on Pine St. and throughout the town. Shoppers browsing through these shops will find a selection of wicker, glass, porcelain, brass, oak objects, antique clocks, stained glass, furniture and jewelry.

In the north end of the downtown area, between Sir Francis Drake Boulevard and San Anselmo Creek, is picturesque Creek Park, designed by former San Anselmo planning commissioner Dan Goltz and landscape architect Paul Leffingwell. This park contains two acres of land with grassy knolls, benches, picnic tables, and a lovely arbor.

The trains are gone but not forgotten. The old train depot along Center Boulevard adjacent to Creek Park is now a bus stop.

The San Anselmo Community Center is located at 237 Crescent Road in the old seventeen-room Robson-Harrington house. Built in 1910 by lumber magnate Edwin Kleber Wood, the estate was sold in 1922 to Mr. and Mrs. Kernan Robson, who added extensive gardens, orchards, a vineyard, and unusual walls made of bricks. The bricks with melted glaze were salvaged from San Francisco after the 1906 earthquake and fire.

Still here, today, are arches, tile fountains, and Italian pottery and ceramic works. The grounds cover two-and-a-half acres with both palm and redwood trees in front, a large lawn area in back, fourteen picnic sites, barbecues, and a small plaza with benches.

*San Francisco Theological Seminary in San Anselmo.*

Below the plaza is a children's playground.

The house itself is open only by appointment. Over the years this community center has been used for meetings, classes, conferences, a variety of cultural events, parties, and receptions. The grounds are open until 9:00 P.M. (453-1602)

To get there, turn west on Woodland Avenue off San Anselmo Avenue. Woodland jogs to the right and runs into Crescent before making a left turn. Continue straight on Crescent until you reach number 237.

## The San Francisco Theological Seminary

San Anselmo became an important spot on the map of Northern California when the San Francisco Theological Seminary moved there in 1892. This seminary of the United Presbyterian Church was founded by Dr. William Anderson Scott, who was sent to the booming frontier town of San Francisco to establish a church and a Presbyterian college and seminary.

Scott ran into some problems in San Francisco—he was hanged in effigy twice and run out of town for opposing the Committee of Vigilance and for mentioning Jefferson Davis and Abraham Lincoln in the same pastoral prayer. Scott managed to recover,

*Outside dining in San Anselmo.*

however and achieve his goal. The Seminary began classes in San Francisco in 1871.

In 1873, Scott's daughter, Louisiana, married Arthur Foster, president of the North Pacific Coast Railroad. Foster later donated nineteen acres in San Anselmo for a new seminary site.

In 1891, stonemasons began construction of two buildngs out of hand-cut blue stone quarried in San Rafael. Montgomery Hall and Scott Hall still tower today, like medieval castles, above the town of San Anselmo. The buildings were paid for out of a $250,000 gift from Alexander Montgomery, a San Francisco businessman. When Montgomery died in 1893, he left $50,000 for a crypt to be built for his remains inside a memorial chapel.

Today the San Francisco Theological Seminary is the second largest Presbyterian seminary in the United States. About eight hundred students per year come here from all around the world to receive their training.

The twenty-one-acre campus is located at 2 Kensington. To visit, turn west off Sir Francis Drake Boulevard onto Bolinas Avenue, the street that divides San Anselmo from Ross. A self-guided walking tour and free brochure may be obtained in the reception area of the office located on the corner of Kensington and Bolinas. It is open from 9:00 A.M. to 5:00 P.M. Monday through Friday. For more information call the Office of Seminary Relations, 258-6500.

## Following Sir Francis Drake Boulevard to Fairfax

Look northwest from the Hub and you will see Red Hill, a mound of earth scarred by cracks of red dirt eroding down the sides. There are some duplexes built on this hill which native San Anselmo residents watch with more than casual interest. The whole top of the hill gave way in 1967 after a heavy rainstorm and slid down on four similar apartments. Fortunately, they were unoccupied at the time.

Below the hill, at 892 Sir Francis Drake Boulevard, is the Red Hill Shopping Center, which contains a wide variety of stores, large and small.

The four tennis courts at Memorial Park are just northwest of the Red Hill Shopping Center. This nine-acre park contains two Little League baseball fields and a regular baseball field with a 400-foot outfield and bleachers that will seat up to 300 people. There are also a soccer field, which sometimes doubles for a football field, a children's playground, and a few picnic tables.

The American Legion Log Cabin is located here at 120 Sonoma Avenue. Turn northeast off Sir Francis Drake Boulevard onto San Francisco Boulevard. Go two blocks, then turn right on Sonoma Avenue. The Log Cabin was built in 1934 by volunteers for use by the American Legion, Boy Scouts, and other groups in the community. This popular center is still in full use today. (459-9932)

A good hiking area over hilly terrain is Sorich Ranch Park, which can be reached by following San Francisco Boulevard to the end. Here are sixty-three acres of open space, but the facilities are limited to one picnic table.

Another hiking area farther southwest is Faude Park, a fifteen-acre parcel of open space donated in 1973 to the town of San Anselmo by C. Frederick Faude, a resident of Marin County for many years. The park may be reached by following Sir Francis Drake Boulevard to the first stop light past Drake High School. Turn right on Broadmoor Avenue and follow it to the end. Turn right on Indian Rock Road and go to the top of the hill, then turn right on Tomahawk Drive for one block to the entrance of the park.

Faude Park is good for hiking, but there are no facilities available. The land is hilly open space with a scattering of trees and is used mainly by local residents.

Butterfield Road leads from Sir Francis Drake Boulevard into Sleepy Hollow, an area of ranch-style homes, many with their own corrals and stables. At the end of Butterfield Road is San Domenico School, a Catholic girls' school on what was once an old dairy ranch, then a golf course.

# Fairfax

**M**r. Alfred Taliaferro sailed to California from Virginia in 1849 to seek gold. He eventually built a home in Fairfax on thirty-one acres of the old Sais Ranch, in the area now known as the Marin Town and Country Club.

In 1855, this property was acquired from Taliaferro by his good friend and fellow Virginian, Charles Snowden Fairfax, for whom the town was named. Fairfax, officially Lord Fairfax, Tenth Baron of Cameron, was born in 1829, a member of the State of Virginia Fairfax family. His ancestor, through his mother's side of the family, was Thomas, Lord Culpepper. He had received the land in Virginia in 1649 as a royal grant by Charles II, King of England. The land, known as the Northern Neck of Virginia, "bounded by and within the heads" of the Potomac and Rappahannock rivers, passed to Thomas, Lord Fairfax, Sixth Baron of Cameron. Thomas's niece, Anne Fairfax, married their next-door neighbor, Lawrence Washington, older brother to George. Lawrence built the family home at Mt. Vernon. (In 1747, George Washington, age 15, had been employed to survey the Fairfax land, more than five million acres.)

Charles Snowden Fairfax moved to California in 1849. Unsuccessful at mining, he entered politics and was elected to the state assembly in 1853, serving as speaker in 1854. In 1855, he married Ada Benham. Their Fairfax home, called Bird's Nest Glen, was situated in a lovely sylvan valley. The family was famous for its Southern hospitality. Entertainment was lavish and bottles of champagne were kept cooling in the creek for refreshment during summer walks.

A famous duel was fought near Fairfax's estate in January 1861. His two friends, Daniel Showalter, a Democrat from Kentucky,

*Fairfax when the train ran through the town around 1920.* Arrigoni Family Collection.

and Charles Piercy, a Republican from Illinois, had disagreed politically. The three men ate lunch together before the duel and Fairfax tried to dissuade them, but they persisted. Charles Piercy was killed by a shot from Showalter's rifle. The Kentuckian was indicted for murder by the Marin Grand Jury but fled the county before he could be arrested.

Bill Allen, President of the Fairfax Historical Society, believes the actual site of the duel was in San Anselmo. He writes, "John Murray, son of William Murray, who settled where Murray Park is today, remembers seeing, as a boy, the combantants leave the Fairfax estate, and walk down the open field towards Landsdale. After the duel was over and all the participants had departed, he visited the spot where the duel was fought. He remembers seeing some of the blood spilled when Piercy was shot. The location according to John was the location of the old Landsdale Yolanda School."

Charles Fairfax continued his political career. He was elected to the Marin County Board of Supervisors and also spent five years as clerk of the California Supreme Court. In 1868, he put his affairs in order including having the title of Bird's Nest Glen cleared, then went east to the Democratic Convention being held in New York. Already suffering from tuberculosis, Lord Charles Snowden Fairfax died at the home of his mother in Baltimore, Maryland on April 4, 1869. (Although Charles never claimed the title Baron of Cameron, his nephew later went to England, assumed it, and the titled family line continued. They now reside on an estate north of London.)

After Charles's death, the thirty-one acre estate was sold by Ada Fairfax to Mary and Peter Owens. The site was later sold again to George Wright, then to Emma Woodward and in 1905 to Charles and Adele Pastori. Pastori was a well-known chef, and his wife Adele, was a former opera singer at La Scala in Milan, Italy and in England. Her daughter, Tina, claimed that her mother lost her voice singing on the English operatic stage because of the English fogs. Charles and Adele opened an Italian restaurant, providing outstanding cuisine to visitors coming by train from San Francisco.

After Pastori died, the restaurant burned but was rebuilt by Adele. In 1925, the Emporium Stores purchased the property to use as a club for employees. Between 1937 and 1943, it was leased to the Marin Boys School. In 1943, Max Friedman bought it and a year later opened the Marin Town and Country Club for dancing, swimming and wading (in seven separate pools), picnicking, and baseball. The club remained open until 1972.

Over the years, the town of Fairfax became well-known for picnics held in the Fairfax Park and the Pavilion, built in 1921, on the site of an ancient Indian mound. To raise money for equipment, members of the Volunteer Fire Department brought in big bands to play in the Pavilion in the twenties and thirties. They also sponsored a bang-up Fourth of July picnic.

In the Manor Hill area of Fairfax, a funicular railroad was opened in 1913 to provide access to building lots. It was modeled after funiculars Edward S. Holt had seen in the mountains of Europe. With his partner, Prentis Gray, he organized the Fairfax Incline Railroad Company. The car, built on three levels, held twenty-six passengers for the ride up the 500-foot hillside. To help sell lots adjacent to the funicular, auctions were held with big barbecues, beer drinking, and entertainment. The lots sold for $200 and $400. In 1929, the funicular was declared unsafe and was abandoned in 1930.

Fairfax, today, still maintains its small-town atmosphere. Where the old station stood in the middle of town, there is a parking lot landscaped with trees, bushes, flowers and benches. On the corner of Broadway Street and Bolinas Avenue stands a popular

*Funicular runs up Manor Hill off Scenic Road in Fairfax around 1914.*
Arrigoni Family Collection.

old-fashioned soft drink bar called The Corner Cafe where the
Fairfax Park Annex Building once stood. It was removed in 1919
and replaced with the present day Alpine Building which was
opened originally as a grocery store and ice cream parlor. Old
photographs remain of early western films being shot in this area
by the Essanay Film Manufacturing Company. Many movies, featuring Bronco Billy Andersen, were made here, and the wild west
locations were filmed on Bolinas Road, past Deer Park Villa.

Other studios who used Fairfax to shoot included the
Keanograph Factory between 1913-1915, the Testa Photo Studio
in 1921, and the Navarra Picture Corporation in 1922. An epilogue
to this story is that in February 1989, filmmakers George Lucas
and Steven Spielberg were back in Fairfax at Deer Park School
for five days shooting scenes for a new movie starring Harrison
Ford and Sean Connery. The film was called "Indiana Jones
and the Last Crusade," and was the third in a trilogy which included "Raiders of the Lost Ark" and "Indiana Jones and the
Temple of Doom."

The downtown shopping area of Fairfax runs along Sir Francis
Drake Boulevard, Broadway Street (which parallels Sir Francis

*The Fairfax Library.*

Drake), and southwest on Bolinas Road. Fairfax has many unique shops, selling everything from antiques to fine-conditioned
used clothing such as the popular shop, Savvy, 1828 Sir Francis
Drake, Savvy, owned by Cynthia Shone, also offers salesman's
samples, jewelry and accessories.

People also come from all over the county to shop at the well-
stocked Fairfax Lumber at 109 Broadway which has been in
business over 75 years. Larry McFadden, president, and his
friendly staff offer a full-service lumber yard, hardware supplies
and nursery.

Residents patronize the local variety store at 61 Broadway for
the same reason: it supplies everything imaginable.

One of my favorite restaurants in the county is Pucci's, owned
and operated by Enrico and Tony Pucci at 35 Broadway. Pucci,
a superb cook, serves homemade Italian pastas, desserts and a
variety of fresh seafood, meats and vegetarian specialties such
as eggplant parmigiana, ravioli with spinach and ricotta.

Another Italian restaurant, Deer Park Villa, owned by the
Ghiringhelli family, has been in business for fifty years serving
outstanding selections of veal, seafood, pastas, beef and chicken.
Their park-like setting on Bolinas Road provides a popular place
for weddings, anniversary parties and other celebrations.

Finally there is my favorite gourmet grocery, Food Villa, at 1966 Sir Francis Drake Boulevard owned by Larry Galetti. It is a friendly small-town grocery where you never have to wait in line to check out. Larry displays some fascinating old Fairfax photos and sets up a toy train at Christmas to the delight of his customers. The grocery also has an excellent meat department owned by John Puccinelli who makes his own sausages. You can even sign up your children to play Little League here.

The lovely Fairfax Library, a branch of the Marin County Library system, is located at 2097 Sir Francis Drake Boulevard, just northwest of the downtown area. This was the side of the old Buon Gusto Restaurant, originally the "Firenze Villa" owned by P. Recommi. He sold it to a Mr. Andreazzi, owner of a restaurant called Buon Gusto in San Francisco. In 1913, Mr. Andreazzi sold Buon Gusto to the great-grandfather of former Fairfax Police Chief Chuck Grasso. The restaurant was purchased in 1922 by Fiori Giannini, whose family ran it for another forty-four years. His daughter, Eleanor McArdle Jean, sold the property to the county in 1976 for a library.

The library is on three-and-a-half acres of rolling oak-studded hills with lovely views. The building, designed by architect Woody Stockwell is constructed of warm woods, lots of glass to allow an open outdoor feeling, and a wide deck with a rustic view. In the meeting room is a beautiful mural painted by Glen Dines, local author and artist. A plaque on the fireplace notes that it was donated by the Peter Arrigoni family in memory of Peter's mother, Rose Divita Arrigoni, 1910-1975.

Many people come to Fairfax for the excellent riding stables in the area, the tennis clubs, and the famous Meadow Club, a private golf course with a beautiful old clubhouse used by local residents for wedding receptions and parties. The club members celebrated their fiftieth anniversary in 1977.

Other visitors come to picnic in the 4.7-acre Fairfax Town Park on Bolinas Road and Park Road adjacent to the town hall, police and fire station. The park has a creek and majestic old redwood trees, picnic tables, a children's playground, and tennis courts.

The fifty-three-acre Deer Park is reached by driving four-tenths of a mile south on Porteous Avenue off Bolinas Road. This is also the location of the Deer Park Elementary School now used by the Fairfax-San Anselmo Children's Center. Picnic tables are scat-

tered under tall redwoods beside a creek. Facilities include
barbecues and privies. There are several scenic hiking trails, but
beware of poison oak. Open 7:00 A.M. to 10:00 P.M.

# The Water District Lakes

F ive pristine alpine lakes are maintained by the Marin
Municipal Water District on watershed land. Two additional
lakes, Nicasio and Soulajule, are located on private watershed lands devoted primarily to agriculture. The lakes are
reservoirs for the county's drinking water, so no boating and swimming are allowed. Fishing is permitted and avid fishermen can
always be found along the banks.

The most popular fishing lakes—Bon Tempe, Lagunitas, and
Alpine—are also the easiest to reach. Drive south on Bolinas Road
from Fairfax for one and a half miles. Turn left at a sign that says
"Crest Farm." You will pass through a gate which is open from
8:00 A.M. to sunset. Crest Farm is a private residence on the
right; continue straight to reach the lakes. Half a mile later you
will arrive at The Sky Oaks Ranger Station (459-0888 or 459-5267)
where you will be charged an entrance fee of $3 per vehicle (up
to eight people per vehicle allowed). A sign will direct you to the
lakes, just a short hike.

You can reach all the lakes (except Nicasio and Soulajule) from
this trailhead on connecting trails. Phoenix Lake is also accessible through the town of Ross. Kent Lake may be reached by hiking east from Sir Francis Drake Boulevard near the town of
Lagunitas.

The lakes are regularly stocked with trout. Special fishing regula-
tions apply to Lake Lagunitas. At Lake Lagunitas you will find
several picnic areas with tables scattered among redwood trees.
A picturesque covered spillway leads up to the lake. You may walk
up the trail next to the spillway or use the road which leads up
the left side of the dam from the parking lot, marked "Protection
Road." Horse trails encircle both Lakes Lagunitas and Bon Tempe.

Alpine Dam, built in 1917 primarily by Italian-American labor
and raised twice to its present level, may be reached by driving
south on Bolinas Road from Fairfax for a distance of six miles.
This road continues to Route 1 on the Pacific coast near Bolinas.

It is a beautiful ride, but the road is narrow and exposed to strong winds. It may be closed for several days at a time in summer and fall because of fire hazard. The dam itself is an interesting structure, with a cubist honeycomb design on the south side. It has been compared to an ancient amphitheater.

*Downstream face of Alpine Dam looking south—July 7, 1918.* From the collection of Nancy M. Skinner.

# San Rafael 8

## From Mission Town to County Seat

S an Rafael, seventeen miles north of San Francisco, is the oldest and largest of Marin's cities, and also serves as its county seat. The downtown area, built up around the old mission, is nestled below San Rafael Hill. In the last three decades, the city, with a population of 48,885, has spread beyond the downtown area to the adjacent hills: to the southeast on either side of the San Rafael Canal; to the east along Point San Pedro Road; to the north to Santa Venetia and the Frank Lloyd Wright-designed Civic Center; and beyond to the large residential areas in Terra Linda, Marinwood, and Lucas Valley.

The city of San Rafael had its beginnings in 1817 with the founding of a Spanish mission (the twentieth in the chain of twenty-one in California), built as a northern outpost against the threat of a Russian invasion into Spanish territory. Already the Russian American Company had established a fort in Sonoma County, and Russians were occupying Bodega Bay on the north. They were occupied with the slaughter of sea otters.

Initially, the Mission San Rafael Arcangel, named for Saint Raphael, the angel of bodily healing, was an *asistencia* or "helper" mission used as a sanitorium for Indians from the Mission San Francisco de Asis (Dolores).

When the Spanish founded the San Francisco mission in 1776, they used Indian labor to do the actual construction. Many were Coast Miwok Indians who were taken from their homeland in Marin (see Miwok Indian Village, Kule Loklo, Chapter 11).

*West End, San Rafael looking down 5th Street. (4th Street on the right) Mansion Row is upper left known then as 6th Street. Across the street in front is "H" (1880s).* Courtesy Marin Historical Society.

By the time the mission was complete, the Spanish had converted many of the Indians to Catholicism. Despite their supposed spiritual health, the Indians were often sick and many died from their forced dislocation. Changes of food, clothing, housing, and an unfamiliar damp climate proved deadly to them. In addition, thousands died of tuberculosis and the so-called "childhood diseases" such as measles and chicken pox. In 1812, at Mission Dolores, every child under twelve years died, and Presidio soldiers were sent out to dig mass graves. Final records show that out of 6,536 Indians baptized at the San Francisco mission, 5,037 died.

Father Gil y Toboada, a padre with some medical knowledge, took over the asistencia in San Rafael from 1817 to 1819. A hospital, chapel, priests' quarters, and storeroom were built of adobe. Reportedly, the mission building consisted of a chapel and a long single-story structure forming an L shape. It had a red tile roof with rafters held together by strips of rawhide.

Father Gil began planting an orchard of pear trees. The surrounding hills were stocked with cattle and sheep, horses and hogs. Indians were taught to care for the animals and to farm, cook, clean, spin wool, and make clothes.

In 1822, the little asistencia became a full-fledged mission. That was also the year that Spain's rule of California was assumed by

Mexico. As the Spanish missions grew in power, their rivalry with the new Mexican authories became intense.

By 1928, the Mission San Rafael Arcangel could boast of 1,140 Indian converts living there. The mission lands thrived. Two years later there were 8 buildings, 2,000 horses and cattle, fields of wheat, barley, and corn, plus 10 acres of orchards and vineyards.

Not all the Indians gave in without a struggle to serving the Spanish padres. An Indian named Pomponio, a San Rafael area native, defied the Spaniards and even cut off his own heel to escape a leg iron. In 1823, Pomponio was captured for the second time and and executed in Monterey. Around the same time, a band of a thousand Indians enraged over the killing of an Indian boy by a riotous Mexican soldier, attacked the Mission San Rafael and burned several buildings.

Chief Marin, for whom the county is reportedly named, (the county also may have gotten its title from the Latin word 'Marinera' which was part of a name on a 1775 map), and his war chief, Quintin, attacked the mission in San Rafael. Marin's successful raids resulted in an expedition being sent to subdue him. He was captured in Bodega and taken to the San Francisco Presidio to be converted, but escaped and continued raiding until he was recaptured nine years later. In the end, according to legend, Chief Marin and Quintin were eventually subdued and worked as skilled mariners for the padres. Marin died at Mission San Rafael Arcangel in 1834.

The year 1834 also saw the mission taken over by the Mexican civil government. Rivalry between the Spanish missionaries and the Mexicans had reached a crisis, and the Mexican government had passed a decree of secularization which transferred all mission lands to the state. The Spanish Franciscan friars were exiled and replaced with Mexican Franciscans. General Mariano Vallejo was appointed administrator of the San Rafael mission. He used his position to confiscate much of the mission's equipment and land.

A group of the remaining Coast Miwok Indians was taken to a parcel in Nicasio called 'Tinicasia' (now Halleck''s Valley) given to them by General Vallejo who forgot to file the Indian claim at Monterey. Genial Don Timoteo Murphy, a kind Irishman who spoke the Coast Miwok language with an Irish brogue, was made overseer of the Indians. Murphy, a muscular man who stood at least six feet, two-and-a-half inches (one report says six feet, seven inches) did his best to help the Miwok, but few made the adjustment to "civilized" life.

Murphy was rewarded for his work with the Indians with a land grant of three leagues (nearly 22,000 acres) from the Mexican governor, Micheltorena. The grant was called *San Pedro, Santa Margarita, y Las Gallinas* (Saint Peter, Saint Margaret, and the Hens). This area included what is now known as northeast and east San Rafael to San Pedro Point, and north to the subdivisions of Terra Linda, Marinwood, and Lucas Valley.

In the late 1830s and 40s, despite Murphy's kind efforts, the Indians were taken advantage of in every way possible. Some Indian children were forcefully taken from their parents and sold as servants to California ranchos farther south.

The end of the Coast Miwok Indian came during the Gold Rush, 1849-55, with three laws passed by the new California state legislature. The first law stated that an Indian could not testify in court. The second declared that any white man could bring an Indian to court and have the Indian declared a vagrant, thus subjecting him to sale by auction to the highest bidder. The third law stated that any native child or adult could be bound over to a white citizen. This made it possible for the Indians to be used as slave labor. The Indians, already decimated by illness, now had no rights in this new society, no way to defend themselves against the white man and keep their way of life intact. A civilization that had evolved over thousands of years was thus destroyed in half a century.

By 1840, the Mission San Rafael Arcangel was all but abandoned. The only life came from the orchard trees that continued to bear fruit. In 1846, the California Bear Flag replaced the Mexican flag and was in turn replaced by the Stars and Stripes.

Prosperity came to San Rafael with the Gold Rush. Saloons, hotels, and boardinghouses were built almost overnight. Streets, identified by numbers and letters, were laid out and lots divided up. In 1851, Marin became one of the twenty-seven original counties in California, and San Rafael was awarded the county seat. One of the old mission buildings was converted into a town meeting hall, court, and jail. In 1853, when Don Timoteo Murphy passed away, the new county government was moved into this two-story adobe house on the corner of Fourth and C streets.

The last old mission building was razed around 1860 for salvageable timbers. The remaining orchard became a campground for passing gypsies and a park for picnicking and for political rallies.

In the 1860s, the town continued to grow. The first public school opened in San Rafael in 1861, and a newspaper began publication. The Civil War broke out, creating conflicts between Marin citizens, some sympathizing with the North, others loyal to the South.

By the end of that decade, the San Rafael and San Quentin Railroad was completed, making fast access to San Francisco a reality. Suddenly, San Rafael became the retreat of wealthy residents of San Francisco. Elegant new mansions were built, many near the center of town. Fashionable resort hotels were constructed, including the luxurious 200-room Hotel Rafael built on a twenty-one-acre site by James M. Donahue and William Tell Coleman in what is now the Dominican area. Patrons of Hotel Rafael enjoyed leisurely meals, attended dances, and played tennis. They could also go to see productions staged in Gordon's Opera House at Fourth and D streets. (This later became a movie house, the Star Theater.)

In keeping with the town's prosperous look, a new Marin County courthouse was dedicated August 3, 1872, and construction began. Completed in March 1873 at a cost of $51,000, it was designed in a Greek Revival style with tall columns and an imposing set of steps. The building lasted nearly one hundred years, finally being destroyed by fire in 1971.

In 1874, San Rafael incorporated. For the next several decades, it experienced the same spurts of growth as did other areas of the county. A tent city was erected in San Rafael for survivors of the 1906 earthquake and fire in San Francisco. Many refugees stayed permanently, increasing the population of San Rafael by 60 percent. Other boosts in population came with the building of Hamilton Field between 1933 and 1935, the opening of the Golden Gate Bridge in 1937, and World War II. New housing developments were welcomed with enthusiasm.

Throughout all these years, the trees in the old "Priest's Orchard" on the former mission grounds continued to bear fruit. In 1929, Richard Lohrmann, a San Rafael nurseryman, took a graft from one of the last pear trees just before an apartment house was built on the orchard site at Fifth and Lootens streets. By 1934, there was only one pear tree left.

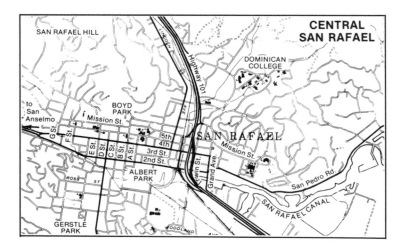

In 1946, the Marin Historical Society began to campaign to resurrect the mission, and three years later a replica of the Mission San Rafael Arcangel was built with money from the Hearst Foundation.

The last mission pear tree was knocked down by a bulldozer in 1963 in the interests of progress and a new parking lot. The graft the nurseryman had taken grew into a tree which can now be seen adjacent to the Jose Moya del Pinto Library at the Marin Art and Garden Center in Ross.

# Central San Rafael

T he downtown area of San Rafael is crisscrossed by a grid of one-way streets. At the center of town, on the spot where the old courthouse once stood, is a high-rise bank building building with a grassy plaza in front. The mission is a block away, and behind it is "Mansion Row." Many of the old elegant estates remain as private homes, clubs, schools, and community centers. In town there are also parks, children's playgrounds, and a wildlife center.

The main shopping area in central San Rafael is along Fourth Street. There is a wide variety of shops and restaurants, and a large Macy's department store. A favorite shop of Marin County residents is the Cottage Bookstore at 1225 Fourth Street.

For many years, if you happened to be on Fourth Street on a Friday or Saturday evening, you might be surprised to see teenagers in cars cruising along the thoroughfare and up side streets. This 1950s custom was revived after movie producer George Lucas, a resident of Marin, used Fourth Street to film *American Graffiti.*

## The Mission San Rafael Arcangel

The white adobe building with its red tile roof on Fifth Avenue and A Street is the replica of the Mission San Rafael Arcangel. Signs will lead you there from the Central San Rafael exit off Highway 101. The mission is a good place to begin a walking tour of downtown San Rafael.

## Mansion Row

"Mansion Row" in San Rafael was the street behind the mission where many elegant homes were built. Several of these are now open to the public. From the mission, walk west on Fifth Avenue to B Street and turn right one block to Mission Avenue. Begin at the Gate House, which houses the Marin Historical Museum, then continue walking west past Maple Lawn, now privately owned by the Elks Club, and go on to Falkirk, the San Rafael Community Center. Just beyond is Foster Hall, part of the coeducational high school, Marin Academy.

Along the way you may also want to visit the San Rafael Library, a block south on Fifth Avenue, and the San Rafael City Hall, just to the east of the library.

At 1125 B Street (where B Street ends at Mission), is the former gate house or guest lodge to Maple Lawn, an estate built by Mrs. Theodocia Cook Arner, sister to Seth and Dan Cook. These two brothers came out from New York in 1850 and made a fortune in silver in the Comstock Lode in Nevada. Maple Lawn, named for the Japanese maples planted on the estate grounds, was built in 1875. Three years later, Seth Cook purchased six more acres from Joseph Angelotti. The Gate House, built on this site, is a High Victorian Gothic-style structure, constructed in 1879 by Ira Cook, the two brothers' father, who moved out to join them. Eventually this house, then called "Park Lodge," was given to Ira Cook's granddaughter, Louise Arner Cook, and her husband, John Franklin Boyd.

*Gate House to Maple Lawn, the old Louise Boyd Estate in San Rafael. Now the Headquarters of the Marin Historical Society.*

Park Lodge was described by the *Marin County Journal* at that time as being the "most perfect and costly of its size in the town...rich in finish and ornamentation....Enclosed with an iron fence, having granite piers, and the large gate, forming the main entrance to the grounds, [the house] will be very imposing."

Today, the Gate House is the home of the Marin County Historical Society Museum, which contains a fascinating collection of artifacts, photographs, and drawings of Marin's early pioneers. One room exhibits an antique baby cradle and clothes about one hundred years old such as women's satin gowns, parasols, shoes, gloves, scarves, and hats. You may also see a 1859 sewing machine, the first typewriter used in the Marin County courthouse, and a ballot box used to select juries a century ago. On the main floor are bronze busts of Mr. and Mrs. Peter Donahue, who built the railroad in Marin, and a fog bell from the ferryboat named for their son, the *James M. Donahue*. There is also an excellent collection of Indian artifacts— arrowheads, spears, fishing sinkers, pipes, mortars, and pestles.

Finally, one should not miss the fine exhibit devoted to Louise Boyd, whose family once owned all this property. Miss Boyd became an internationally renowned explorer, and her strategic maps of the Arctic regions were used by the United States government during World War II. The exhibit shows her as a child, an adolescent, a young woman, and an adult explorer. Awards presented to her from all over the world are displayed on the museum walls.

The Marin County Historical Society Museum is usually open on Wednesdays, Saturdays, and Sundays from 1:00 P.M. to 4:00 P.M. At this writing, the former gate house is closed for earthquake safety repairs. Phone first before visiting to be certain it has reopened. (454-8538)

Behind the Gate House is Boyd Park, presented to the city of San Rafael in 1905 by Louise Arner Boyd and her husband John in memory of their sons, Seth Cook Boyd and John Franklin Boyd, who both died at an early age. Robert Dollar later donated two parcels of land on the east slope of San Rafael Hill, adding ten acres to the park.

Today, Boyd Park is a marvelous green oasis in the midst of busy downtown San Rafael. On its 17.5 acres are a children's playground, tennis court, twenty-one picnic areas, barbecues, and restrooms.

Continue west on Mission Avenue past Maple Lawn—the Boyd estate now owned by the Elks Club—to Falkirk, Cultural Center of San Rafael, at 1408 Mission Avenue. There was once a house here owned by railroad magnate James B. Walker. It was purchased by Ella F. Nichols (Mrs. Trenor) Park, who auctioned off Walker's furniture and had his house removed. In 1888, she built a mansion typical of the Queen Anne style with porches, gables, dormers, and rounded and slated bays, at a cost of $30,000. The architect was Clinton Day, who also designed the famous City of Paris department store in San Francisco and the Stanford University chapel in Palo Alto.

The mansion was purchased in 1906 by Captain Robert Dollar, who owned a worldwide steamship line. Captain Dollar named the estate "Falkirk," after the place of his birth in Scotland. He lived in the house until his death in 1932. The estate remained within the family until purchased by the city of San Rafael in 1974.

Falkirk has seventeen rooms and is surrounded by eleven acres of gardens and hillside. The interior of the mansion has fine wood paneling of Sierra pine, burled ash, and redwood. There are lovely stained glass windows, damask-patterned brocade stretched over

*Falkirk Cultural Center of San Rafael.*

the walls in the parlor, an ornate Persian rug, and white lace curtains.

The mansion is used today by a variety of Marin County groups for meetings, musical concerts, lectures and the Marin Poetry Center. On the second floor is an exhibition gallery with changing contemporary art exhibits.

Mary Case Dekker and her husband, Fred, of San Rafael were directly responsible for saving Falkirk. Upon hearing that the old mansion might be torn down, Mrs. Dekker organized the San Rafael Preservation Committee in May 1972. This group later was absorbed into Marin Heritage, which worked with the city of San Rafael in preserving the mansion.

You may visit Falkirk from Monday through Friday from 11:00 A.M. to 4:00 P.M., Thursday until 9:00 P.M. and and Saturday from 9:00 A.M. to 11:00 A.M.

Restoration is still going on with an emphasis on the gardens. A new outdoor sculpture by artist Heather McGill of Oakland is a three-section piece around a pool capped by a redwood pyramid structure. The work is incased in copper and provides a place to sit.

The facilities at Falkirk are available to rent for meetings, retreats, weddings or community functions. Call 485-3328.

At the west end of Mansion Row is Marin Academy, the third school to be located on this historic spot at Mission and Cottage avenues. The Mount Tamalpais Military Academy opened in 1890 in the Gilbert House. In 1892, Trustee A. W. Foster donated to the school the adjoining three-story mansion built by Thomas O'Conner in 1870. It was known thereafter as Foster Hall.

This school was taken over by new owners in 1925 and renamed the San Rafael Military Academy. Four surplus World War I army barracks located in Vallejo were floated up the San Rafael Canal and brought onto the Academy grounds to be used as dormitories. They are gone today.

When the San Rafael Military Academy closed in 1971, the property was purchased by a group of parents who wanted to form a coeducational private high school. Thus Marin Academy began classes in the fall of 1972. It is a college preparatory school, grades nine through twelve, and is committed to a strong academic program as well as outdoor sports and activities.

At the heart of the 9.5-acre campus is Foster Hall, a lovely old building with white columns and a broad front porch. The driveway encircles a lawn, shaded by mature sequoia trees. Foster Hall itself is said to be haunted, and faculty members living in the second-floor apartments have become well-acquainted with the "spirits" of the house—a woman in a long dress and a child.

For tours of the school or for other information, call 453-4550.

*Marin Academy on "Mansion Row" in San Rafael.*

## San Rafael Improvement Club

At Fifth and H streets, just west of Mansion Row, is a building that was originally the "Victrola Pavilion," representing the Victor Talking Machine Company in the Panama-Pacific International Exposition of 1915 held in San Francisco. The building has been described by one architect as "an irregular-shaped Neo-Classical-Revival style structure with fluted Doric columns, a Doric frieze, and simple pediment."

When the exposition was over, Leon Douglass, a resident of San Rafael and chairman of the board of directors of the Victor Talking Machine Company, had the building dismantled, placed on rafts, and floated to San Rafael. A few weeks later, in January 1916, the San Rafael Improvement Club (which had been organized in 1902 for the purpose of planting trees and annihilating mosquitoes) arranged to buy the building for a clubhouse. A large fund-raising drive was launched to build a foundation on property leased from A. W. Foster. The pavilion was completely reconstructed, and a roof, back wall and extra pillars were added for support. A circular front and large plate glass windows completed the conversion to a clubhouse. This was all done within six months for only $3,000. The formal opening was June 3, 1916. In 1922, A. W. Foster deeded the property to the club for $10, and the club is still in use today.

## Dominican College

Dominican College is a four-year coeducational liberal arts college which the Dominican sisters began as a school for girls in Monterey around 1850. The school moved to Benicia, then to San Rafael in 1889. A convent was built at 1520 Grand Avenue on ten acres purchased from William T. Coleman.

The convent was a white, four-story Victorian building constructed of redwood. It remained in use until July 12, 1990 when the upper stories were set on fire by a crew using a blow torch to remove old paint. The five-alarm fire caused an estimated one-million dollars in damage.

Other buildings were gradually added to the school. The brown-shingled Meadowlands, located on Palm Avenue and Olive Street, was purchased by the Sisters in 1918. Meadowlands was a summer home for Michael de Young, cofounder of the San Francsico

*The main convent house (or motherhouse) of the Dominican order in San Rafael, built in 1889. Located on the Dominican College campus.*

*Chronicle.* For a time the Meadowlands library was turned into a chapel by the Sisters; the main rooms were used for classrooms, and the upper floor was a residence. In 1924, a wing of twenty-seven bedrooms with adjoining baths was added, and eventually Meadowlands developed into the students' favorite residence hall. Over the years it has also been used as a religious retreat and convention center.

Across Grand Avenue from the original convent is an area of twenty-eight acres called Forest Meadows. Tucked in among the trees is a small amphitheater where Dominican College holds graduation exercises every spring. There are also several tennis courts. Forest Meadows has been used by many groups over the years for outdoor drama productions, summer camp, and group picnics.

Today, Dominican College covers nearly eight acres of campus and woods in an exclusive part of San Rafael. A wide variety of students come to Dominican from all over the world for bachelor and master's degree programs. In keeping with a recent trend, nearly one-third of those enrolled are women returning to school, to seek careers after raising a family, or to pursue a change of careers.

*The Marin Wildlife Center across from Albert Park, San Rafael.*

Dominican College invites the public to its many and varied programs and events. The outstanding music department presents a large number of productions and concerts yearly. There are also continually changing art exhibits, drama productions, dance concerts, and guest lecturers, many free of charge. (457-4440)

From Central San Rafael exit off Highway 101, signs will direct you to the campus.

### Marin Wildlife Center

To reach the Marin Wildlife Center, drive south on B Street, then east (or left) on Albert Park Lane (a one-way street) to number 76. Walk across a small bridge that spans a freshwater creek to reach the museum grounds.

The facilities here have had a variety of names and purposes. They began in July 1953 as a Junior Museum with the idea of creating exhibits and putting a small collection of animals on display for children. An old parish hall from St. Paul's Episcopal Church, owned by the Optimists Club, was leased for $1 per year. Two new homes, condemned because they were sliding down hillsides, were purchased for $1 each. Weekend work parties and donations by local contractors, labor unions, and tradesmen put the whole thing together for less than $5,000. The doors opened May 22, 1955.

Through the years financing has been primarily a continuing problem for the museum. It is supported by the efforts of members and volunteers, and by fund-raising activities.

In 1961, the name of the museum was changed to the Louise A. Boyd Natural Science Museum in honor of the famous Artic explorer. Until her death in 1972, Miss Boyd came often to visit the museum and donated several of her awards and mememtoes.

In 1978, the name of the museum was changed again, this time to the Marin Wildlife Center. Today, the center sponsors hikes and wildlife classes for clinic volunteers. Docents lead tours of the museum by appointment. Staff members answer hundreds of telephone calls weekly, giving information on ecology and on the handling of injured wildlife. The clinic cares for thousands of wild animals every year and claims a release rate of rehabilitated animals of over 50 percent, a phenomenal accomplishment.

A walk through the grounds will acquaint you with the animals the Wildlife Center has taken in but for various reasons has been unable to release. There are four pelicans including Groucho and Chico, each missing part of a wing, Goldie the eagle, gulls, hawks, ravens and many other birds.

The clinic is open for animal care every day from 8:00 A.M. to 5:00 P.M. For emergency service, call 454-6961. Regular museum hours are Tuesday through Saturday from 9:00 A.M. to 5:00 P.M.

### Albert Park

The 11.5-acre Albert Park is adjacent to the Marin Wildlife Center. Facilities here include baseball and softball diamonds with viewing stands, four tennis courts, four picnic areas (no barbeques), a basketball court, children's playground, and the San Rafael Community Center. The land was given to the city of San Rafael in 1937 by Jacob Albert, a Marin businessman. Albert owned the large Albert's department store, eventually bought out by Macy's, and he built the first "skyscraper" in Marin, the present Albert building on Fourth and B streets. He also donated the site of the Boy Scout Hall on Second and A streets and contributed most of the funds for construction.

*Jostling at Albert Park, San Rafael.*

A supreme community effort to refurbish Albert Park was led by Dolly Nave in the early 1980's. Dolly and her husband, Richard, raised five boys and spent 28 years involved with Little League Baseball. As much of the time was spent at Albert Park, Dolly found herself running the snack bars and hiring young people to staff them as part of an out-of-school work opportunity.

In 1977, a master plan had been drawn up to refurbish the playing fields in the park which would have included proper drainage and irrigation. The estimated cost was $400,000.

Some years later, $100,000 was set up by the city of San Rafael as part of the city's interest in refurbishing the fields. When Dolly got involved as coordinator and manager of the project, she enlisted the aid of a group of 88 people and managed to obtain $525,000 in donated labor, material and equipment from the business community.

The results were impressive. The playing fields were done over using a sand turf. All new irrigation equipment and drainage lines were installed, and the area was subjected to hydroseeding. A batting cage was added for rental funds.

In the softball area, the grandstand was repaired and repainted and a press box added. The baseball stadium was given a new roof, and a PA system and score board were installed. New dressing rooms and restrooms were built. The old bathrooms were also painted along with the light standards. Security lighting was installed in the park. A paved area was put in around the baseball and softball grandstands and walkways. Finally, a cage-type sand box for small children was built and park benches added. The tennis courts were also resurfaced and landscaped. All this work was completed by 1985.

Major contributors to the Albert Park project included T & B Sports; Ghilotti Brothers who provided the grading; Maggiora-Ghilotti who supplied the drainage lines; Ray Forester, drainage; James McDonald, architect for the press box; Brian Whittenkeller, landscape architect; McPhails-Shamrock, drainage material and sand; Joe Pedrolli and Son, masonry for the tennis area; Dean Rhodes, engineer for the field; Jack Estes and Gene Carter, surveyors; Thomas Swan, signs; DeMello Roofing, the roofs on the press box, stadium, two snackbars, and the new bathrooms; Zappetini and sons, the park benches; Cagwin and Dorward, irrigation and hydroseeding; Muzinich Plumbing, bathrooms; Marvin Larsen, basalt; San Marin Lumber, wood; and Denny Coleman, painting.

## Gerstle Park

Gerstle Park is a lovely, quiet area for resting or for playing. There are four picnic areas, one holding 200 and another accommodating 80 people. There is also a tennis court hidden in a redwood grove, a basketball court, and a children's playground. To get there, drive south on D Street to San Rafael Avenue. Turn right and go two blocks.

The park was once the grounds of a summer home called "Violet Terrace," where four generations of the Gerstle family lived, beginning in 1881. Lewis Gerstle emigrated from Bavaria, lived for a while in San Francisco, and then moved to Sacramento, where he met Louis Sloss. The two men became fast friends and established a partnership which continued throughout their lives. They even married sisters—Lewis Gerstle wed Hannah Greenbaum, and Sloss married her older sister, Sarah.

In 1897, when the Alaskan Gold Rush was on, Gerstle and Sloss formed the Alaskan Commercial Company. They secured a lease from the government to conduct sealing operations off the Pribilof Islands and made a fortune.

The Sloss family bought property in San Rafael adjoining Violet Terrace so the two families could spend summer vacations together. The children would race from one house to another, through orchards and under arbors.

Lewis Gerstle died in 1902, but his widow Hannah continued to enjoy the house for summer vacations until her death in 1930. At that time, the Gerstle heirs gave the property to the city for a park. Caesar Bettini, a gardener, was kept on to tend the estate. (His son Paul eventually became mayor of San Rafael.) The house was used as a retirement center, then as lodging for the Army Air Corps from Hamilton during World War II. In 1955, it was destroyed by an arson fire.

On the park's six acres are nearly fifty different species of trees, including a variety of acacia, laurel, myrtle, an assortment of fruit trees, oak, redwood, basswood, buckeye, madrone, magnolia, maple, redbud, silk tree, smoke tree, toyon, and walnut. The Sloss house served as a lodge for the park until it burned in 1955.

For a permit to rent a picnic area in Gerstle Park or any other San Rafael park, phone Karen Limb at 485-3333.

# East San Rafael

On the east side of town a canal comes in from the bay. The San Rafael Canal parallels Point San Pedro Road and is lined with homes, condominiums, yacht clubs, boat yards, and restaurants.

The canal ends near the freeway behind the Montecito Shopping Center, built in the late 1950s and completely remodeled in the 1980s. This was once a municipal yacht harbor but was filled-in, all in the name of progress.

Beyond the canal, Point San Pedro Road heads east, following the shoreline of San Rafael Bay; it passes the Peacock Gap and Country Club and arrives at McNear's Beach County Park. The road then becomes North San Pedro Road as it curves northwest to China Camp State Park, now following the shore of San Pablo Bay. Eventually the road turns inland and runs through Santa Venetia, ending at the spectacular Marin County Civic Center.

The entire loop, beginning and ending at the freeway, is about ten miles and takes just over a half hour by car. This lovely, scenic ride is especially popular with bicyclists.

## San Rafael Canal Area

South of the San Rafael Canal is a residential section known as "The Canal." Tucked in among the commercial estabishments on East Francisco Boulevard is tiny Beach Park. Farther on is Dominic's Harbor Restaurant, serving seafood and Italian-style food. It looks out over the canal, and many people come to Dominic's by boat.

Two small neighborhood parks are located in "The Canal." Pickleweed Park, at the junction of Kerner Boulevard and Canal Street, consists of 6.2 acres running between Canal Street and the San Rafael Canal. Park facilities include benches, a sport field, play equipment, rest rooms and The Pickelweed Park Community Center, 485-3077.

Tiny Schoen Park, about one-tenth of an acre, overlooks San Rafael Bay on East Canal Street. It has a picnic area, some play equipment, and benches.

## Peacock Gap Golf and Country Club

On the north side of the canal, Point San Pedro Road heads to the east, past yacht harbors, the Marin Beach and Tennis Club, and the Loch Lomond marina and shopping center. The Peacock Gap area is 3.5 miles from the Montecito Shopping Center.

Turn left on Peacock Drive to get to the Peacock Gap Golf and Country Club. Here is an eighteen-hole golf course covering 128 acres of rolling hills, with lakes and creeks. The clubhouse at 333 Biscayne Drive has a restaurant, bar, and banquet facilities, and is open to the public. (453-4122)

## McNear's Brickyard

On Point San Pedro Road, a block or so past Peacock Drive, you will see the entrance to McNear's brickyard. The pioneers in Marin soon discovered that the clay soil was ideal for producing bricks.

In 1869, John A. McNear and his brother George bought 700 acres in this area for $35,000. When their partnership dissolved, John kept the property in Marin and increased his holdings to 2,500 acres; his land ran from McNear's Point to Santa Venetia near the

*Patent Brick Yard, McInnis Park, 1880s.* California Room, Marin County Library, Marin County Civic Center.

Civic Center, In 1889, he acquired the Fortin Brick Company brickyard which was being worked by Chinese labor.

This impressive private company continues today but according to Scott McNear, a fifth generation member of the family, the ore has run out. In November 1988, the family purchased 362 acres off the Petaluma-Point Reyes Rd. just outside of Hick's Valley and plan to mine the clay there for their San Rafael kilns.

## McNear's Beach

McNear's Beach, a popular picnic and swimming area for the past century, lies in a sheltered cove on San Pablo Bay. In 1970 the county of Marin purchased the old resort and, after some remodeling, the beach was opened to the public.

The park covers approximately 70 acres and includes large areas of green lawns, picnic sites, a new 500-foot concrete pier with wood railings, 3,000-square-foot swimming pool, two tennis courts, a swimming beach, restrooms, changing rooms, and a snack bar.

Fees to use the park are $3 per car on weekdays, $5 on weekends and holidays, and $1 in winter. The summer season is from April to October. Walk-ins are $1.

McNear's Beach is about half a mile beyond the brickyard. Turn right on Cantera Way and follow the long drive lined with eucalyptus trees into the park.

## China Camp State Park

Half-a-mile beyond McNear's Beach is China Camp State Park. This location began as a Chinese settlement in the 1860s after the American Civil War. It was a debarkation and relay point for coolie laborers being smuggled in at night to work on the con-

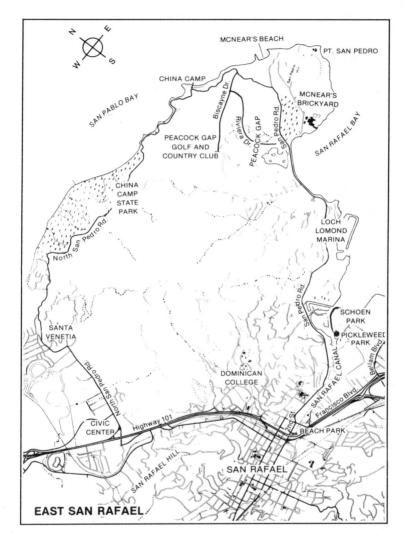

EAST SAN RAFAEL

struction of the Central Pacific Railroad.

After the completion of the railroad in 1869, the Chinese returned to China Camp and began shrimp fishing. The *1880 History of Marin County* describes China Camp at the time:

> . . .*you hitch your team to a fence, and a walk of two or three hundred yards brings you upon the scene of the fishing grounds*

*of Point San Pedro. This industry is entirely in the hands of Chinamen, who conduct a very extensive business, employing upwards of two hundred and twenty-five men. The land occupied by the fishermen is owned by McNear & Bro., and leased to Mr. Richard Bullis for one thousand dollars a year, and by him leased to the Chinamen for nearly three thousand dollars.*

*From ten to fifteen acres are occupied, the shore line serving for houses, boat building, shipping, etc., and the side hill for drying the fish, and preparing them for market. Shrimps constitute the principal catch, and of these from twenty to thirty tons per week are taken. The shrimps are dried on the hillsides, threashed, "a la Chinois," to get off the hull, winnowed through a hand mill, and sent to market.*

*The fish sell for eight to fourteen cents per pound in the San Francisco market, at wholesale, and the hulls are shipped to China, and sold for manure where they bring twenty dollars per ton, affording a profit over all expenses of five dollars. It is said to be an excellent fertilizer.*

*Other kinds of fish are taken in great quantities, as flounders, perch, etc., and some of which are used only for dressing soil. The stakes to which the fishers attach their nets extend out into the bay a mile or more.*

*There are thirty-two houses on the beach, and more all the time building. Two boats are now on the ways, one forty feet long, and the other thirty. Nine hundred cords of wood have been used this season, which they buy in Redwood City and ship themselves to their fishing grounds. Captain Bullis makes a weekly trip to the city with a cargo, the law requiring a white captain on a forty-foot craft.*

In the 1906 San Francisco earthquake and fire, Chinatown burned to the ground and thousands of Chinese refugees fled to China Camp. Shanties built on stilts filled the shoreline and extended out into the water. The beach and hillsides were covered with makeshift camps. Many of the refugees stayed at China Camp while others eventually returned to San Francisco to help with the rebuilding of that city.

In 1910, the state of California planted bass in the shrimping area and put restrictions on the nets, thereby wiping out the

*The old pier at China Camp State Park.*

industry practically overnight. A disastrous fire in 1913 burned most
of the shanties, and the Chinese began to leave.

Then, in the 1920s, Frank Spenger invented a special cone-shaped
net that allowed large fish to escape but retained the shrimp. Quan
Hock Quock, using a fleet of thirty-six motorboats equipped with
this new net, reportedly hauled in a thousand pounds of shrimp
per boat. He also operated a small store built out over the water
adjacent to the pier.

Henry Quan and his wife Grace took over the shrimping business
and store after the death of Quan Hock Quock. Although mud
began to cover the shrimp grounds, the Quan heirs remained for
many years.

In 1954, a movie was filmed at China Camp, *Blood Alley,* starring John Wayne and Lauren Bacall. For years after, hundreds of
people came out to see the site of what was to become a film
classic.

China Camp is now part of a 1,476-acre park. The land was purchased by the state of California between the years 1976-78 from
Hawaii developer Chinn Ho, who donated the thirty-six acres that
contain the shrimp village. The Marin Chinese Cultural Group
believes this site to be the only remaining authentic Chinese fishing
village left in California.

The village is located about half a mile beyond the park boundary sign. Parking is in a gravel lot overlooking the bay. From there, a walk leads down a dirt road to the village itself. Park hours are 8:00 A.M. to sunset, and there is no entrance fee.

The village is a photographer's delight. A long, rickety wooden pier stretches out into the bay. On shore are shacks and dilapidated old buildings, dinghies and fishing boats. There is a small beach with a few picnic tables. (No fires or barbecues are allowed.)

Thirty walk-in campsites on the Back Ranch area north of the village and more picnic sites along the bay front have been added in the past few years. A museum and store are open on weekends. Phone 456-0766 for more information.

As you leave the village site, the park continues along San Pablo Bay to Rat Rock Cove, where wooden shanties were once built out over the water. These houses burned around 1904. North San Pedro Road continues to follow the shoreline, past the Back Ranch Meadows and through a broad pickleweed marsh, still part of the park. Watch out for deer crossing the road.

# North San Rafael

After leaving China Camp State Park, North San Pedro Road goes on to Santa Venetia, a residential area named after Venice, Italy. In 1914, a real estate developer had planned to use Las Gallinas Creek to create a canal lined by elegant homes. There would also be a palatial clubhouse, miles of bridle paths, and authentic gondolas as a final perfect touch. World War I and the Depression killed this romantic plan. Houses were eventually built here, but on a more modest scale.

As you drive through Santa Venetia, look off to the right for a golden spire to appear over the treetops. Then, the blue dome and roof of the Marin County Civic Center comes into view.

Just beyond the Civic Center is Highway 101, which at this point climbs Puerto Suello Hill, the geographic division between Central and North San Rafael. From the crest of the hill there is a sweeping view of the Las Gallinas Valley, originally a land grant of 22,000 acres of old mission land, and known today as the residential areas of Terra Linda, Marinwood, and Lucas Valley.

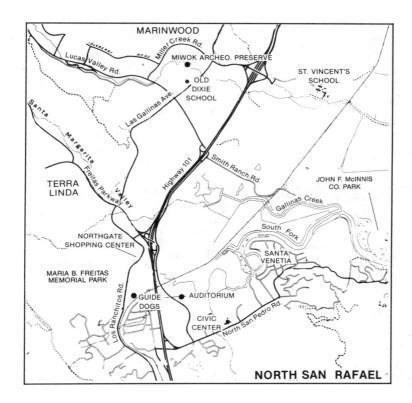

## Marin County Civic Center

The famous architect Frank Lloyd Wright designed the unusual and beautiful Marin County Civic Center as his last commission.

The 160-acre site was purchased by the county of Marin in April 1956. Another 80 acres were later added. Presentation plans were submitted to the county by Wright the following March, and were followed a year later with additional plans for a fairgrounds with an amphitheater, pavilion, playground, lagoon, and general civic area.

Wright's plan was to unite three isolated hillcrests by way of one horizontal building line. The two buildings (administration building and hall of justice) would span the valleys in between and blend into each hill by means of a series of gracefully-moving arches. They would have the effect of floating from hill to hill.

Not everyone liked the new plans, or the cost, and a bitter fight

*The Marin County Civic Center designed by Frank Lloyd Wright.*

ensued. Soon the lines were drawn. Against the Wright plan were members of the American Legion, an irate taxpayers' group, County Supervisor William Fusselman, and George Jones, the powerful county clerk. Supporting the plans were Supervisors Vera Schultz, Walter Castro, William Gnoss, and James Marshall, plus Planning Director Mary Summers and conservationist leader Caroline Livermore.

Proponents of the plan gave slide shows around the county in an effort to consolidate public support. As people took sides, animosity grew; intrigues, plots, and counterplots developed.

Then, Frank Lloyd Wright died suddenly on April 9, 1959. If the Civic Center were built, the people of Marin would have his last masterpiece. Six days later, the board of supervisors voted to continue working on the project with the Wright Foundation, and plans proceeded to submit the blueprints out to bid. Architect Aaron Green, representing the Wright Foundation, estimated the administration building would cost $3,379,000, and the bids received were right in line. Groundbreaking ceremonies were held in February 1960.

Disaster struck when in the June elections two of the supervisors supporting the plan—Vera Schultz and Jim Marshall—were defeated in their reelection campaigns by anti-tax candidates

J. Walter Blair and George Ludy. Suddenly, Fusselman had a 3-2 majority on the board of supervisors opposing the new Civic Center. Mary Summers, planning director for the county for twenty years, resigned in protest, as did County Counsel Leland Jordan and County Administrator Donald A. Jensen.

The bulldozers were working and the steel girders were up in January 1961 when the new board of supervisors was sworn in. Fusselman, a candy-maker from San Anselmo, was elected chairman. On January 10, a stop-work order on the Marin County Civic Center was voted through the board. The Civic Center Committee was dismissed, and discussion began on the possibility of converting the administration building into a county hospital.

Marin citizens erupted with rage at this high-handed action. People who had paid little attention to local politics suddenly found their county the laughingstock of the whole Bay Area and demanded that something be done about it. A grand jury investigation was called for. Meetings turned into shouting matches.

An *Independent Journal* ballot showed disapproval of the stop-work order to be running 8-to-1. Picket lines were set up.

Finally, upon receiving an independent committee's report that converting the administration building into a hospital would cost

*Marin County Civic Center.*

*Inside the Marin County Civic Center looking down from the fourth floor of the Administration Building.*

more than finishing the original building, Supervisor George Ludy changed his vote, and construction was allowed to continue.

But the political controversy had not ended. In another attempt to foil the plans, the board voted, on a motion from J. Walter Blair, to abolish the office of county administrator. Again, the citizens of Marin took up arms. Blair was recalled by his Mill Valley district—the first successful recall election against a supervisor in California history—and Peter Behr, a lawyer and recent Mill Valley councilman, was elected. The result of the election was the completion of the entire Civic Center complex. (Peter Behr's popularity in the county continued. He went on to the state senate, where he served eight years until his voluntary retirement.)

Marin County was rocked to its foundations by the Civic Center controversy, and afterwards much was changed. The result was the demise of one kind of leadership in the county and the rise of another force, that of citizen involvement and participation.

As you begin your tour of the Civic Center, stop for a look at the original Frank Lloyd Wright model on display on the ground floor of the administration building, which is the closest to San Pedro Road. Then, as you explore the grounds, you can see which parts of the original dream came true. (Tours are also conducted through the Civic Center Volunteer Office which has been run for the past ten years by Joan Brown. She will supply docents for groups or individual tours. 499-7407)

This complex was the culmination of the majority of Wright's ideas and shows his fascination with the use of circles, long horizon-

*The County Civic Center Auditorium.*

*Marin County Civic Center.*

tal lines, contrasting textures, and crescent shapes. These motifs
are built into the outside of the buildings: wide crescents look
like half-moons stretched over driveways that pass right through
the buildings. On each consecutive floor going up, the crescent
shapes used in balconies become smaller. On the top floor, they
turn into round circles, a motif continued in the blue round and
horizontal roof.

The exterior color, a buff pink, is continued inside and contrasts
with a highly polished brick-red floor, gold/brass-colored fixtures,
and ornamental grillwork. The gold/brass color is also used in the
futuristic-looking spire built in the shape of a four-sided needlelike
pyramid that towers majestically above the complex.

Wright liked the use of balconies, fountains, and patios, and
incorporated these features into his design. As you enter the administration building, you are struck by its vast openness—three
floors of balconies illuminated by a crescent-shaped skylight.
Exotic tropical and subtropical plants grow in profusion down the
middle of the ground floor and continue into the hall of justice
building. There are massive schefflera (the Australian umbrella
tree), dieffenbachia, bird of paradise, wandering Jew, and Maranta
(prayer plants that fold up at night).

There are two exhibition galleries—one in the connecting hall from the administration building to the hall of justice, and another on the third floor of the administration building outside the board of supervisors' chambers. Supervisors' offices look down on a landscaped patio with a circular fountain next to the cafeteria. This cafeteria is open to the public and has excellent, inexpensive food. You can eat lunch outside, around the fountain.

The main branch of the county library is on the fourth floor of the administration building. It features an extensive collection of books and the unique Anne Kent California History Room, which contains a variety of books on history, old photographs, and Marin County historical documents.

On the south end of this building, the fourth floor opens up to the hillside where there is an attractive, carefully labeled "drought garden" containing plants that require little water. A short path leads to the top of the hill—an excellent spot to take photographs. There is a beautiful view all the way to the bay, and a unique perspective on the rooflines of the buildings.

Connecting with the administration building is the hall of justice, with its long halls and round courtrooms. It is now open to the public, but for years it was closed off and resembled an armed camp. During a trial in 1970 involving San Quentin inmates, this visionary building was the scene of a shootout. Guns were smuggled into the courtroom, hostages were taken, and a Marin

*The Marin County Civic Center Lagoon.*

County judge was killed in the melee that followed. For years after this incident, the doors to the court floors were kept locked, the halls patrolled by armed deputies, and metal detectors used to screen everyone entering.

In addition to the two main buildings, the Civic Center complex contains a post office (the only one ever designed by Wright), landscaped lagoon (a favorite spot for feeding ducks), exhibit building, two theaters (including the 2,003-seat Veterans Auditorium and the Showcase Theater next to the Exhibition Hall), and fairgrounds.

When addressing the citizens of Marin with his preliminary plans, Frank Lloyd Wright had this to say about his design for the Civic Center:

> *Beauty is the moving cause of nearly every issue worth the civilization we have, and civilization without a culture is like a man without a soul. Culture consists of the expression by the human spirit of the love of beauty.*
>
> *We will never have a culture of our own until we have an architecture of our own. An architecture of our own does not mean something that is ours by the way of our own tastes. It is something that we have knowledge concerning. We will have it only when we know what constitutes a good building and when we know that the good building is not one that hurts the landscape, but is one that makes the landscape more beautiful than it was before that building was built. In Marin County you have one of the most beautiful landscapes I have seen, and I am proud to make the buildings of this County characteristic of the beauty of the County.*
>
> *Here is a crucial opportunity to open the eyes not of Marin County alone, but of the entire country, to what officials gathering together might themselves do to broaden and beautify human lives.*

## Guide Dogs for the Blind

North of the Civic Center and to the west of Highway 101, at 350 Los Ranchitos Road, is Guide Dogs for the Blind, an institution that trains dogs to aid people who have lost their sight and prepares people to use these highly trained dogs.

The eleven-acre campus contains kennels, an office building, and student dormitories. The dogs—Labradors, German shepherds, or golden retrievers—are often seen in downtown San Rafael as they are being trained to lead people across streets in heavy traffic conditions.

The public is invited to the monthly graduations, at which time they may tour the kennels and see a demonstration of working guide dogs. Call 499-4000 for pre-arranged tours.

## Northgate Shopping Center

The popular Northgate Mall Shopping Center is farther north on Los Ranchitos Road and is also accessible from the Freitas Parkway exit off Highway 101. Opened in 1965, it is one of the largest shopping centers in Marin, covering an area of forty-five acres with over 100 department stores, shops, and restaurants. Anything you want to buy—clothing, furniture, books, or gifts— can be found at Northgate.

The shopping center was completely remodeled in the 1980s with a grand opening in 1987. Well-known department stores such as Sears and The Emporium are located here.

## Maria B. Freitas Park

Beyond the shopping center is the Maria B. Freitas Park which is also called the Water Park. Stay on Freitas Parkway, then turn right on Montecillo Rd. toward Kaiser Hospital. The park is located near the hospital's Parking Lot 2. It contains a gazebo, a children's wading pool and small barbeques.

## John F. McInnis Park

At the end of Smith Ranch Road, eight-tenths of a mile from Highway 101, is the John F. McInnis Park, named in memory of a former San Rafael city councilman and Marin County supervisor who died in office in 1972. The park covers an area of 441 acres beyond the Marin County Civic Center. It contains two softball diamonds, one with lights and bleachers. There are also two soccer fields, four tennis courts, an equestrian area, a canoe launch, picnic tables, a golf driving range and restrooms.

The rules say no open fires, group use by permit only, and pets must be under owners' control.

## Miwok Archeological Preserve of Marin

Located along Miller Creek near Las Gallinas Avenue, is a site where the Coast Miwok resided for more than two thousand years. This village, called Cotomkotca, was a political and cermonial center as well as a burial site. More than 500 old Coast Miwok village sites have been identified in Marin and southern Sonoma counties, mostly near San Francisco, Drakes and Tomales Bays. Nearly 90 percent of these have been destroyed by road and structure building.

To get to the preserve, take the Marinwood exit off Highway 101 to Miller Creek Road, then turn left at Las Gallinas. The site is behind the Miller Creek Middle School at 2255 Las Gallinas, beyond the basketball courts. You will see a round mound surrounded by a wire fence with a double gate. It is identified as "MRN 138" which means "Marin" plus the number of the archeological site.

These mounds are the remains of a Coast Miwok dialectic troupe or tribelet. At this place, archeologists have found human remains as well as animal, bird and fish bones, bone tools and ornaments, stone arrow and spear points, acorn grinding mortars, and shell tools and ornaments. All are clues to the way of life of these early Marin citizens.

Primitive beads were made from olivella shells, a small snail. After about 1200 A.D., the Coast Miwok used clam shells to make small round beads called clam disc beads, or money beads. Strung with abalone ornaments, these became ceremonial jewelry. They were also used as a medium of exchange and traded as far as western Nevada. Wide belts made of thousands of clam beads were used as dance regalia. Bird feathers were used in dance skirts and headdresses, ear ornaments and belts, as well as basket ornaments.

The Miwok did not make pottery but were expert basket makers. Their waterproof baskets were used for cooking, and a wide variety of carrying baskets served every purpose pottery served in other cultures. Cordage and net making were also highly developed arts.

After archeological studies were completed, all the remains were reinterred. The sign at the site says: "This is their resting place— here they will remain." Also found at Miller Creek were six ceremonial structures and a floor covered with a thousand pounds of a fallen clay roof. This village was a ceremonial center for all the tribes living in the Gallinas Valley.

To arrange for a tour, contact the Miwok Archeological Preserve of Marin at 2255 Las Gallinas, San Rafael 94903.

## Old Dixie School

In front of the Miller Creek Middle School is the historic Old Dixie School, built by pioneer James Miller in 1864. The school originally stood north of Miller Creek Road on Highway 101 but was moved to this location in 1972.

The little white schoolhouse with its high, black-trimmed windows makes a picturesque sight surrounded by green lawn and a picket fence. It is furnished as an old-fashioned school complete with textbooks (including replicas of the McGuffey Readers), slates, slate pens, desks, a blackboard, antique clock, pictures of Presidents Washington and Lincoln, a thirty-seven star flag, and a school bell.

The building is used as a community meeting house for several groups. To arrange for a tour, call the Dixie Schoolhouse Foundation at 472-3010 or 479-8678. Members of this organization are trying to arrange for funding for permanent staffing so the schoolhouse may be open to the public on a regular basis.

## St. Vincent's School

On the east side of Highway 101 at the Marinwood exit is St. Vincent's School, a California Historical Landmark.

When pioneer Timoteo Murphy died in 1853, he left 317 acres of land to the Roman Catholic archbishop of California, Joseph Alemany, to establish a "seminary of learning." On January 1, 1855, the Daughters of Charity of St. Vincent de Paul came to Marin from San Francisco to establish a school for six orphaned girls. This did not work out, and the children returned to San Francisco that same year, but the name "St. Vincent" remained.

The girls were replaced by 14 orphaned boys at the new "St. Vincent's Orphan Asylum of San Francisco," a name used until 1975. The orphan asylum grew rapidly, and by 1890 there were 600 boys living at St. Vincent's. Buildings were added and a large farming operation developed.

*St. Vincent's School, San Rafael.*

From 1868 to 1890, the Domincan Sisters taught at St. Vincent's before moving into their new convent facilities on Grand Avenue in San Rafael. The strict Christian Brothers were brought in and stayed from 1894 to 1922. At that time Dominican Sisters from the Mission San Jose took over and are still teaching at St. Vincent's.

Today, the number of children living at St. Vincent's School is limited to sixty. They are neither orphans or deliquents, but boys ages seven to fourteen who have emotional and social adjustment problems.

The boys now live in cottages which provide a more home-like atmosphere than the old dormitories. On weekends they may participate in a "Visiting Family Program" in which they are invited into homes of people interested in the school. It helps prepare the boys for the adjustment they will make when they are placed with a foster family or return to their own homes after leaving St. Vincent's.

The entrance to St. Vincent's is a lovely, eucalyptus-lined drive. It is like taking a journey into the past, into a quiet world of Spanish missions, formal gardens, palm trees, and fountains.

A sign in the front parking lot, half-a-mile from the freeway, advises you to check in at the main office. To reach it, walk straight back under a long, cool portico, then turn left. In this area there are extensive gardens, benches, iron gates, graceful archways, colorful bougainvillea, statues of lions, and a round fountain with water lilies. Old buildings of yellow stucco with green tile roofs surround a central court, reminiscent of a California mission. As you stand in this quiet spot, remember that 50,000 boys have lived here in the last hundred years.

At the main office you can arrange for a tour of the Chapel of the Most Holy Rosary. This familiar landmark, the richly-carved spires and ornate church facade seen fleetingly through tall eucalyptus trees from the freeway. It was completed in 1930, part of a large building program initiated by Father Francis P. McElroy.

In front of the chapel, up under the eaves, are dozens of swallow nests. Hundreds of the industrious birds swoop around with great speed. Unlike the swallows at the famous Mission San Juan Capistrano in Southern California, the birds at St. Vincent's never leave. When the church was cleaned and painted in 1979, they hovered around nervously and watched the progress. The minute the paint was dry, the swallows began rebuilding their mud nests exactly as they were before.

Inside the chapel, one is immediately impressed with fifteen beautiful stained glass windows depicting the life of Jesus. Paintings marking the Stations of the Cross line the wall, and the ceiling is ornately carved and painted. The center aisle is inlaid with tile, and there is generous use of intricately-carved white marble and stone along the walls and in the high columns. The altar is also of white marble, carved in a simpler design.

As you leave the quiet beauty of the chapel and look again at the graceful old buildings, cool porticos, fountains, and flowers, it seems a long way to the hurtling tempo of the twentieth century.

# North Marin                                   9

## *The Old West*

N ovato, Marin's northernmost city, lies in a sheltered inland valley surrounded by hills. Away from the coastal fog, it is warmer here than in the rest of the county.

This is a sprawling western town with wide streets and boulevards. The actual city limits encompass twenty-three square miles, while the Greater Novato Area is a tremendous seventy square miles, taking in Hamilton Air Force Base, Ignacio, Black Point and adjacent Green Point, several large residential areas, parks, and the county airport.

Novato has seen tremendous growth in recent years. With the creation of extensive parkland in West Marin, the ranch land in the northern part of the county was the last area open to development. While many new homes and industrial parks have been built here, Novato still retains its friendly, small-town atmosphere, and there is a strong sense of community.

## Hamilton Field

I n 1929, the federal government decided a major military installation was needed in Marin, and a site known as Marin Meadows in North Marin was picked to build an air base. President Hoover signed the bill and work began in December 1933. Coming in the heart of the Depression, these new jobs were a great boon to residents of the county.

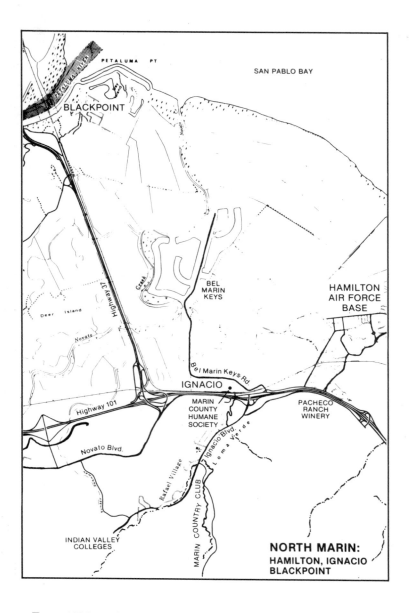

From 1935 to 1940, Hamilton Field was used as a bomber base. Then it became a fighter base and was particularly important to the country throughout World War II as a jumping-off point to the

Pacific. In 1947 it was renamed Hamilton Air Force Base. Hamilton eventually occupied 2,010 acres and became the home of the 78th Fighter Wing (Air Defense), including the 83rd and 84th Fighter Interceptor Squadron, part of the U.S. Air Force Aerospace Defense Command.

The Air Force has declared the base surplus, but it is still being used by the Army (Sixth Army Flight Detachment) and an element of the Coast Guard. The Navy operates an exchange, a commissary, and a housing office at Hamilton. In addition, all the services use the base from time to time for reserve training.

In 1979 and 1980, the facilities at Hamilton were used as temporary housing for Asian refugees awaiting resettlement around the country. Future use of the base has become a hotly-debated issue in Marin.

# Ignacio

Adjacent to Hamilton Field is Ignacio, at the Highway 101 exit just past Hamilton. This area was named for Ignacio Pacheco, who received the Mexican land grant *Rancho de San Jose* in 1840. The grant, consisting of 6,659.25 acres, may have been named for Pacheco's birthplace, the village of San Jose in Santa Clara County.

Pacheco's parents had come to California from Mexico with the de Anza expedition in 1776. Ignacio grew up to become a Mexican army sergeant and later a justice of the peace in San Rafael.

Today, the Ignacio area contains apartments, industrial parks, and some interesting restaurants. The Alvarado Inn is named for the Mexican governor of California (1836-42), Juan Bautista Alvarado.

A new enterprise in Ignacio is winemaking. This is actually a return to an old Marin tradition started by the Spanish padres. Herbert Rowland, a direct descendant of Ignacio Pacheco, and his family have created the Pacheco Ranch Winery across from Hamilton Air Force Base. Rowland planted several acres of Cabernet Sauvignon grapes which now produce 1,000 cases a year. Local connoisseurs approve the production and look forward to more fine Marin wines.

*Nave Patrola in the 1983 Elk's Parade, 4th and A Streets, San Rafael.*

The winery also ferments a small quantity of Sonoma County Chardonnay grapes in unusual 120 gallon French oak puncheons that provide a very subtle oak undertone to this wine. You are welcome to stop by the ranch by appointment. (883-5583)

Ignacio is also the location of a large bowling complex called Nave Lanes built by "Papa" Bill Nave and his sons Bill, Bob, and Rich in 1958. The Nave family has been in Marin since "Grampa" Pete Nave arrived in 1880 from a little town outside Genoa, Italy. In 1890, he purchased land from Ramon Pacheco which was part of the Pacheco land grant. It was fondly known as the "cabbage patch" for all the vegetables he raised and delivered to local stores by cart. Today, it is the site of the Nave Shopping Center in Novato.

The architect for Nave Lanes was Gordan Phillips, a former pupil of Frank Lloyd Wright who used many of the same features incorporated in the Marin Civic Center. It is easy to recognize similar curves, round holes, round pillars, even a stucco atrium.

Rich Nave, a San Rafael City Councilman between 1983-1987, his brothers Bob and Bill, other members of the family and friends organized the "Nave Patrola." This "Italian" military marching unit has delighted residents of Marin for the past twenty years in parades from Pt. Reyes to San Rafael and all over the state of California.

## Indian Valley Colleges

Indian Valley, a two-year comprehensive community college, opened in 1975 (interim classes began in 1971) under the name Marin Community College District, which also operates the College of Marin in Kentfield. It is located at the west end of Ignacio Boulevard, to the northwest of the private Marin Golf and Country Club.

The campus covers 333 acres of rolling, oak-studded hills and contains clusters of two-story wooden buildings nestled beneath the trees. Architects Neptune and Thomas of Pasadena, California won an Award of Merit in 1977 for their design of the college.

The school has an enrollment of 2,000 to 2,500 credit students and also schedules community education and services on campus. There are three colleges within the school: the College of Social and Behavioral Science, the College of Arts and Humanities, and the College of Natural and Physical Environment. Each has its own administration, learning center, counseling offices, and student lounge. In 1988 the students voted to rename the centers Miwok, Ohlone and Pomo.

Indian Valley Colleges has the only olympic-size swimming pool in the county. It is open to the public; phone 883-3473 for the hours. There are also six tennis courts, hiking and bicycle trails.

## The Marin Humane Society

The Marin Humane Society, organized over eighty years ago, is located at 171 Bel Marin Keys Road, to the east of Highway 101 (take the Ignacio exit, bear right at the fork, then make an immediate left on Bel Marin Keys Road). Marin has nearly double the national average of domestic animals. Under a contract with the county of Marin, the Humane Society has responsibility of Animal Control Services; so if your pet has roamed, this may be where you can locate him.

The Humane Society maintains a strong adoption program and has found homes for thousands of dogs and cats over the years. They also operate a spaying clinic to help control animal population. Classes are given at the Society's headquarters and throughout Marin schools on the care and handling of animals.

The Humane Society is open Monday through Saturday from 10:00 A.M. to 5:30 P.M. and 7:00 P.M. on Wednesdays. To hear the lost-animal recording, call 883-4625 from 5:30 P.M. to 9:00 A.M. For additional information, call 883-4621.

# Black Point

T his hilly, wooded point of land fronts on the Petaluma River near where it flows into San Pablo Bay. Black Point was settled in 1853, and most of the pioneers were engaged in wood cutting and dairying. A few schooners were built here, and in the 1860s, fine oak was sent to Mare Island for the construction of naval ships. The thick oak forests were soon gone, but the area remained an important shipping point on the Petaluma River. A branch railroad connected it with Ignacio.

Black Point today is a residential area with many unusual homes scattered through the hills. The widely known Renaissance Pleasure Faire, held here annually in late summer and early fall, is a recreation of Elizabethan England, and fair-goers are encouraged to dress up in period costumes. Arts, crafts, and jewelry are displayed and sold, and an interesting variety of old English dishes are available, plus beer and wine. Performing minstrels, a parade featuring the queen, and other entertainments run continuously.

To get to Black Point, drive north on Highway 101 and then east on Route 37 (just north of Ignacio). Turn off on the Black Point-Atherton Avenue exit. When the fair is going on, you will see tents, banners, and a field of parked cars off to the right.

The Black Point Public Fishing Access is a mile farther on the Petaluma River. Operated by the county of Marin, this one-acre site under the Petaluma River bridge contains one ramp, two docks (one private), picnic tables and a parking lot. This public fishing access was developed by the Wildlife Conservation Board. The other side of the river is Sonoma County and the Port Sonoma marina.

# Novato

T he Novato area was originally part of five Mexican land grants. The first came three years after the secularization of the Spanish missions, when the Mexican govern-

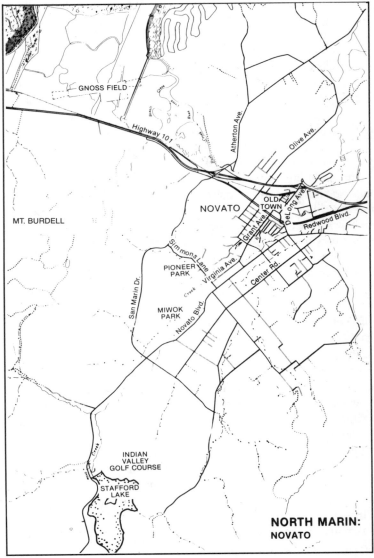

**NORTH MARIN:**
NOVATO

ment was strengthening its hold on California by awarding land
to citizens who had proven their loyalty and dedication to Mexico. According to the *1880 History of Marin,* the first grant here
was *Rancho de Novato,* awarded in 1839 to Fernando Feliz, whose
family had come to California from Mexico with the de Anza ex-

pedition of 1776. Feliz was born in Los Angeles Pueblo in 1795. He served in the army and was awarded with this land grant of 8,876.02 acres.

The other land grants were: *Rancho San Jose,* 1840, awarded to Ignacio Pacheco in exchange for a Sonoma grant he had obtained; *Corte Madera de Novato,* 1840, 8,878.02 acres awarded to John Martin, a Scotsman who married a native woman, Tomasa Cantura; *Rancho Olompali,* 1843, 8,877.43 acres awarded to Camilo Ynitia, a native American and son of the Miwok chief, Olompali; and *Rancho Nicasio,* 1844, 56,621.04 acres awarded to Don Pablo de la Guerra and John Cooper.

The early land grantees set about their peaceful business of building homes, raising families, planting crops, and tending their animals. They raised cattle and hunted the plentiful local game, such as elk, bear, deer, and game birds. Generally, the land barons lived a very good life, entertaining often at gay fiestas in their adobe haciendas. The men have been described as tall and vigorous. Their typical Spanish costume was a wide-brimmed hat, short, decorated jacket, and deerskin leggings. The black-haired Spanish women wore loose, short-sleeved gowns of silk, crepe, or calico, complemented by colorful belts and jewelry. As they had Indian maids to cook and clean their houses, the ladies spent their time knitting and doing needlework.

The only flaw in the serenity of rancho life was the continuing migration into California of American citizens. Tension and jealousy grew into hatred; the Mexicans feared an American takeover of California, and the new settlers feared they would be expelled by the Mexican California officials.

Violence broke out in 1845 when Captain Elliott Libbey, of the American ship Tasso, was stabbed and beaten in Yerba Buena. Groups of Americans began forming makeshift armies whose members patrolled the northern countryside.

In June 1846, Mexican General Vallejo and others were captured in Sonoma by these American vigilantes in what came to be called the Bear Flag Revolt. By July, a state of war existed between the United States and Mexico.

The American troops were led by Captain J. C. Fremont. The Mexican leader was Jose Castro, lieutenant colonel of cavalry in the Mexican army and acting commandant of the Department of California.

A memorable quote from the *1880 History of Marin* gives us a picture of Fremont's party:

> *There were Americans, French, English, Swiss, Poles, Russians, Prussians, Chileans, Germans, Greeks, Austrians, Pawnees, native Indians, etc., all riding side by side and talking a polyglot of lingual hash never exceeded in diversibility since the confusion of tongues at the tower of Babel.*
>
> *Some wore the relics of their home-spun garments, some relied upon the antelope and the bear for their wardrobe, some lightly habited in buckskin leggings and a coat of war paint, and their weapons were equally various.*
>
> *There was the grim old hunter with his long heavy rifle, the farmer with his double-barreled shot-gun, the Indian with his bow and arrows; and others with horse-pistols, revolvers, sabres, ships' cutlasses, bowie-knives and 'pepper-boxes' (Allen's revolvers).*

Thus was the war won. The United States acquired California in a settlement with the Mexican government at Guadalupe Hidalgo on February 2, 1848.

Novato was soon transformed from a sleepy Mexican community to an American frontier town. Within a year, Americans and European immigrants were rushing to California as part of the gold rush. Settlers built saloons, hotels, and stores. The beef and timber industries grew to serve both the local population and the thousands pouring into San Francisco. The oak and laurel in the area were cut and exported by the pioneers, and the supply was soon exhausted.

As Novato is farther inland than other portions of Marin and free from strong sea breezes, the early pioneers found its milder climate perfect for growing fruit. Joseph B. Sweetser and Francis De Long bought 15,000 acres in the mid-1850s. De Long eventually bought out his partner and by 1880 had 20,000 apple trees, 3,500 pear trees, 3,000 apricot trees, 200 cherry trees, 600 peach trees, 500 almond trees, and a vineyard with 8,000 vines. Dr. Galen Burdell's wife planted an orchard of tropical fruit with orange trees from Los Angeles, Japan, Florida, and Tahiti.

The center of town was originally around Novato Creek on the old county road now called South Novato Boulevard. Local products were shipped out by barge and scow to San Francisco and

*Trains arrived in Novato in 1879.* Arrigoni Family Collection.

to points east and west. These same water transports brought supplies to Novato and the North Marin area.

Trains came to Novato in 1879, connecting Sonoma County to Novato, Ignacio, and San Rafael. The railroad enabled school children to attend high school in San Rafael, and workers could commute to San Francisco by a variety of connections.

Produce could now be shipped quickly, and it found a ready market. Frank Gnoss, a Swiss immigrant to Novato, raised hens and planted fruit trees such as peaches and apricots. (Two of his sons have served as county officials: William A. Gnoss was a county supervisor from 1952 to 1971, and George Gnoss was county clerk from 1962 to 1974.)

The area around the railroad station—where there were hotels, a blacksmith, a grocery, livery stables, and a cheese factory— was then referred to as : "New Town," and the area around Novato Creek became "Old Town." The first Novato school was built in 1859, and the picturesque Presbyterian church was erected in 1896. The school was located at the corner of Grant Avenue and US 101 at what is now called Redwood Boulevard.

In 1918, an area of lots named the Sweetser Subdivision Number One, in the district of First through Seventh streets, was offered for sale. The population of Novato continued to increase, especially in the 1930s, with the construction of Hamilton Field, though the

Depression nearly wiped out Novato's big orchards and poultry farmers. Prices for products dropped so low that orchards were left to die, and many small farmers lost their land.

After World War II, tract homes began to be built for the big population boom. The freeway was constructed and ran right through the heart of town (the bypass was not built until the 1970s). In 1948, the North Marin Water District was formed, making Novato independent of the Marin Municipal Water District. A drive to incorporate the city began in the 1950s and finally succeeded in 1960. The city now could exercise control over the housing development. Novato continues to grow but does so in an orderly, planned fashion.

## Old Town Novato

Old Town Novato is the part of town that grew up around the old train depot at the east end of Grant Avenue at Railroad Avenue (it was known then as "New Town"). The picturesque depot, painted in mustard and brown colors, was built in 1917 to replace an earlier station. It closed in 1959 as there were no more passenger trains running through Novato, although occasionally

*Gina Burrafato at the old Novato train station.*

a freight train still passes through.

Near the train station, at 701 Scott Court, is the historic Flatiron Building. This elongated, triangular-shaped structure has had a checkered career as a Wells Fargo office, drugstore, newspaper office, antique shop, real estate office, bookstore operated by the John Birch Society, and sandwich shop.

The remodeled stores of Old Town Novato are along three blocks of Grant Avenue east of Redwood Boulevard. There is a western theme, even an antique metal hitching post. On this tree-lined street are antique shops, a saddle shop, restaurants, and many specialty stores.

## Novato's Municipal Buildings

Two blocks north of Old Town are several historic buildings now being used by the community. When in 1960 Novato voted to incorporate, the old Presbyterian church, located at the southwest corner of Sherman and De Long, became its city hall. The interior was remodeled for offices and the outside painted red with white trim. The entrance foyer is now decorated in a turn-of-the-century decor with old photos of the Novato area and two heavy wooden church pews for seating.

North of the city hall are two houses also taken over by the city for offices. One was the church parsonage, used for many years by the police department, which is now occupied by the finance department. The other house, north of the church, contains the parks and recreation department.

The Novato Community House, built in 1923, is west of the city hall on Machin and now houses the city council chambers. Painted a deep red to match the city hall, the Community House still has iron horse-head hitching posts in front. This building has always been the nucleus of Novato's cultural and social life. Senior citizen groups meet here for bingo, cards, and pool, and the Novato Community Players present their productions here. Preschool children also use the facilities for a variety of programs.

Across De Long Avenue from the city hall is the Novato History Museum and Archives, founded and directed for many years by Novato volunteer city historian, Peg Coady. The Novato Historical Guild, which she organized, runs the museum. Peg now lives in Auburn, California and the Novato Museum has been directed by

*The Novato City Hall.*

Jacqueline Moore since 1982.

This pioneer house, built around 1850, was once the home of Henry Jones, the local postmaster. Its style of architecture is called "eclectic pioneer," which incorporates various European architectural styles remembered by the pioneers and used when they built their homes.

*The Novato History Museum.*

The house was originally located in Old Town. On June 11, 1972, it was donated to the city by Fabian Bobo and moved to its present location where restoration began. The museum opened on June 6, 1976. The archives and collection of artifacts cover the period from post-Indian to the present and include a section upstairs designated the "Hamilton Field Room." It contains a collection of photos and artifacts about the former active air base. The museum also has many oral history tapes made by members of Novato pioneer families.

You may visit the Novato History Museum on Thursday and Saturday from 10:00 A.M. to 4:00 P.M., except holidays. For an appointment for groups on other days, call 892-2358 or 897-4320.

Next door to the museum, at 807 De Long Avenue, is the Novato Chamber of Commerce, located in what was a Queen Anne-style cottage purchased in 1902 (or 1904) by Charles Edgar Carlile. Close to the house is a three-story wooden water tower.

Restoration began in 1973 by Landmark Associates. The water tank was moved slightly and connected to the house, and unique offices were built in them both. The "tank house" now features a circular staircase, exposed beams, redwood walls, and three offices on three separate levels; the house has five offices.

## Pioneer Park

About a ten-minute drive from Old Town is Pioneer Park and the old Pioneer Cemetery. Go west on Grant Avenue, which runs into Virginia Avenue at a slight right angle. Virginia Avenue ends at the park, whose entrance is on Simmons Lane.

The five-acre Pioneer Park was established as part of efforts to restore the old cemetery which had been heavily-damaged by vandals. The original plan was to level off the knoll and remove all the old headstones, but a citizens group formed by Peg Coady worked to save the historical cemetery. (In 1974, Peg Coady and Will Lieb won an award from Novato for the "best citizen project of the year" for their work.)

The entire project of creating the park and restoring the cemetery was completed with a $2,600 budget plus thousands of hours of volunteer time. Today, the results can be enjoyed—well-groomed, sloping lawns, picnic tables under tall shade trees, a children's playground, a gazebo, and several tennis courts. The park is open between 6:00 A.M. and 10:00 P.M. Note that dogs must be on a lease, and fires may be built only in barbecue pits.

The old cemetery is at the top of a knoll and can be reached by climbing stairs made of railroad ties. Towering above the marble gravestones are two obelisks marking the burial sites of the cemetery's earliest occupants, Mrs. Charlotte C. Haven (1861) and Maria Ingalls Sweetser (1876). Other members of the Sweetser family, who originally owned the land, as well as many prominent Novato pioneers are buried here.

Walking among the gravestones and reading the names and epitaphs of these early settlers, you can begin to imagine what it was like one hundred years ago in the frontier town of Novato.

## Miwok Park

Miwok Park, which includes a Coast Miwok village archeological site, is just west of Pioneer Park at 2200 Novato Boulevard. Here, on thirty-four acres are lawns and shaded picnic areas, a creek, a banquet-sized barbecue with sink facilities, and a preschool children's playground.

A garden identifies "California Native Plants used for tools, food, shelter, clothing and basketry by Coastal Indians." Remains of the archeological dig have been moved inside, but occasionally arrowheads and other artifacts are found under the trees along the creek.

The Marin Museum of the American Indian (formerly the Miwok Museum), was opened in 1973 as the Novato Prehistory Museum in a small two-story house donated by Crocker Bank. The museum contains artifacts found in the archeological site, plus collections of Indian art of the Americas from Alaska to South America. There are tools and baskets, mortars and pestles, collections of obsidian arrowheads and clam shell beads, a quiver with bow and arrows, and fishing equipment. A display shows the uses the Indians made of tule, a low, bulrush marsh plant. Tule was woven into receptacles for serving food, deer-mask hunting disguises, and leggings and moccasins. It was also used for constructing houses and building canoes.

Beside the permanent exhibit showing the life of the Coast Miwok, there are changing exhibits on other North American Indians. Current programs include demonstrations in basket weaving, puppet shows of Indian tales, Indian games, a Miwok discovery hunt and hands-on activities such as grinding acorns in authentic stone mortars.

Admission to the museum is free, although a small donation is requested. Hours are 10:00 A.M. to 4:00 P.M. Tuesday through

*Indian Valley Golf Course.*

Saturday, and noon to 4:00 P.M. on Sunday; closed Monday and most holidays. Special tours and field trips may be arranged. (897-4064)

# Indian Valley Golf Course

Opened in 1958, this 212-acre public golf course is most famous for its elevator (which looks like a tram) running between the thirteenth green and the fourteenth tee. The clubhouse, with a fully-stocked pro shop plus the "19th Hole" Bar and Restaurant, has a lovely view of Stafford Lake.

The turnoff to the Indian Valley Golf Course is 1.8 miles west of Miwok Park on Novato Boulevard (which becomes Hicks Valley Road). As you turn left on the mile-long road leading to the clubhouse, you pass the Novato Creek Dam which forms Stafford Lake.

A practice range and putting green are available. (897-1118)

# Stafford Lake County Park

The entrance to Stafford Lake County Park is on Hicks Valley Road, approximately half a mile beyond the entrance road to the Indian Valley Golf Course.

The park covers 139 acres, and many picnic areas lie scattered about on the manicured lawns sloping down to the lake. Several of the picnic tables are protected from wind by semicircular wooden structures. Stafford Lake is the winter home of a flock of Canada geese.

Other facilities here include a softball diamond, volleyball court, children's playground and restrooms.

The park is open from 6:00 A.M. to 8:00 P.M. There is a $3 parking fee on summer weekends and $1 the rest of the time. Rules prohibit boats, pets, open fires, swimming, and wading. There is a large picnic area capable of accommodating over three hundred people, but a permit must be obtained.

For more information call the Marin County Parks and Recreation Department at 499-6387.

*The children's playground at Stafford Lake County Park.*

# Gnoss Field Marin County Airport

T he Marin County Airport, originally called the Novato Airport, was started by Paul W. "Woody" Binford, a flight
instructor in World War II. In 1946, Woody leased farmland
two miles north of Novato, built a dirt runway and a T-hangar, and
with one airplane—an Aeronca Champion—began teaching students
to fly.

In 1947, Binford took in a partner, Jack Lewis, who added his
own plane, and the two men built a second hangar. Binford had
found that the angle of the runway was not quite right for the heavy
winds whipping around Mt. Burdell; so they carved out another
one 3,000 feet long in an east-west direction.

Now the airfield met the requirements of the Civil Aviation
Administration (now the FAA), and they could teach flying to ex-
GIs, who could use service benefits to pay for lessons. Eventually
the flying school grew to six planes and fifty students.

In 1949, the government changed the rules; GIs enrolled in flight
training now had to prove they were specifically going to use the
skill in their vocation. This killed the program, and by October
1949, Binford and Lewis had given up their lease on the land. Harry

Tollefson, another flight instructor from World War II, took over and ran the airport facilities until the county of Marin bought him out in 1968.

The new Marin County Airport was named "Gnoss Field" for North Marin's popular supervisor, William Gnoss, who had worked hard for many years to expand aviation in Marin. At the dedication ceremonies, Woody Binford flew the first plane into the airport—a large, single-engine Navion that seated four people. Bill Gnoss was his special passenger.

The current major runway was paved in 1968 with asphalt six inches thick. The runway lies north to south, is 3,300 feet long, 60 feet wide, and stands one foot above sea level. The biggest problem pilots face here are strong rolling gusts of wind from the western hills especially in the spring. The master plan at Gnoss Field called for a second large runway to be built in an east-west direction, and a control tower to be constructed; but neither project has been undertaken to date. A rotating beacon of light showing the location of the airport shines from sunset to sunrise. The runway and taxi ways are lit all night, and there are red and white vertical approach beams.

Gnoss Field has one fixed base operator: Marin Air Service (897-7101). It is both a Cessna and a Piper dealer. The operator has fuel available and provides service maintenance.

Marin Air Service operates a radio called "unicom" on a VHF frequency of 123.0. Pilots may call in for information on gas, overnight parking availability ($4.00 to $6.00 per night), and weather conditions. Pilots headed for Marin may also get weather information from the Oakland Terminal Control, which will also notify them if Gnoss Field has closed down for any reason. Unicom operates in summer from 7:30 A.M. to 7:00 P.M., and from 8:00 A.M. to 6:00 P.M. in winter. Fuel is available until 8:00 P.M.

A new restaurant, the Marin County Cafe, has recently opened on weekdays from 8:00 A.M. to 2:30 P.M. They will expand their hours in the future.

To drive to Gnoss Field, take the Atherton Avenue turnoff north of Novato on Highway 101. (A blue and white sign prior to this turnoff says "Airport.") Turn right on Atherton, then left on Binford Road (named for Woody Binford), which is a frontage road east of the freeway. The airport is approximately one-and-a-half miles north.

# Rancho Olompali

**M**arin County residents who have been involved with archeological study of the Miwok Indians claim that the Indian mounds at Rancho Olompali, north of Novato, are even older than Site #38 at Miller Creek, which goes back 2,600 years. Archeologists have spent several years at Olompali, but much more research needs to be completed. Some people claim the Indians occupied the site between approximately 1300 and 1852 AD.

An interesting theory on the history of Olompali was put forth in 1979 by Dr. Robert C. Thomas, an East Bay physician. In his book *Drake at Olomp-ali,* he claims that Sir Francis Drake, on his circumnavigation of the world in 1579, anchored his ship, the *Golden Hinde,* in the Chol-Olom harbor on the Petaluma River, then sojourned for a month on the Rancho Olompali site.

Thomas traces his ancestry back to Camilo Ynitia, son of the Miwok chief Olompali, who received the rancho as a Mexican land grant in 1843. Thomas's great-grandmother was Maria Antonia Ynitia, daughter of Camilo Ynitia. He uses family legends to bolster his claim, to the point of recalling the Indians' reaction when the ship arrived—they thought it was a ghost ship manned by strange aliens. Thomas also suggests the name Novato originated with Drake, who called the area "Nova-Albion" and added the Indian word "ko" to identify the native people. "Nova-Albion-Ko" became shortened over the years to "Nova-Ko" which eventually became "Novato." (Another theory is that Novato was named by a priest at Mission Rafael in honor of Saint Novatus.) One piece of evidence supports Thomas's claim: in 1974 an Elizabeth I coin dated 1567 was unearthed at Olompali by anthropologist Charles Slaymaker.

Slaymaker is now a researcher at the University of California at Davis where he is still cataloguing artifacts he collected at Olompali between 1972 and 1977. There are between 50,000 to 100,000 beads, bones, bottles and other specimens.

Ruins of adobe buildings used by the Indians still stand at Olompali whose principal village was called "A 'palako'ta." When the adobe was built is in question, but it was most likely in either 1776 or 1828. An account in the *1880 History of Marin* states that members of a Spanish expedition taught the Indians to make adobe during a stop there in 1776. Subsequent historians claim it would have been impossible for the adobe bricks to have been mixed, formed, sun-dried, and placed in construction in the short time the Spanish were there.

Probably these Indians learned the construction of adobe when they helped build a new church for the San Rafael mission. After its completion in 1824, some of the Indians were allowed freedom. They returned to Olompali and constructed the first adobe there sometime before 1828.

The application for the Olompali land grant was actually made by Mariano Vallejo, commandant at Sonoma, in the name of Camilo Ynitia. It was awarded on October 22, 1843.

James Black, originally from Scotland, who at this time was county assessor as well as county coroner, set the grant at 8,456 acres. Camilo Ynitia, a good friend of James Black, sold him the property in 1852 for $5,000 in gold coin.

Black gave the property to his daughter Mary when she married Dr. Galen Burdell, a dentist, in 1863. The couple moved onto the property three years later. In 1874, they visited Japan and came back with plants and Japanese gardeners who laid out the first formal garden in Marin.

In 1913 their son James and his wife Josephine remodeled the old timber house into a twenty-six-room stucco mansion incorporating the old adobe within its walls. This house remained in the Burdell family until 1942. After changing hands several times, the house burned in 1969. Only the original adobe walls survived.

For about a year previous to the fire and for a short time thereafter, the mansion and surrounding acreage were occupied by a hippie commune called the "Chosen Family." The commune was financed by its founder, houseboat-builder and real estate speculator Donald C. McCoy, Jr. Among the inhabitants were former show people and school teachers—even a former nun. McCoy's relatives fought in the courts to prevent him from spending his entire fortune on the venture, and the police made raids on the dwellings in search of drugs. Because the members of the commune frequently wore no clothing, especially around the pool, the Chosen Family became a curiosity, but the members were rarely seen in town except for occasional visits to the local ice cream parlors.

Tragedy and near tragedy always hovered close to the Chosen

Family. One day, one of the small children fell off a tricycle and drowned in the pool. Commune members escaped injury when the house burned, but Novato Fire Chief George Cavallero died when his car plunged off Highway 101 as he sped to the fire following a fire truck. With hopes for an idyllic life dashed by internal problems and sad events, the Chosen Family left Olompali not long after the fire.

In 1972, the Rancho Olompali was designated a Historic Place on the National Register and became a State Historical Landmark. The property is now owned by the state of California but remains undeveloped. One day it will be a park of 760 acres but lack of state funding has delayed the opening for fourteen years already. Some restoration of the formal gardens has been accomplished by Marin County youths working for the Youth Conservation Corps.

Another group of some 800 members called "Olompali People" are pushing for an improved access road, the restoration of historic buildings and the opening of a visitor's center in the wood-frame house built by Galen Burdell in the mid-1880s. They raised $70,000 for Olompali's master plan.

The future Olompali State Historic Park is also remembered as the site of the only battle of the Bear Flag Revolt fought in Marin. William Todd, believed to have been the nephew of Abraham Lincoln, was taken prisoner along with other Americans and held by the Mexicans at Rancho Olompali. (Todd had designed the flag for the revolt, which is now the California state flag.)

Charmaine Burdell, the granddaughter of James Burdell, lived at Olompali as a child. She is very interested in history and has investigated Olompali's original owner, Camilo Ynitia. Since it was not the custom to give land grants to Indians, she believes he may actually have been the son of a Spanish officer.

Someday when Rancho Olompali is a park, you will be able to explore this historic spot, remembering the very different lifestyles of the people who lived here and enjoyed the lovely formal gardens, the magnificent old magnolia tree, agaves, pomegranate trees, date palms, and majestic royal palms. There is also a handsome circular fish pond with a miniature volcanic rock mountain in the middle, once topped by a stork. As a child, Charmaine Burdell swam in this fish pond; when it was emptied, she used it for roller skating.

The old adobe walls built by the Indians are fenced-in and protected under a makeshift wooden roof. This is all that remains

*Geese and ducks at Stafford Lake County Park.*

of the Miwok who lived quietly on this land until the Spanish padres came and changed their lives. The marsh where the Indians once canoed was filled years ago to make way for Highway 101. The roar of traffic on this nearby freeway brings us back to the twentieth century.

# West Marin 10

## The Pastoral Inland Valleys

T he pastoral valleys of West Marin have changed very little in the past 130 years. Today, there are dairy ranches and a scattering of small towns. Visitors and residents delight at the open hills and fields dotted with grazing cattle, horses, and deer.

The valleys were part of two Mexican land grants awarded in 1844: *Rancho de Nicasio*, granted to Pablo de la Guerra and Juan Cooper; and *Rancho Canada de San Geronimo*, given to Rafael Cacho.

Early California pioneers ranched this country, hunted the plentiful game, and fished for steelhead trout and salmon in Lagunitas Creek. The trains reached the valley in 1875, and many travelers decided that this was the perfect vacation spot. Early settlements were tracts of summer homes; later these were converted to year-round residences.

The peaceful, rural existence continued undisturbed until 1967 when suddenly there was talk of an eight-lane freeway going through the Ross Valley and continuing west. It threatened to open up West Marin to big real estate development.

For the next six years, preservation of this land became a dominant issue in Marin politics. The freeway was stopped, and in 1972, in a series of controversial votes, the Board of Supervisors created a new agricultural zoning which provided that only one residence could be build for every sixty acres. This applied to a large portion of West Marin's 350,000 acres.

In 1973, a countywide masterplan was adopted, and a new community plan was then developed for West Marin. Put into effect in May 1978, the plan limits development to one unit per twenty

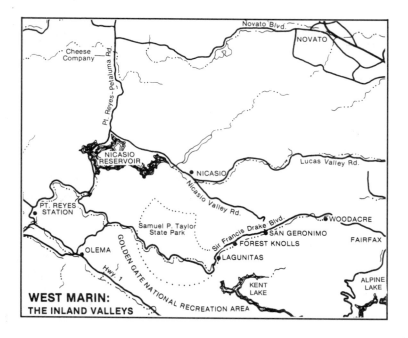

WEST MARIN:
THE INLAND VALLEYS

acres, assuring that the rural flavor of these valleys will be preserved.

The West Marin valleys are just over the hill from Fairfax. After passing through the town of Fairfax, Sir Francis Drake Boulevard begins the climb up and over White's Hill. This mile-and-a-half of curvy two-lane road is a continuing problem for the highway department, as it cracks and slides regularly. The hill was an even larger problem in the early 1870s when the railroad was being built. Rather than going over the top, railroad officials used Chinese labor to build a 1,200-foot-long tunnel through the hill near the summit. In 1904 they opened a second tunnel, 3,190 feet long, and eliminated a 4.7-mile climb. Both tunnels are closed today.

As you cross White's Hill, you leave the suburbs behind. The open hills are before you, gold in summer and fall, green in winter and spring. Though only seven miles from the freeway, the valleys are a peaceful change from busy, suburban Marin.

As the road levels out at the bottom of White's Hill, a sign points to the left. This is San Geronimo Drive, leading to the tiny hamlet of Woodacre.

# Woodacre

The land around Woodacre was once owned by Adolph Mailliard, grandson of Joseph Bonaparte, Napoleon's brother. Adolph maintained three dairy ranches and a mansion here. (The Mailliard home later became the Woodacre Lodge and the Woodacre Improvement Club until it burned in 1958. The family remained prominent in Marin affairs for many years. Adolph's great-grandson, William Somers Mailliard, represented Marin in Washington, D.C. as a congressman from 1955 to 1974.)

When the North Pacific Coast Railroad arrived in 1875, the valley was suddenly opened up to San Francisco commuters. Two stations were eventually built in Woodacre: the Woodacre Lodge Station (near the old grocery store on what is now Railroad Avenue, south of Carson Road) and the Woodacre Station (to the northwest, just south of Park Street). The tracks came straight from the tunnel through White's Hill and into the heart of town. Carson Road crossed under the tracks and was called the "subway." You can still see evidence of the abutments.

In 1907, the railroad changed to a broad gauge and became the Northwestern Pacific. Two commute trains ran morning and evening with a midday freight; train time to San Francisco was one-and-one-half hours.

In 1913 the Lagunitas Development Company built a summer-home tract here, and Woodacre could then be called a "town." The Improvement Club was organized in 1924, and a post office was opened a year later.

Train service was discontinued in 1933 and since then, although the population has increased, little else has changed. Woodacre is still a small country town, and it is not at all unusual to see kids riding horses down the middle of the main streets.

The Woodacre Improvement Club (also known as the San Geronimo Valley Swim and Tennis Club), offer sports facilities which include two tennis courts, an adult pool, a children's pool, ball fields, and a clubhouse. The pool is open to the public for a fee on Tuesdays only. For information call 488-0708. In Woodacre's small business center, you'll find the Woodacre Market and Deli, open every day from 9:00 A.M. to 7:00 P.M.

*The train station in Woodacre.* Old postcard, courtesy of Bill Allen.

# San Geronimo

F rom Woodacre, Sir Francis Drake Boulevard continues on through the rolling hills of this lovely valley.

Just past the town, on the parallel San Geronimo Valley Drive, is the San Geronimo Water Treatment Plant. It was built in 1962 by the Marin Municipal Water District and serves the residents of the San Geronimo Valley and all areas north of Corte Madera to Hamilton Air Force Base. It is open to the public by appointment from 9:00 A.M. to 3:00 P.M., and an interesting tour acquaints visitors with the procedures for purifying and filtering water. Large groups may also make appointments by calling 488-9184 or the District office at 924-4600.

Farther on is the tiny town of San Geronimo, on the south side of Sir Francis Drake Boulevard. Adjacent to the Valley Community Church is the old railroad station. The building was moved west from its original site for the safety of the children who attend the church nursery school.

Half a mile west of the San Geronimo train station was a gold mine begun in 1878 by Adolph Mailliard. By 1880, the mine was being operated by fourteen men who worked in three shifts of eight hours each, plus two engineers who worked twelve-hour shifts. *The 1880 History of Marin County* reported that the value of the ore averaged from $30 to $40 per ton although it had yielded up to $90. The ore contained gold, silver, iron, manganese, antimony, and tracings of nickel.

On the north side of Sir Francis Drake Boulevard is the clubhouse of the San Geronimo Golf Club. This attractive golf course, covering 150 acres of the old Roy Ranch, began operation in 1965. A subdivision was created at that time, allowing a few homes to be built around the golf course on lots of one to ten acres. The golf course was closed for several years, then reopened in 1988. For information: on the golf fees call the pro shop at 488-4030; restaurant, 488-9849. In May 1990 the golf course was sold to the Japanese C & N Corporation, but the facilities are still open to the public.

Here at the golf course, Nicasio Valley Road intersects Sir Francis Drake and leads north toward the town of Nicasio, at the geographic center of Marin County.

# Forest Knolls

Continuing west on Sir Francis Drake, Forest Knolls is approximately one mile away. This is another area where one-time summer homes are now year-round residences.

*Rick Seramin plays the San Geronimo Golf Course.*

Located on the main road is the Forest Knolls Garage and Chevron gas station operated by the Yerion family since 1947. For sale inside are beer, candy and chips.

The House of Richard is an interesting shop, with natural foods, a deli, ice cream parlor, handcrafts, imports, clothes, rugs, seeds, baskets, and cosmetics. Nearby are a few antique and specialty shops.

# Lagunitas

L agunitas is just a short distance past Forest Knolls and marks a change in terrain—from open hills to redwood forest. Again, as a result of the railroad, people began buying cottages in this area around 1905.

# Samuel P. Taylor State Park

T he road is now shaded by thick stands of redwood trees, with lush ferns growing beneath. Seven-tenths of a mile past Lagunitas, a sign welcomes you to Samuel P. Taylor State Park. The Irving Picnic Area, the park office at the main entrance to the camping area, and the Madrone Picnic Area are all just off Sir Francis Drake Boulevard.

Picnicking, hiking, swimming in the creek, and camping under the redwoods are just as popular here today as they were over a hundred years ago when the North Pacific Coast Railroad deposited vacationers at the two-story hotel and into the Camp Taylor grounds.

At that time there was a paper mill here, built along the creek by Samuel Penfield Taylor, a transplanted Easterner. It supplied newsprint, bags, manila wrapping, election ballots, and other paper products to San Francisco.

Taylor's first mill opened in 1856 using a waterwheel. A larger mill was built in 1884 using steam power. Chinese supplied rags from San Francisco for the paper, and some of them worked at the site.

A small town emerged known as "Taylorville," which consisted

*The old paper mill at Samuel P. Taylor State Park.* Courtesy of Bill Silverthorne Photo Collection.

of about a hundred families, a boardinghouse, store, hotel, post office, blacksmith, and a carpenter.

Taylor died in 1886, leaving his widow, son, and brothers to run the business. Using the land as collateral, Mrs. Taylor borrowed money from Alexander Montgomery; but when the country suffered a depression in 1893, she was unable to repay the loan. After Montgomery died, his widow Elizabeth married Arthur Rodgers, who eventually gained control of the property by foreclosure.

The land became a park in a very roundabout way. Boyd Stewart, a West Marin rancher from a pioneer family, remembers the story well. In 1924, a year after his family bought their ranch, Boyd, then a student at Stanford, was sent by his father to visit Elizabeth Rodgers in her suite at the Fairmont Hotel in San Francisco.

Boyd was understandably nervous. He was to discuss a mutual boundary between their lands which had not been clearly established. At that time, Mrs. Rodgers owned about 25,000 acres in the Camp Taylor-Devil's Gulch area. When Stewart told her what he wanted, the widow consulted a set of books and thumbed through several before finding the papers that identified this property. Then she asked him to do something for her. She had decided she would give the land encompassing Camp Taylor to

*Ranger Nedra Martinez and Park Aid Erica Smolowe welcome visitors to the Samuel P. Taylor State Park.*

the county for a park. Boyd was to present the offer to the Marin County Board of Supervisors.

Stewart carried out her request, but the Board of Supervisors refused the offer, preferring instead to collect the taxes. Rebuffed,

Mrs. Rodgers countered by refusing to pay taxes on the parcel. This eventually resulted in default of the land to the county.

The Marin County Conservation League then became interested and urged the county to forego the taxes and let the state take over the land. The League put up money for legal fees, waged a large campaign, and emerged victorious; the area became a state park in 1945.

Today there are 2,600 acres, many picnic sites, sixty campsites, two group camp areas located in the Madrone Group area which have a combined capacity of 75 people, a picnic area for groups of up to a hundred people, and a special area set aside for backpackers and bikers. Facilities in the park include rest rooms, hot showers, picnic tables, and barbecue pits. Horsemen use the Devil's Gulch Camp, which has a hitching rack, watering troughs, and camping facilities for up to 25 people and their horses. Reservations are necessary and can be made by contacting the District headquarters for the Devils Gulch Camp and Redwood Grove Picnic areas at 456-5218; for camping reservations call MISTRIX at 1-800-444-7275; for Samuel P. Taylor State Park, 488-9897. The fees at this time are: day parking, $3.00; weekends, $4.00; hiking and biking, $2.00 per person.

Dogs with licenses and proof of rabies vaccination are allowed in the park, but they cannot be taken on the trails and must always be on a leash.

The old mill burned in 1915, and all that is left are rock walls covered with moss and fallen leaves. The mill site is a short distance north of the main picnic area adjacent to the creek; a sign marks the trail down to the ruins. At the site there is an historical plaque and an exhibit of old photographs of Taylorville in its heyday. A line of iron strips in the ground between the mill and the creek once held a redwood pipe that brought water to the waterwheel.

Other trails follow Paper Mill Creek and the old narrow-gauge railroad bed. One takes you up Barnabe Peak which is 1,498 feet high and has a wonderful view.

The Paper Mill Dam and Fish Ladder are marked by a plaque stating that this was the first fish ladder of its kind on the Pacific Coast. It was designed and built by Stephen Schuyler Stedman in 1887. Duplicates were later constructed elsewhere in California, Oregon, and Washington.

From Samuel P. Taylor Park, Sir Francis Drake Boulevard leaves the thick forest and winds through open hills, meeting Highway 1 at the town of Olema (see Chapter 11).

# Nicasio

To reach the town of Nicasio, return to Nicasio Valley Road at the San Geronimo Golf Club. This road goes north through ranchland and redwood trees to Nicasio, approximately 4.2 miles from Sir Francis Drake Boulevard. Lucas Valley Road intersects Nicasio Valley Road about half a mile before the town; this connects with Highway 101.

Nicasio was once a populous village inhabited by the Nicasio Indians, a powerful tribe numbering many thousands. Then the Spanish and the Americans came, and by 1880, only eight wickiups (tule huts) remained.

By the late 1800s, ranching, dairying, and logging the redwood forests were important enterprises in this area. The village of Nicasio was thriving. There was a three-story hotel with twenty-two rooms, a bar, dining room, kitchen, and parlor. Other buildings sprang up—a Catholic church, blacksmith shop, store, meat market, livery stable, and boardinghouse. The post office was established in 1870, followed later by a racetrack and a creamery. A stagecoach from San Geronimo connected Nicasio to the rest of Marin. Nicasio's great ambition was to be the county seat, but this did not happen. It lost that bid to San Rafael in 1863.

Then the railroad came to Marin and roads began to be built, but not to Nicasio, isolated in the center of the county, away from the harbors and centers of commerce. The town was locked in time, and today Nicasio appears more rural than it did in 1880.

In the center of town is a large open square donated by William J. Miller for the courthouse that was never built. Today it is used for baseball games and town barbecues. St. Mary's Catholic Church stands facing the square. This small white church was built in 1867 of locally-milled redwood. In 1967, St. Mary's parishioners celebrated their hundredth anniversary and were presented by the Native Sons and Daughters of the Golden West with a plaque declaring the structure a historical monument.

*The pioneer Nicasio School.*

Across the square is Druid's Hall, built in 1933. It is used for private meetings of the Nicasio Grove of the Druid's Lodge. The building next door was a pioneer butcher shop that opened for business one hundred years ago.

The only commerce left in Nicasio is the Nicasio Land Company owned and operated by Peter Edwards, and a bar and restaurant called Rancho Nicasio, once the site of the Nicasio Hotel. The post office and a public telephone are located in this building.

The old Nicasio School, just north of town on Nicasio Valley Road, was built in 1871 to replace an earlier version erected in 1866. It was declared an historical site in 1959. The building was remodeled and painted red by its owner, the late local judge and avid horseman, Ray Shone. The old school is still a private residence of the Shone family.

Nicasio is the home of artist, George Sumner, who came to national prominence in 1985 with his painting titled "Sweet Liberty." This picture was reproduced as the official poster commemorating the centennial of the Statue of Liberty, July 4, 1986. Sumner is also famous for his "environmental-impressionist" paintings of whales, dolphins and seascapes. You may tour his studio by appointment, 332-0353.

## Nicasio Reservoir

Just past the old Nicasio School, the Nicasio Reservoir begins. Built in 1960 by the Marin Municipal Water District, the reservoir at maximum covers 869 acres of the Nicasio Valley.

The Water District maintains a 100-foot-wide strip around the reservoir and allows fishing and hiking from sunrise to sunset. Fish are stocked by the California Department of Fish and Game and include bass, bluegill, and catfish. The latter, newly introduced, are expected to thrive in the warm, slightly muddy water. Also found are large carp introduced from Europe centuries ago. They are especially popular with Asians. They were probably introduced when fishermen brought them as minnows for bait.

The Nicasio Point Nature Preserve, northeast of the dam site and just off the Point Reyes-Petaluma Road, consists of twenty-two acres of open space. It was donated to the county of Marin in 1968 by William Field. The County Parks Department once envisioned a regional park in this area, but tight budgets precluded its development. There are no public facilities here, but hikes are welcome.

## Marin French Cheese Company

Founded in 1865 by Jefferson Thompson and still run by members of the family, the Marin French Cheese Company produces the

*Gina Burrafato at the Marin French Cheese Company.*

*Dairy cattle can be seen throughout West Marin.*

world famous "Rouge et Noir" brand of Camembert cheese based on the famous "Camembert veritable" of Normandie, France. A brochure from the company states that this variety of cheese was named by Napoleon after the tiny hamlet of Camembert in Orne, France, where it originated.

To get to the cheese company, continue on the Nicasio Valley Road 2.7 miles past the reservoir to the intersection of the Point Reyes-Petaluma Road. Turn right and drive 3.2 miles. The curvy road follows a picturesque creek called Arroyo Sausal which flows through hilly ranch country.

Visitors are invited to sample cheese and tour the factory from 10:00 A.M. to 4:00 P.M. daily. There are large picnic areas next to a duck pond where picnickers can enjoy their cheese along with wine, beer, soda, bread, and other snacks sold inside.

In 1977, a plaque was placed here, dedicated to the California Pioneer Cheese Makers by the Petaluma Parlor of the Native Daughters of the Golden West. The Marin French Cheese Company is open daily from 9:00 A.M. to 5:00 P.M.; it is closed on selected holidays. (707) 762-6001.

From here you can retrace your steps and go on toward Point Reyes, or continue north a short way to Novato Boulevard. Turn right, or east, to arrive in the town of Novato and Highway 101, a distance of about nine miles.

# West Marin

# 11

The Rugged Pacific Coast

T he coast of Marin is separated from the rest of the county by high mountains, hills, and the San Andreas Fault. It is an area of inspiring beauty, a world apart. This is a wild and rugged place, with towering cliffs, white beaches, pristine lakes, and thick forests.

Most of the acreage lies within the boundaries of the Golden Gate National Recreation Area and the Point Reyes National Seashore. Except for enclaves of private land at Muir Beach, Stinson Beach, and Bolinas, the Marin coast line is preserved for public use.

A drive from Muir Beach to Tomales, with time out to explore the Point Reyes peninsula, is an unforgettable experience. Highway 1, the Shoreline Highway, goes up the coast from Muir Beach to Stinson Beach. This narrow road winds along the ridges high above the ocean, and the scenery is breathtaking, the equal of Big Sur. Because of the 1989 earthquake which caused severe cracking and a landslide in January 1990, the road is temporarily closed.

North of Stinson Beach and the Bolinas Lagoon, the road takes an inland route through the rolling hills of the Olema Valley, following the San Andreas faultline. From the little town of Point Reyes Station, Highway 1 continues north along the eastern shore of Tomales Bay. Sir Francis Drake Boulevard, which joins Highway 1 at the town of Olema, goes up the opposite shore of Tomales Bay, then turns west toward the ocean, ending at the remote tip of the Point Reyes promontory.

# Muir Beach

**B**egin your drive up the coast at Muir Beach, which is quite close to Mill Valley in Southern Marin. This semicircular cove on the Pacific Ocean has a lovely sandy beach, creek, lawn, and picnic area with barbecue grills and privies. It is a popular place to fish for surfperch and various species of rockfish. Swimming is discouraged as there are no lifeguards on duty. Dogs are allowed but must be kept under control. Camping is prohibited.

## Muir Beach Overlook

One and a half miles north on Shoreline Highway is Muir Beach Overlook. Turn left at a sign that reads "Vista Point" (the street is also called Muir Beach Overlook) and go through a residential area to the parking lot. From this small park there are spectacular unobstructed views of the ocean with San Francisco to the south and Duxbury Reef to the north. Whale watching is good from this overlook in December and January when the gray whales are migrating south to their spawning lagoon in Mexico. You can see them spouting far out to sea as they swim by (bring your binoculars).

Military buffs will want to explore the World War II gun emplacements in what were called "Base End Stations." Built in 1940, the stations were used as range finders for coastal defense artillery batteries. They became obsolete after the war.

Picnic tables and privies are available here for public use. Several

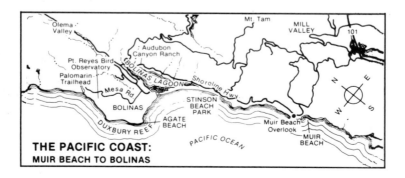

THE PACIFIC COAST:
MUIR BEACH TO BOLINAS

steep paths lead down to rocks below, but watch out—it's a dangerous climb.

# Stinson Beach

Continue another five-and-one-half miles on Highway 1 to Stinson Beach. The vistas along the way are breathtaking, but the narrow, curvy road needs full attention; so stop at one of the turnouts to enjoy the view of this rugged coastline. As you continue down the road, suddenly you see Stinson Beach below you—a three-mile crescent of white sand, one of the finest beaches in Northern California.

Route 1 becomes the main street of the charming shoreline village of Stinson Beach. You will be delighted with the antique stores and art galleries, many featuring works of local artists. Of special note is sculptor Peter Allen whose exquisite marine mammal carvings out of one-hundred-year-old redwood and impressive bronze sculptures are on exhibit at the Stinson Beach Art Center Gallery, 3448 Shoreline Hwy. (868-0553). Stinson Beach Books is also well worth a stop; besides books and cards, it carries an extensive selection of posters.

## Stinson Beach Park

Beyond the town is the Stinson Beach Park, once known as Easkoot's Beach. Captain Alfred Easkoot, the county's first surveyor, ran an overnight "tent camp" here in the 1870s and '80s. He supplied dressing rooms and organized parties and fishing trips.

Around 1880, Nathan Stinson and his wife Rose opened a resort that became known as Willow Camp. A dance floor was the main attraction, and guests flocked to the area by wagon and stageline.

This was followed by another tent city erected in the early 1900s by Archie Upton, Nathan Stinson's stepson. Upton gave beach property to the county in 1932; seven years later, Marin County bought Willow Camp from Eve Stinson Fitzhenry. The area was maintained as a county park until the state of California took it over in 1950. It is now part of the Golden Gate National Recreation Area.

Stinson Beach Park is a popular area for swimming, picnicking, surf fishing, and sunbathing. The beach can become crowded on

*Stinson Beach*

a hot day (a rare occurrence), but you can always find a spot for a solitary walk.

Bird watchers are delighted by the many species here—gulls, sooty shearwaters, pelicans, western grebes, swallows, killdeer, willets, and sandpipers. In winter, thousands of fluttering monarch butterflies cluster in the trees near the beach, displaying their brilliant orange-and-black wings.

Lifeguards are on duty at the beach during the summer and some holidays. Facilities include a snack bar in summer, tables, charcoal-grill stoves, and rest rooms. Hours are 9:00 A.M. to 6:00 PM in winter, 9:00 PM in spring, and 10:00 PM after Memorial Day. Call 868-0942 for information or emergencies and 868-1922 for weather reports, tides, and surf conditions. No camping or pets are allowed.

# Bolinas Lagoon

Just past Stinson Beach, Highway 1 curves around the 1,034-acre Bolinas Lagoon. This quiet body of water, a Marin County Nature Preserve, is one of the most important of the state's surviving lagoons. It is one of the least disturbed tidelands of California, a rich feeding ground for migrating Great

Blue Herons, Great Egrets, ducks, and other waterfowl.

In the early 1800s, the Bolinas end of the lagoon was a harbor for small ocean-going vessels. "Lighters," or very shallow-draft scows, were used for carrying wood down and across the lagoon to be loaded onto larger vessels at Bolinas.

Later, the lagoon began to be filled up by sedimentation from erosion caused by heavy logging and excessive grazing and planting. The Bolinas mesa was an area of intensive potato growing from around 1860 to the 1920s. Farmers planted their potatoes in straight rows instead of following the curvature of the hills, and soil washed down the furrows into the lagoon during winter rains. Tidal mud flats now comprise around 70 percent of the lagoon's acreage.

Located within the lagoon are Kent and Pickleweed islands, both wildlife sanctuaries. The islands have a permanent colony of harbor seals numbering between forty and fifty, which increases to around one hundred after pupping season in June, July, and August. More fish are also found in the lagoon during the summer months. The seasonal migration is thought to originate from San Francisco Bay but may also include seals from other coastal hauling-out grounds such as Drake's Estero.

Pickleweed Island, only one hundred meters from Highway 1, has been used both as a whelping site by the females and a retreat by mothers and pups who prefer to haul out away from the main herd on Kent Island.

To view Pickleweed Island from the edge of Bolinas Lagoon, follow the Shoreline Highway 1.7 miles from the entrance of Stinson Beach Park. There is a small parking area on the right, adjacent to the point where a creek flows under the highway and into the lagoon. Walk across the road past two large posts for the best view of the island. Caution: Signs there warn against disturbing the marine mammals, and a fine of up to $10,000 will be levied for each violation.

In the late afternoon the seals often swim out through the entrance of the lagoon into the ocean to feed. People strolling along Stinson Beach at this time can see seal heads bobbing up and down as the marine mammals swim and fish along the shoreline.

## Audubon Canyon Ranch

The world-famous Audubon Canyon Ranch is located on the

Bolinas Lagoon 3.3 miles from the Stinson Beach Park entrance.

Operated by the Marin, Golden Gate, Sequoia, and Madrone Audubon Societies, the 1,000-acre ranch was purchased in segments over an eighteen-year period in order to preserve the famous heron and egret rookery. Visitors may climb the half-mile Rawlings or Alice Kent Trails, a steep 250 foot rise, and look down on the nesting birds from a special observation point called Henderson Overlook. Mounted telescopes are available for closer viewing.

The four canyons in the ranch are rich in wildlife. As you hike, watch for band-tailed pigeons, hawks, screech owls, vultures, squirrels, gray foxes, raccoons, badgers, bobcats, and deer. Over ninety species of birds have been identified at the ranch, of which sixty remain year round.

Several trails lead hikers through forests of Douglas fir, redwood, and other native California trees. Wildflowers present an array of mixed colors in the spring—purple and white iris, blue hound's-tongue, blue lupine, and orange poppies.

Headquarters for the ranch is a two-story 1875 white frame house. Historical and environmental exhibits, and a nature bookshop are housed in an old milking barn.

Volunteer Canyon borders on Highway 1 and is open to the public by special arrangement. This is the location of another pioneer house, built around 1852. The canyon was named in honor of the volunteers who fought to save the Bolinas Lagoon from a disastrous oil spill in 1971.

The Audubon Canyon Ranch is open 10:00 A.M. to 4:00 P.M. weekends and holidays from around the middle of March to the middle of July. This is the time of year when the white Great Egrets and Great Blue Herons are nesting in the tall redwood trees. Facilities here include picnic tables and rest rooms which are wheel chair accessible as are the displays. Group tours are conducted Tuesday through Friday; reservations may be made by calling 868-9244. There is no charge, but contributions are welcome.

# Bolinas

The beach town of Bolinas was the busiest spot in Marin in the 1850s. Now it lies hidden down an unmarked road on the west side of the lagoon adjacent to the ocean. Road signs mysteriously disappear in the vicinity of Bolinas as soon as they are put up. The little town is surrounded by parkland and, while not unfriendly, the residents value their privacy.

To visit Bolinas, follow Highway 1 to the north end of the lagoon, just over a mile past the Audubon Canyon Ranch. Turn south, or left, on the Olema-Bolinas Road which is opposite the sign marking the "Rancho Baulines." Historians disagree on the origin of the name "Baulinas" or "Baulenes." In her book, *Bolinas, A Narrative of the Days of the Dons,* Marin W. Pepper states that the name meant "whales playground" in the Indian language. The Spanish word for "whale" is "ballena." Others say that the word simply refers to the Indians who lived in that area. Some sources trace the name to a pilot on the Vizcaino expedition.

The original settlers were a Mexican family. In 1836 Rafael Garcia was awarded a Mexican land grant of nearly 9,000 acres, which he called the *Rancho Tomales Y Baulenes.* A few years later, Garcia turned the area over to his brother-in-law Gregorio Briones and moved north into the Olema Valley. The earliest days were bucolic, with the main occupations being dairy ranching and cattle raising.

When the gold rush boom hit California in 1849, Bolinas was affected immediately. There was a virgin forest here, and lumber was urgently required in the exploding city of San Francisco. Thirteen million board feet of lumber were cut during the next thirty years. Sawmills, wharves, lumber schooners, and steamers became part of Bolinas.

Along with lumber, other exports—firewood, dairy products, potatoes, chickens, and eggs—brought in big profits. Hundreds of thousands of murre eggs from the Farallon Islands were collected by Bolinas residents and sold, nearly wiping out that unique bird colony.

At this time Bolinas was connected to the rest of the county by boat, wagon road, and horse trails. A road, part of the Shoreline Highway, was opened in 1870. The railroad never made it this far.

Today the way to Bolinas is the same—by water or by the single road. When driving into town, watch on your right for the old Bolinas School built in 1907. At first glance, Bolinas will remind you of a small New England village.

On Wharf Road, which is at the end of the Bolinas-Olema Road, are a variety of shops. Some of these buildings date back to the 1880s. A row of summer homes built on pilings juts out over the

water. In the 1906 earthquake, buildings in this area were dumped right into the Bolinas Lagoon.

Also on Wharf Road is the College of Marin Marine Biology Laboratory, located in an old Coast Guard station that began operation in 1917. The street ends at the public beach.

On Brighton Avenue (turn right at the intersection of the Olema-Bolinas Road and Wharf Road) is the small Bolinas Park which has a tennis court, picnic tables, restrooms, and a drinking fountain.

## Point Reyes Bird Observatory

On the way out of Bolinas, a side trip to the Point Reyes Bird Observatory will be of interest to all bird lovers. Founded in 1965, this private, nonprofit organization of ornithologists, both professional and volunteer, operates a bird observatory which is open year round. The purpose of the organization is to do ecological research on migration patterns, nesting, and breeding habits of various species of landbirds, shorebirds, and seabirds. They also provide conservation and environmental education and participate in the study of marine mammals.

To reach the Point Reyes Bird Observatory Palomarin Field Station, turn southwest on Mesa Road from the Olema-Bolinas Road. In the winter, watch for monarch butterflies in the eucalyptus trees along here. Proceed for about four miles to the site, which is the old Palomarin Ranch and a former religious settlement. The last half-mile of road is gravel.

The station is open seven days a week from dawn to dusk. Admission is free. Inside the visitors' room are interesting displays of bird nests, wildflowers, bird skulls, and information on the Farallon Islands. (Personnel from the Point Reyes Bird Observatory also reside at a field station on the Farallon Islands, twenty-five miles off the Golden Gate, studying seabirds and marine mammals. They are the sole guardians of this natural resource for the United States Fish and Wildlife Service.)

Visitors may pick up brochures and pamphlets with valuable information about wildlife in the immediate area and about the activities of the organization. A phone is available at the station, but there are no public restrooms.

◄ *The rugged coastline of the Pacific Ocean.*

Banding work is done from 7:00 A.M. to 11:00 A.M. daily from April through November and on weekends the rest of the year. (868-1221)

## Palomarin Trailhead

Past the Point Reyes Bird Observatory is the trailhead at Palomarin. From here you have access to miles of trails in the southern end of the Point Reyes National Seashore, trails that lead inland and along the coast.

It is just 2.5 miles on Coast Trail to Bass Lake, passing Abalone Point where it is still legal to dive for the succulent mollusks. Coast Trail then passes two lakes: Pelican and Crystal. Wildcat Camp, near the beach, is 5.4 miles from the trailhead; Glen Camp, in a protected spot between two ridges, is 7.4 miles. The trail continues along the ridges above the ocean to Coast Camp, 12.5 miles away.

To reserve a campsite or obtain a trail map, phone Mon. through Friday from 9:00 A.M. to noon, 663-1092. Campers may only stay one night. Parking and privies are available at the Palomarin trailhead.

## Duxbury Reef and Agate Beach

Named for a steamer that grounded on it in August 1849, Duxbury Reef is often called a "living marine laboratory." Accessible only during a minus tide, the reef reveals a myriad of sea treasures. Tidepool collecting is illegal, though, as this area is now a marine preserve.

Save your collecting for adjoining Agate Beach, a favorite spot for beachcombers. Agates and glass fishing balls can be found here after a storm, and other treasures have been salvaged by residents following the frequent shipwrecks over the years.

To get there from the Bird Observatory, take a right turn on Overlook Drive from Mesa Road (left if you are going directly to the reef from Mesa Road off the Olema-Bolinas Road). Then turn right on Elm and go to the end, where there is a parking lot. Again, do not depend on road signs, as the ones installed—like those leading to Bolinas—are often torn down.

Duxbury Reef is the largest shale intertidal reef in North America, running a mile long and 2,000 yards south into the sea. Its rocks are 28 millions years old, though it has been only a million

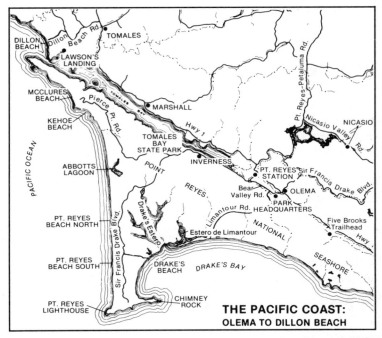

THE PACIFIC COAST:
OLEMA TO DILLON BEACH

years since the reef was lifted up by an upheaval along the San Andreas fault. The soft shale is especially fine for boring clams such as the rock piddock.

Be sure to check a tide table, for the reef can be explored only at low tide. You will see countless numbers of marine creatures: barnacles, periwinkles, rock snails, and black turban snails. Carpets of sea anemones look like squishy beds of sandy gravel and bits of shell because the tiny animals attach these materials to their outer surfaces to reflect heat and retain moisture.

Starfish are plentiful on the reef, as are purple urchins which look like lovely violet-colored flowers. Small limpets are found in many varieties, including the slipper, button, plate, dunce cap, and the owl limpet (though the latter is not common on this reef). Also visible are massive beds of California sea mussels and a few red and black abalone.

The priceless Duxbury Reef was endangered in January 1971 when a big oil spill occurred in San Francisco Bay. The reef took the brunt of the first heavy waves of oil that swept the Bolinas-Stinson area.

The great mussel beds were saturated with oil, and patches of tar were flung over the millions of barnacles, limpets, and urchins. Iridescent oily film spread colorfully across the surface of the tidepools. Surf grass and kelp lay in black streaks in the reef's crevices; mats of straw, brought in to absorb the oil, clogged the homes of rock crabs and starfish.

Volunteers began working round the clock to save the reef. They dug the oil out with pitchforks, shovels, and their fingernails. With the volunteers was Gordon L. Chan, a biology and zoology teacher at the College of Marin, who had been studying the reef since 1959. He looked for his huge pet sea anemone, Big Tony, whom he had been hand feeding for thirteen years, and found him still alive, miraculously, after the spill.

To access the damaged caused by the oil, Chan conducted a study of the reef, sponsored in part by Standard Oil, whose tankers had caused the spill. He found, in the years following, that life on the reef was gradually returning to normal. Today it has fully recovered and is again rife with sea life.

# The Olema Valley

From the Bolinas Lagoon, the San Andreas Fault runs northwest through the Olema Valley. Highway 1 follows the fault zone, winding through stands of eucalyptus and over the rolling hills. During the 1906 earthquake, buildings, fences, trees, and the road in the valley were heavily damaged and visibly dislocated. At one time, this slender tranquil valley abounded with wild game. Now, cows and horses graze on the hills. Although this is parkland, ranching continues here on a lease-back basis.

West of the faultline is the Point Reyes peninsula, heavily forested and foggy, a contrast to the sunny, open hills to the east. The ocean is cut off from view by the Inverness Ridge, but there are trails—mostly long and steep—that ascend to the ridgetops and lead to fishing lakes and to the coast.

## Dogtown

Woodville, originally named by lumbermen, was nicknamed Dogtown for the dogs that hunters used to track bear and deer. The village is located a curvy half-mile through fragrant eucalyptus trees past the intersection of the Bolinas Road and Highway 1.

In the 1800s, there was a lumber mill here. Reportedly over six million feet of virgin redwood were cut, sawed, and shipped by schooners to San Francisco. With all this activity, a saloon, blacksmith shop, grocery, and department store flourished.

In 1863, two copper mine companies were organized to bring out low-grade copper ore from the William W. Wilkins property at Dogtown. The mine did not produce much ore, through the Union Company dug down to 700 feet.

Wilkins lost a few head of cattle down the mine shaft and went to court in 1904 to clear his land of what was clearly a losing operation. He succeeded in getting a judgment, and peace returned.

The mine was reopened during the First World War when copper was so scarce that even this low-grade ore was mined. A reported 22,500 pounds were taken out by the Chetco Company during those years and ferried aboard the schooner Owl to the town of Pittsburg.

Today the old Wilkins Ranch is part of the Point Reyes National Seashore. You make hike into the area marked by a gate north of the Connolly property (a dangerous spot to park, so leave your car farther up the road).

The mine is about a mile northeast of Dogtown in an area old maps call "Copper Mine Gulch." Follow the small stream to the mine. Remnants of the old road are visible, though covered with fallen trees. Pieces of an old boiler and bits of other machinery may still be found on the site. The actual mine shafts have been sealed to comply with a federal law. These shafts are extremely hazardous and, during winter, full of water.

The name of the town was changed back to Woodville well over one hundred years ago to provide "a better image." It was renamed Dogtown by a resolution of the Marin County Board of Supervisors a few years ago.

## Twin Lakes

As you continue along Highway 1, 2.8 miles past Dogtown, you may notice cars parked and people carrying picnic hampers headed up the hill to the east. They are going up to the ponds of the old Borello Ranch, called Twin Lakes but often referred to as the Hagmaier or Sieroty ponds.

A large wooden gate cuts off access by vehicle to an old ranch road, so visitors must hike in; it is about a five-minute walk. To reach the lake on the north, head up the old road, then turn left and walk down the hill. To arrive at the south lake, keep hiking uphill, then turn right and go down. This lake may also be reached by walking through a flat pasture to the right of the road. A fast-flowing creek runs adjacent to the pasture.

When you arrive at the lakes, do not be surprised if you encounter someone sunbathing "au natural."

GGNRA rangers warn that there are no lifeguards on duty here, and the water can become stagnant in the summer. Except for garbage cans adjacent to the gate, there are no facilities here.

## Five Brooks Trailhead

The Five Brooks Trailhead is located at the site of the old Five Brooks Stables. Facilities include a parking area and privies. Hikers may pick up a number of trails here to Bear Valley, Glen Camp, Wildcat Beach and Palomarin.

## Stewart Ranch

The Stewart Horse Ranch is the private operation of a second- and third-generation Marin County family who raises Angus cattle and Morgan horses and operates under the name "Woodside." The ranch begins two and one-half miles past Twin Lakes, and the main ranch house is eight-tenths of a mile beyond.

The National Park Service rents the Stewarts approximately 1,000 acres in this location, in Tennessee Valley, and in Green Gulch. Like other private ranchers within the Golden Gate National Recreation Area, the Stewarts retain grazing rights through a lease with the government on the land they once owned.

The family also retains a lifetime residency in the redwood ranch house, built in 1863 and 1864 by Horatio Nelson Olds, who had large land holdings in this area. The Stewart family bought the ranch in 1923, rebuilt the ranch house fireplace, and added barns.

Boyd Stewart, who has lived all his life in West Marin, was a leader in the movement to create the park. He claims that talk about the park began as long ago as 1932. Stewart also notes that the ranches in the area are over 120 years old. The land was bought (not homesteaded) in the period when the great land grants were broken up.

## Olema

The town of Olema was named after the Coast Miwok Indian village of Olemaloke, which meant "Coyote Village." This tiny hamlet, at the intersection of Highway 1 and Sir Francis Drake Boulevard, 2.5 miles past the Stewart Ranch, gives little hint of the bustling activity that went on here 120 years ago.

Historical accounts of pioneer days in Olema mention two churches, seven bars, and a race track. Other services included a post office, grocery store, butcher shop, two hotels, stables, an express office, and a dry goods store. Druids Hall was built in 1881.

The old Olema butcher shop, "Gamboni's," shall forever remain a historical relic. In 1967 the front of it was carted off to Washington, D.C., to be used in a display in the California section at the "Hall of Everyday Life in the American Past" in the Smithsonian's Museum of History and Technology.

Today in the town of Olema there are two restaurants, a grocery store, and a campground. The Olema Inn, the old Nelson's Hotel, built in 1876, which once served as a local bank and stage stop, was remodeled and now contains six rooms all with private baths. It features a restaurant with an outdoor deck and garden. The hotel was closed for a couple of years, but opened in the spring of 1989.

A second hotel, the Point Reyes Seashore Lodge (10021 Coastal Highway), opened in June 1988. It contains 21 rooms plus a sitting room downstairs with a stone fireplace and a lovely view of the valley.

The Olema Store sells beer and wine, picnic supplies, "healthy munchies," and also has a boutique.

The Olema Ranch Campgrounds are open to the public and provide gas, a post office and laundromat. The current owner, Horst Hanf, a San Rafael contractor, wants to add approximately twenty bungalows in a two-and-one-half acre field east of the entrance.

# Point Reyes National Seashore

Just past Olema is the headquarters of the Point Reyes National Seashore. Some thirty-five miles north of San Francisco, this wild sweep of land has been described as an "island in time."

The triangular-shaped Point Reyes peninsula, separated from the rest of the county by that fissure in the earth known as the San Andreas Fault, is indeed different from the "mainland." Not only the soil and plants but the granite and shale rocks here differ completely from the mixture of sandstone, chert, and serpentine found in the rest of Marin.

Geologists explain that the "island" is moving northwest an average of two inches per year and may have moved 300 miles in the past 80 to 100 million years, lurching ahead whenever there is an earthquake. Rocks matching those on Point Reyes are found an incredible distance south in the Tehachapi Mountains.

Point Reyes was named by Sebastian Vizcaino, who sailed along the California coast in early 1603. On January 6, the twelfth day of Christmas, he passed the peninsula and called it "Punto de los Reyes" for the Feast of the Three Kings.

At that time, there were reportedly over one hundred Miwok Indian villages here. When the Spanish came, the Indians were sent to the missions and few ever returned.

In the days of the early settlers, Point Reyes contained rich cattle and dairy ranches which supplied products for San Francisco. Like the Bolinas area, it was also logged. A few attempts were made at developing the land, but these failed, perhaps because the peninsula is isolated and the weather is often cold, windy, and foggy. In any case, Point Reyes made it to the second half of the twentieth century as undeveloped as it was one hundred years ago.

In 1935, the federal government began taking a look at this land for a park. In September 1962, a bill was finally signed authorizing the creation of the Point Reyes National Seashore, to include nearly 64,000 acres of the peninsula. The area is now 75,000 acres. The plan for the park is to keep it wild, with few roads, some leased ranchland, and much of the area formally designated as Wilderness.

Before setting out to explore Point Reyes, visit the park headquarters at the old Bear Valley Ranch. Here you can pick up general directions and maps for the hundred miles of trails and obtain information about fishing, clamming, and horse rentals. You may also make reservations for the four hike-in campgrounds Monday-Friday, 9:00 AM to noon only at 663-1092, 663-1092.

*The Bear Valley Visitor Center at the Point Reyes National Seashore.*

The headquarters is open from 9:00 A.M. to 5:00 P.M. The administration office is 663-8522; recorded general information, 663-9029.

To get there, drive northwest from Olema and turn left on Bear Valley Road. The distance from the intersection to the parking lot is seven-tenths of a mile.

The Bear Valley Visitor Center was completed in 1983 at a cost of 1.4 million dollars raised entirely through donations. The new center contains a seismograph used for monitoring earthquakes. You can select books, pamphlets, and postcards on the area and study exhibits on geology, natural science, Miwok Indians, early explorers, ranching, shipwrecks, and the park itself. Public telephones, first aid, picnic tables, and restrooms are also available. There are food concessions in the park only during the summer months; so you may want to bring your own. The nearest stores are in Olema or Point Reyes Station.

The trails that begin at the headquarters lead throughout the park, connecting with the Five Brooks and Palomarin trailheads. You can hike or ride horseback through dark forests and open meadows, up the ridges, and down to the beach. There is an easy, level walk along the Bear Valley Trail, to the ocean, 4.5

*The country club built by the Pacific Union Club, 1895. It was located in Bear Valley in the Divide Meadow.* Courtesy of Nancy Skinner.

miles away. For the more ambitious, Sky Trail leads up to Mt. Wittenberg for an exhilarating view of the Pacific Ocean, Tomales Bay, and the entire peninsula; farther on, this trail connects with Coast Trail, following the cliffs along the shore.

For a short walk near the headquarters, try the Earthquake Trail, the self-guided Woodpecker Nature Trail, or the trail to Kule Loklo, a replica of a Coast Miwok Indian village. The Morgan Horse Farm is also open to the public.

## Earthquake Trail

If you've ever wanted to know more about earthquakes and what causes them, walk the Earthquake Trail, which begins near the picnic area at park headquarters. This self-guided walk takes you right along the edge of the notorious San Andreas Fault.

Along the 0.6-mile trail, which is paved and wheelchair accessible, you will see the scars of the disastrous 1906 quake; this area, known as the old Skinner Ranch, was near the epicenter. In front of the main ranch house, the ground reportedly moved fifteen feet, nine inches. The garden path that led to the front steps of the farmhouse moved over to face a wall. A cow barn was torn in two when the east side was dragged sixteen feet.

As you walk along, interpretive signs explain the geology of this area and give interesting facts about earthquakes. You will see more evidence of 1906: a fence that was offset fifteen feet, a creek bed that shifted, and an exhibit about the internationally famous cow that was "swallowed up" at the Shafter Ranch, south of the Skinner place.

The cow story is questionable, but the official commission investigating the incident at the time wrote: "A fault crevice was momentarily so wide as to admit a cow which fell in head first and was thus entombed. The closure which immediately followed left only the tail visible." The trail is open daily from sunrise to sunset.

## Miwok Indian Kule Loklo Village

Indians have lived in Marin County for at least 5,000 years and in California for at least 10,000. The earliest dated site in Marin is on de Silva Island at the north end of Richardson Bay Bridge.

The Miwok derive their name from a Sierra Miwok word meaning people, although the Coast Miwok used other terms for themselves. Linguists used the term for several groups with similar languages.

They were hunters and gatherers using spears and bows and arrows to kill deer and elk. Arrows were tipped with obsidian, a volcanic glass for which the Miwok traded seashore products to inland tribes. Their diet also included fish and shellfish, wildfowl, root vegetables, greens, berries and nuts. Food was abundant and varied. A mainstay of their diet was acorns which were ground, leached and cooked in baskets to make the starchy bland food which is represented in our diets by potatoes, rice, bread and pasta.

The Coast Miwok constructed canoes by tying together bundles of tule rushes. These light craft were used for fishing and transportation on bays, but not on the open ocean. Dome-shaped houses constructed of tules and more permanent houses of redwood bark slabs were used for shelter. A men's sweat house also served as a dormitory where men stayed when they were restricted from contact with women before important activities such as hunting and dancing. Smaller women's sweat houses also existed.

The principal structure in the village was the dance house or roundhouse, a round semi-subterranean structure with a long low entryway. A central hearth was used for fires on ceremonial occasions and dances, most of which were religious. Some dances took place outdoors on the round dance ground.

At Point Reyes, a replica of a Coast Miwok village has been constructed by the joint efforts of the Point Reyes National Seashore and the Miwok Archaeological Preserve of Marin; it is called Kule Loklo, which means "Bear Valley" in the Bodega Miwok language. The village was constructed with traditional materials and methods. Basket making and bread making are often demonstrated on Saturdays. There is also a regular program of interpretive walks to the village.

The dance house is open to the public when the village is staffed. Visitors can enter the shelter through a low tunnel. Upon reaching the main room it is possible to stand upright. A small stone fire ring is in the center beneath an opening in the roof for the smoke to escape. Logs for sitting encircle the fire. Park rangers at Kule Loklo demonstrate Miwok crafts and explain the way of life here centuries ago. Call the Park at 663-1092 for information. School groups may visit with prior reservations.

In 1776, there were 3,000 Coast Miwok living in this area. Then the Spanish missionaries arrived and recruited the Indians for slave labor and forced religious conversion on them. In less than sixty years, only 300 were still alive. Today there are no full-blooded Coast Miwok left, but hundreds of their descendants live in the Bay Area, particularly in Sonoma County, very much aware of their ancestry. Many Coast Miwok people married Pomo people in the 19th century. The two Park rangers assigned to Kule Loklo are of Coast Miwok/Pomo descent.

In mid-July a traditional "Big Time" takes place at Kule Loklo with craft demonstrations, traditional dancing and food, and Indian goods for sale. A fall Acorn Festival, a thanksgiving for the acorn crop, is also open to the public.

The Miwok Archeological Preserve of Marin sponsors adult classes in traditional central California Indian skills at Kule Loklo in the spring and fall. Contact them at 2255 Las Gallinas, San Rafael, 94903.

## Morgan Horse Farm

The Morgan Horse Farm here in Point Reyes began with donations of Morgan colts from local ranchers with the intention that the grown horses would be used by park rangers.

The Morgan breed began in the state of Vermont in the early 1800s with a prodigious horse known as "Justin Morgan." He was only fourteen hands high and was thought to be a blend of thoroughbred and Arabian with some other elements. Today's Morgan horses are known for intelligence, good disposition, endurance, and extraordinary longevity.

Use of the Morgans has vastly improved the quality of contact with visitors to the parks, the rangers declare. People seem more comfortable talking to a ranger on horseback than they would be if the ranger were in a vehicle.

The Morgan Horse Farm has several interesting displays including an old hay rake, grain driller, mower, and blacksmith shop with an anvil and forge. During summer weekends, visitors may be treated to a horse training and riding demonstration.

## Limantour

On Bear Valley Road, about a mile northwest of the park headquarters, you will find the the Limantour Road which winds its way over Inverness Ridge and down to the beach at Limantour Spit.

It is a lovely, scenic drive to the beach about eight miles away. Going up the summit you pass through forests of Douglas fir and bishop pine.

Along the way, you may be surprised to see what appear to be white deer. These are fallow deer, seen in white and also other colors. Imported to Marin in the 1940s, they are originally from the Mediterranean area of Europe. They have large palmate antlers, which are flat, like those of a moose, with up to fifteen points per side. The deer weigh from 130 to 170 pounds. They are usually seen in small herds or family groups of ten to fifteen. They breed in December, and the fawns are born in April or May.

The axis deer, another exotic species of deer that inhabits Point Reyes, were imported from India. These deer are reddish-brown with lines of conspicuous white spots, looking much like giant fawn. The average adult weight is from 200 to 240 pounds, and they have long slender antlers, most with three points per side.

The axis deer are a herd animal and appear in groups of 5 to 150. This is a tropical species, and the deer breed at any time of the year. They have a strange but distinguishing bark when alarmed or when calling to other herd members.

*The schooner, Pt. Reyes which was owned by ranchers from Pt. Reyes. Approximately 1910-1932.* Courtesy of Nancy Skinner.

Also seen with the fallow and axis are the common California black-tailed deer, a subspecies of the mule deer. Their coat is a tawny yellowish-brown color in summer, with the winter coat being longer and grayer. They breed in the fall—October and November—and fawn are born in the spring. They do not form herds, although a buck may have a small harem during rutting season.

Other animals you might spot here and throughout the park are skunks, rabbits, bobcats, foxes, and raccoons. There are even mountain lions in Point Reyes.

Limantour Spit is a narrow strip of land with a gorgeous white beach. On one side is Drake's Bay and the Pacific Ocean; on the other side is the Estero de Limantour, which is part of the larger Drake's Estero (Spanish for "estuary"). Limantour is named for a French trader whose ship wrecked here in 1841. The beach is a good one for fishing, swimming, and wading. The estero is spectacular for birdwatching, as it provides food and refuge for the 361 bird species found on the peninsula. Visitors may recognize Great Blue Herons, Great Egrets, several varieties of ducks, sandpipers, cormorants, gulls, godwits, western grebes, and willits.

Now under federal protection—which means no clamming or collecting—the mudflats of the Limantour Estero contain string worms, clams, blue ghost shrimp, giant moon snails, sea slugs, and beds of eel grass.

In the Drake's Estero mudflats, clamming is legal with a California fishing license, and you can dig for horseneck and goeyduck clams. Hike along the rocky intertidal area and look for sea anemones, limpets, crabs, starfish, and a large kelp bed.

Drake's Estero is known for sharks, rays, and cod, and also for a colony of seals that haul out on the sandbars within the estero. During the pupping season (March through June), as many as twenty-six pups have been sighted. The seals will tolerate humans at relatively close range—200 meters—without stampeding into the water. This provides a unique opportunity to watch mother-pup interactions. It is important to note that mothers often leave their pups alone on the beach, especially when the pups are quite young. Therefore, if you should find a lone pup, please leave it undisturbed.

With its beach, sand spit, and estero, Limantour is one of the loveliest picnic areas in the park. Facilities are limited to primitive privies (no doors), a telephone, and a gravel parking lot located about a quarter of a mile from the beach; the park service is planning repairs and improvements.

## Point Reyes Hostel

The Point Reyes Hostel is located south of Limantour Road in the former Laguna Ranch main house, about five miles from the headquarters. The hostel welcomes individuals, families, and groups. There are sleeping accommodations for up to 45 people at a cost of $7.00 per person per night. Children under eighteen accompanied by their parents are half price.

Customs are those of the International Hostel Association. Each guest contributes ten minutes of clean-up time in the morning. Guests should bring a sleeping bag, soap, towel, and food. Alcohol and pets are forbidden.

Facilities include hot showers, a large ranch kitchen with utensils, dining room, common room with fireplace, patio, and barbecue.

For reservations phone 663-8811 during the hours the hostel is open—7:30 to 9:30 A.M. and 4:30 to 9:00 P.M. Or write to the hostel at P.O. Box 247, Point Reyes Station, CA 94956.

# Inverness

R eturn on Limantour Road to Bear Valley Rd. Turn left and the road becomes Sir Francis Drake Boulevard. Continue 3.3 miles north past Inverness Park to the town of Inverness situated on Tomales Bay.

The San Andreas Fault runs north under Tomales Bay in a straight line all the way to Bodega Bay. In fact, Tomales Bay was formed when the rift opened up and water flowed in. During the 1906 earthquake, huge mud flows toppled piers, stores collapsed, and houses fell off foundations.

Originally a Mexican land grant to James Barry in 1836, *Rancho Punta de Los Reyes* consisted of eight square leagues adjacent to Tomales Bay and surrounded the area where the town of Inverness would later be developed.

The land grant went through complicated legal entanglements for over twenty years before being acquired in 1857 by two brothers, Oscar and James Shafter, and their law partners.

Thirty-two years later, James Shafter—by then a judge— established the town of Inverness, which he named for the home of his ancestors in Scotland. Judge Shafter died before any substantial development was completed, but houses began to be built within the next five years.

Inverness attracted the wealthy from San Francisco, who came to build summer homes, especially after the disastrous 1906 earthquake. The city refugees must not have realized that the same fault that wrecked San Francisco ran right under the peaceful bay they viewed from their windows.

Many of the well-built summer homes in Inverness are now lived in all year. This lovely little town, about three miles north of Point Reyes Station, is surrounded by parkland (Point Reyes National Seashore and Tomales Bay State Park).

The town offers visitors several motels. The Inverness Store supplies groceries, a full deli with hot and cold food to go, liquor,

*Train crossing north of Tomales.* Photo by Roy Graves, 1929. Bancroft Library.

and such services as making duplicate keys and photocopies. Hours are from 9:00 A.M. to 7:00 P.M. daily. (669-1041)

The Bellweather is one of the most photogenic buildings in the county. Built first as a general store in the 1890s, it was toppled by the 1906 earthquake and was rebuilt. The Bellweather has baskets, pottery, handmade items, and books, maps, and postcards relating to the area.

Marin historian Jack Mason and his wife Jean lived in Inverness in the first substantial house built here (in 1894), which they named "The Gables." Mr. Mason had his own press, North Shore Books, which published his seven books on Marin County history. His home is now a museum. The Jack Mason Museum is open Sat.

10:00 AM to 1:00 PM and Sun. 1:00 to 4:00 PM. It is also open on weekdays except for Thursdays. Call for the hours at 669-1288.

Inverness has been famous for its two Czech restaurants: Manka's at the Inverness Inn and Vladimir's. Milan Prokupek and his wife Manka originated Manka's Restaurant over thirty years ago, while Vladimir's is owned by the Prokupeks' daughter Alena and her Czech husband, Vladimir Nevi. In April 1989, Manka's and the inn were purchased by Ben Grade who has continued the Czech food along with some lighter dishes.

# Point Reyes Promontory

From Inverness, Sir Francis Drake Boulevard continues up the shore of Tomales Bay, then turns southwest and heads toward the ocean. Watch for Mt. Vision Overlook Road on your left. This is a narrow, winding, blacktop road pocked with pits and potholes, but the view of Drake's Estero and Limantour is worth the drive up the mountain.

Another mile and a half down the road is Johnson's Oyster Farm. It is on your left half a mile south on Schooner Bay, part of the Drake's Estero.

The oyster farm, in business for over thirty years, cultivates oysters by suspending them from wooden frames under water. These horizontal trays are more expensive than the sticks people originally used when they started cultivating oysters, but are safer from predators and easier to harvest. The oysters breed in the summer and take three to five years to grow to eating size.

### Point Reyes Beach, North and South

Where the road finally reaches the ocean, ten miles of wind-swept sands face the Pacific. There are north and south entrances 2.5 miles apart, and you will see the signs on Sir Francis Drake Boulevard.

Both beaches provide parking lots, and restrooms. Point Reyes Beach North is 2.8 miles beyond Johnson's Oyster Farm and about eight miles from Inverness.

Signs warn against wading or swimming as the surf is considered extremely dangerous, with riptides and undertows. In any case,

*Pt. Reyes Beach.*

the weather here is really not conducive to swimming. This is a rugged beach, usually cold and foggy, and the coastline is among the most dangerous, having claimed many ships through the years. But this is a fine place to beachcomb, fish, and watch for birds and whales (in December and January).

## Point Reyes Lighthouse and Sea Lion Overlook

Sir Francis Drake Boulevard ends at the very tip of the promontory at Point Reyes Lighthouse. Just before you reach the lighthouse, seven-tenths of a mile past Chimney Rock intersection, there is a wide space in the road with enough room for about five vehicles to park. This is Sea Lion Overlook.

Take the thirty-two steps down to the viewing area, a sandy spot surrounded by railing. You will hear barking coming from Sea Lion Cove below. Steller's sea lions, California sea lions, and sometimes elephant seals are found here. To get a good view of these marine mammals it is best to bring binoculars. Their colors—a dark chocolate when wet and a sandy shade when dry—camouflage them as they swim in the surf or sleep on the rocks.

Beyond the Sea Lion Overlook is the Point Reyes Lighthouse, a very dramatic and exciting place to visit if the weather is clear. The lighthouse sits on the western tip of the promontory, high

*Hiking down to the Point Reyes Lighthouse.*

above the surf. This is one of the windiest, foggiest spots in the entire country; a lonely and treacherous place for ships. Photographs on exhibit inside the Visitors' Center show ships crashed on the rocks or run aground and the rescues being made. Ten major ships are recorded as being wrecked in the Point Reyes area, and another dozen here at the lighthouse.

The first ship lost was the San Augustin at Drake's Bay in 1595. Eleven more ships went down during the 1800s. In 1903, the S.S. Lurline was wrecked at Point Reyes Beach, followed in 1910 by the Annie Smale. The last was the Muleon, which smashed up here in 1931.

The lighthouse was built in 1870 and a revolving three-ton Fresnel lens was installed. Consisting of more than 1,031 pieces of hand-cut crystal, the lens was made in Paris, brought around the Horn in a sailing ship, and hauled from Drake's Bay to the site by heavy oxcarts. The light beamed a one-second flash every five seconds and was visible for twenty-four nautical miles. The source of light was an oil-burning four-wick lamp.

An automated light station was opened in 1975, and it operates a rotating beacon twenty-four hours daily. Also installed here is an electronic diaphone foghorn and a radio beacon.

The old lighthouse, which has undergone extensive repairs, is open to the public from 10:00 A.M. to 4:30 P.M. every day but Tuesday, Wednesday, and Christmas Day. It is closed when the wind exceeds forty miles per hour; so it is wise to phone ahead for weather information to the Lighthouse Visitors Center, 669-1534.

To get to the lighthouse from the parking lot, walk down the old road, a 0.6-mile hike. Then climb down the long stairway—equal to that of a thirty-story building, says the sign. I counted 311 steps from the overlook picnic deck and Visitors' Center down to the lighthouse. The steps originally numbered over 400, but the climb is broken up by three cement ramps and rest areas with benches.

At the lighthouse you can walk around, looking out at the sea. On the rocks below are thousands of California murres, black and white seabirds about sixteen inches high which stand upright, penguin-fashion. In flight, the murre looks like a small loon with a slender head and pointed bill. Gulls and cormorants swoop down on currents of wind out over the glistening water.

From this most western spot in the county you can view the spectacular sweep of the Point Reyes beach, the long, curving line of cliffs toward the north, and the surf crashing upon the rocks. The sea is a vast graveyard of ships.

J. P. Monroe-Fraser wrote in 1880 about a lighthouse:

> When the winds of ocean sweep with fiercest fury across the trackless main, lashing with water into seething billows almost mountain high, when the black pall of night has been cast over the face of the deep, and ships are scudding along under close reef and storm sails, not knowing where they are or how soon they may be cast upon the rocks or stranded upon the beach, when the storm king seems to hold full sway over all the world, suddenly a flash of light is seen piercing the darkness, like a ray of hope from the bosom of God.

## Chimney Rock

On the east end of the Point Reyes promontory is Chimney Rock, a huge sea stack that marks the entrance to Drake's Bay. Go to the Chimney Rock Road intersection, and continue 3.6 miles on this narrow, single-lane blacktop road to the parking lot (no facilities here, just a privy). From this spot it is a thirty-minute hike to the overlook.

On the way, you will pass an old life-saving station built after World War I which then included a five-bedroom house, boathouse, and lookout tower. The Coast Guard took over the station in 1939 and ran it until 1968.

On a metal plaque in the wall adjacent to the steps of the house is an illustration of Sir Francis Drake and an Indian. The inscription reads: "On June 17, 1579, Sir Francis Drake landed on these shores and took possession of the country, calling it Nova Albion."

Past the house, the hike is mostly uphill. On the left are old iron ramps leading down to the water from the boathouse. These were part of the original life-saving station.

About twenty minutes into your hike, you will see a sign directing you to an ocean overlook to the right and Chimney Rock to the left.

At the end of the hike, your reward is a fabulous view of Drake's Bay with its magnificent white cliffs. The huge sea stack at the entrance to the bay is Chimney Rock.

A granite-bouldered reef runs from the steep cliffs in this area out to Chimney Rock. The subtidal area supports a nursery of red abalone, chitons, sunstars, surfgrass, bat starfish, sea urchins, sea cucumbers, and a variety of crabs and snails. This is a natural preserve area that extends all the way to the lighthouse, and the sealife may not be disturbed.

A special warning: Do not try to climb down the cliffs to the beach. They are crumbly and quite dangerous.

## Drake's Beach

On the side of the promontory opposite windy Point Reyes Beach is Drake's Beach, facing on Drake's Bay. Swimming is possible here, as this beach is protected from heavy winds by the sheltering sea cliffs. Many small boats seek the quieter water here.

The Kenneth C. Patrick Information Center is open from 10:00 A.M. to 5:00 P.M. Rangers provide interpretive programs, and there are displays on intertidal creatures and shells to touch. The facilities include a book shop, dressing rooms, rest rooms, and telephone. In winter everything closes down, although it is still possible to use the restrooms.

A popular restaurant called Drake's Beach Cafe is run by Jonne Le Mieux. The restaurant offers fresh oysters, homemade soups

*Drake's Beach.*

such as clam chowder, hamburgers, sandwiches and soft drinks. Drake's Beach Cafe is surprising good for such an out of the way location and is open all year from 10:00 AM to 5:00 PM daily. (669-1297)

Look for a granite cross erected by the Sir Francis Drake Association in 1946, "in commemoration of the landing of Sir Francis Drake...on these shores." Many historians and history buffs believe that this is indeed the spot where Drake came ashore in 1579.

Another plaque near the information center was dedicated in June 1979 in honor of the 400th anniversary of Drake's landing in Marin. A mile east along the beach at Drake's Cove, an anchor and still another plaque have been erected by the Drake Navigator's Guild, whose members believe he landed in that very spot.

The subject of Drake's landing is highly controversial, however. Briefly, the story is as follows:

Sir Francis Drake, admiral of Her Majesty's Navy, knighted gentleman, sea pirate, and adventurer, provided the first known record of Marin on his famous circumnavigation of the world, 1577-80. Acting on private orders from Queen Elizabeth to find

*Barbecuing fresh oysters at Drake's Beach Cafe.*

a suitable site for an English colony in the New World, he enlarged his mission by plundering Spanish ships, cities, and towns along the coast of South America. Although England and Spain were experiencing an uneasy peace, Elizabeth secretly welcomed the Spanish gold.

Drake survived an attempted mutiny, the treacherous water of the Magellan Straits and the loss of four of his five ships and finally arrived in the foggy waters off the Northern California coast in June 1579. He hunted desperately for a safe haven in which to repair his leaky ship.

On June 17, the *Golden Hinde* entered a protected harbor, and Drake's party was able to unload their treasures, overhaul the ship, and repair the leaks. While there, they explored the interior and met with friendly Indians who, according to Drake's reports, offered him their kingdom. He accepted in the name of Queen Elizabeth and left fastened to a large post a plate of brass that claimed the land for his queen. After thirty-seven days of resting and making repairs, they sailed out on July 23, 1579.

Exactly where Sir Francis Drake landed in Marin is a question that has been studied and argued for years. Some historians believe it was here at Drake's Bay, while others think it could have been in the Bolinas Lagoon, Tomales, Bodega, or Half Moon Bay. Others are adamant that Drake discovered San Francisco Bay and landed near San Quentin Point.

Whether or not you believe that Drake landed here, the beach named for him is a lovely spot for a picnic or barbecue, beachcombing, fishing, or just walking.

## Gulf of the Farallones National Marine Sanctuary

Located off the beaches in this area is the Gulf of the Farallones National Marine Sanctuary, 948 square nautical miles established in 1981. This marine region includes the waters of Bodega Bay, Tomales Bay, Drake's Bay, Bolinas Lagoon, Duxbury Reef, Estero San Antonio located north of Dillon Beach, and the Estero de Americano which marks the boundary between Marin and Sonoma Counties.

In the middle of the Sanctuary are the Farallon Islands, a National Wildlife Refuge containing 7,000 seals and sea lions, and 300,000 breeding seabirds.

The islands which are administered by the National Oceanic and Atmospheric Administration are closed to the public.

*The accident-prone "Ida A" out of Pt. Reyes which sailed around the turn of the century, aground on the sand at Ten Mile Beach.* Jack Mason Library.

# Tomales Bay State Park

A fter visiting the remote and rugged Pacific beaches, the warm, sandy coves of Tomales Bay seem especially inviting.

Sheltered from the wind and fog by the Inverness Ridge, the beaches of Tomales Bay State Park are superb for picnicking, swimming, and boating. There are no boat launching facilities here but kayaks, canoes, and small sailboats can be carried in.

Clamming is legal for littleneck, Washington and gaper (or horseneck), but be sure you have a California license and a legal measurer. Fishing is excellent in Tomales Bay, and don't be surprised if you reel in a shark or ray.

To get to Tomales Bay State Park, take Sir Francis Drake Boulevard to the intersection of Pierce Point Road. Drive north for a mile to the park entrance. The park open from 8:00 A.M. to sunset and and charges $3 per car. No dogs are allowed. This 1,596-acre park is not part of the Point Reyes National Seashore but is under the jurisdiction of the state parks department.

Upon entering the park, pick up a brochure, then drive a mile to the popular Heart's Desire Beach. Half-mile trails lead northwest to Indian Beach where Coast Miwok Indians used to camp, and southeast to Pebble Beach.

Shell Beach is separated by private property from the rest of the park but can be reached by turning right on Camino Del Mar, a road three-tenths of a mile beyond Inverness.

Away from the beaches there are trails through the woods. The Jepson Memorial Grove, a virgin stand of bishop pine, can be viewed from a mile-long trail that runs between the picnic area and Pierce Point Road. These craggy, grotesquely-shaped trees, close relatives of the Monterey pine, have survived here from prehistoric times. The grove is named for the botanist who founded the Division of Forestry at the University of California at Berkeley.

Nature lovers will identify many other native California trees in the park; a variety of berry bushes, manzanita, honeysuckle, and fern; and over 300 varieties of wildflowers, including lilies, poppies, wild strawberries, lupine, and iris. Wildlife is plentiful, and bird lovers should look for the rare spotted owl, pelicans, woodpeckers, nuthatches, and many other species.

Facilities in the park include picnic areas, restrooms, barbecue pits, and water. Rangers are on duty daily. A small campground is available for hikers and bikers which costs $2 per night. Spaces are given out on a first-come, first-serve basis. There are no reservations. Vehicles must be out of the park by sunset.

# Point Reyes—The Northern Tip

Nºorth of Tomales Bay State Park, you are back in the boundaries of the Point Reyes National Seashore. Pierce Point Road continues north past Abbotts Lagoon and ends at McClures Beach.

There is a scattering of dairy ranches here, and you will see herds of cattle grazing on the gently sloping hills. Farther north you will see some other large creatures grazing: tule elk, once native to this area, were reintroduced here a few years ago.

### Abbotts Lagoon

This quiet body of water is separated from the ocean by a sandbar, although occasionally there is a break and the saltwater comes flooding in.

Fishing is good here—the catch includes surf perch, sculpins, starry flounders, and large sticklebacks. There are even rumors of some land-locked striped bass.

The still waters of the lagoon are perfect for canoeing, and the upper lagoon has long been a favorite swimming spot.

### Kehoe Beach

The trailhead to Kehoe Beach is two miles past Abbotts Lagoon. The hike to the beach is around half a mile and keeps the shore isolated and wildly beautiful.

### Tule Elk Range

In the northernmost part of the Point Reyes National Seashore is a herd of tule elk brought here from the San Luis Refuge near Los Banos, California, to replace herds that roamed freely here 120 years ago. Legend has it that the last Marin County band of elk swam across Tomales Bay and headed north in a mass migration around 1860.

*The "Samoa," a two-masted steam schooner bringing lumber from Eureka to San Francisco, went aground near Pt. Reyes on January 28, 1913. The people aboard were saved with a "breeches buoy."* Photo courtesy of Nancy Skinner.

The mature bull tule elk weighs up to 425 pounds and has majestic antlers spanning three to four feet. His triumphant trumpeting call can be heard for long distances during rutting season in the fall. The color of these large but docile animals runs from sandy to darker brown with a buff-colored rump.

You enter the Tule Elk Range when you cross the wide cattle guard that runs across the road. High fences mark the boundary of the range.

### McClures Beach

As Pierce Point Road meanders north, there are lovely views of Tomales Bay, the Pacific Ocean, and to the far north, Bodega Bay. The road ends at McClures Beach. There is a parking lot here, also privies and a telephone.

Visitors are greeted by signs that warn of hazardous cliffs, dangerous surf, and sharks. But don't be scared away: the half-mile hike to the beach is worthwhile in spite of these warnings. Many people feel this is the most dramatic and beautiful of all the beaches in Marin. The cliffs are majestic, with towering granite rocks rising straight up and surf crashing against them.

Walk through the tidepools at low tide and look for goose barnacles, sea anemones, sponges, snails, mussels, crabs, and worms. No collecting is permitted.

Birdwatching is excellent, and driftwood may be found after a storm. Surf fishing is permitted, but keep an eye out for incoming tides and watch for "rogue waves"—gigantic waves that sometimes sweep in without warning. And heed the signs—wading and swimming are not a good idea.

## Point Reyes Station

Point Reyes Station, originally called Olema Station, was just a stop on the railroad when the trains began running in 1875. Within a year, Dr. Galen Burdell, a dentist and well-known Marin pioneer, had built a hotel and bar to accommodate the new trade. Then called "Burdell's," the building later became known as the Point Reyes Hotel.

The town grew quickly on Burdell land. Within a short time there

Railroad Depot, Pt. Reyes Station, Cal.

*Train Depot in Pt. Reyes.* Postcard from Jack Mason Museum.

*Train turned over in the 1906 earthquake at Pt. Reyes.* Bill King Photo, Jack Mason Museum.

were a blacksmith, general store, livery stable, grain warehouse, and bank. Life revolved around the train, part of the North Pacific Coast narrow-gauge railroad, which brought passengers and grain into town while exporting cattle, hogs, and dairy products.

The railroad stopped running in 1933, and since then, Point Reyes Station has changed very little. Agriculture is still the main industry, and the town has the appearance of a movie set—"the genuine western town."

To reach Point Reyes Station, follow Sir Francis Drake Boulevard north from Olema (at this point the road is also Highway 1). Just south of town the road crosses a green bridge and then turns left at Ed's Superette Market.

As it goes through the center of town, Highway 1 becomes A Street, also known as Main Street. For three blocks it follows the old railroad right-of-way, ending up at the railroad engine house. As you proceed through town, look for the old train station on your right; still painted yellow, it is now the post office. The old hotel, now closed, stands at A and Second streets.

Take some time to explore Point Reyes Station. Toby's Feed Store sells hay and grain to the local ranchers, but it also has some gift items—flowers, plants, sweatshirts and mugs.

Station House Gifts on Main Street sells books, stationery, cards, art and office supplies, and toys. Stop at the Station House Cafe for fried oysters, fresh from Tomales Bay; or pick up picnic supplies at the Palace Market, which offers fresh seafood, natural foods and a deli. For a casual drink, there's the old Western Saloon.

Also on Main Street in the Creamery Buildings is the studio of an outstanding photographer, Art Rogers. His work can be seen regularly in the *Point Reyes Light*, a weekly newspaper run by David Mitchell. In 1979, Mitchell won the Pulitzer Prize, an honor seldom awarded a weekly paper. It was given for meritorious service for his investigative reporting on Synanon, a drug rehabilitation organization turned religion.

In 1989, a new Dance Palace designed to serve as a community center was built by volunteers. The contractor for the project was Jeff Long who, along with a two-person crew, directed the $650,000 project. The complex includes a 250-seat community theater, smaller meeting rooms, an art room and a kitchen.

Next door is the refurbished Sacred Heart Church which is available as an art gallery or hall for parties. Across the street is a new medical clinic. Town residents helped to build and pay for it.

*Point Reyes Station.*

# The Eastern Shore of Tomales Bay

On the other side of Tomales Bay, Highway 1 heads north along the curving eastern shoreline. About five miles from Point Reyes Station is the Tomales Bay Oyster Company which specializes in homegrown Pacific and French oysters plus live clams, mussels, and fresh scallops. It is open daily from 9:00 A.M. to 5:00 P.M. (663-1242)

Oysters have been cultivated in Tomales Bay since 1875, the year the trains reached here. Two stops on the line were Millerton and Bivalve, towns no longer in existence. At Millerton the oysters were protected from predators by picket fences built out in the water around the beds. Bivalve was established at the turn of the century by the Pacific Oyster Company and was serviced by the railroad, which made daily shipments of oysters to San Francisco.

Two miles past the Tomales Bay Oyster Company is the location of the old Marconi Wireless Company which built a trans-Pacific receiving station here after 1913. The buildings erected were in the Mediterranean style and included a two-story hotel, a warehouse, and administrative residences. These buildings were once occupied by Synanon, a drug treatment community. In 1979, they were purchased by the San Francisco Foundation with money from the Buck Trust. They are now under the control of the Marin Community Foundation and operated by the State Parks Foundation. Eventually they will be run by the State Parks Department. The plans for the complex include remodeling and establishing an Asilomar-type retreat and conference center for no more than 200 people. The Marconi Inn Conference Center (663-9020), will also be used for lectures and classes.

A mile past Marconi is the Marshall Boat Works and an impressive array of fishing boats are anchored near shore. A half-mile beyond is the hamlet of Marshall.

## Marshall

The beginnings of a town—a wharf, hotel, and warehouse—were already in the area of Marshall when the railroad arrived in 1875. The town was named after five Irish brothers, one with a young wife, who had crossed the western plains and arrived

*Marshall Boat Works.*

in Tomales in the mid-1800s.

Today the town has around 150 residents and stretches four-and-one-half miles along Shoreline Highway. Businesses include a fishing supply store, the Hog Island Oyster Company, The Great American Oyster Company, a real estate office and the ever-popular Tony's Seafood Restaurant which was established in 1948. Tony's is run by Anton and John Konatich.

### Audubon Cypress Grove

North of Marshall (eight-tenths of a mile) is the seventy-five-acre Audubon Cypress Grove, most of which will be bequeathed to Audubon Canyon Ranch. This preserve has rich marsh, tidelands, and bird-nesting areas.

Adjacent to the grove is the Caroline Livermore Marshland Sanctuary, thirty acres dedicated to a founder of the Marin Conservation League. The area is identified by a large wooden sign, but it is surrounded by a fence and is not open to the public.

Audubon Canyon Ranch also purchased Hog and Duck islands in Tomales Bay in 1972. Hog Island reportedly received its name when a barge broke up and its cargo of pigs landed on the island's deserted shores. These islands, along with other small pieces of

tideland along Tomales Bay, were purchased to protect the shoreline from development. The land will eventually become part of the state or federal park system.

As you continue north along the eastern shore of Tomales Bay, where the old trains used to run, you will pass a boat works and marine laboratory. Nick's Cove, a seafood restaurant, is a little over three miles from Marshall. It was started in 1933 in an old herring smokehouse by Nick Kajick, an immigrant from Yugoslavia.

Next door to Nick's is the six-acre Miller Park, developed by the Department of Fish and Game and operated by the county of Marin. Facilities include a long fishing pier, concrete boat launch ramp, parking lot, picnic tables, and privies. There is also a lovely view of Hog and Duck islands.

Seven-tenths of a mile north of Miller Park is a place once known as Ocean Roar. From this stop on the railroad, the train turned inland through an area of marsh and tidelands to follow the old estero and creeks up to the town of Tomales. Highway 1 follows the same route, turning inland and heading east toward Tomales. Audubon Canyon Ranch has purchased 118 acres in this area for a wildlife sanctuary.

# Tomales

**B**efore reaching the town of Tomales, Highway 1 is intersected by the road to Petaluma. The original settlement called Lower Town, was at this location. A hotel, warehouses, and a store were built here by an Irish immigrant, John Keyes.

Keyes's house still stands and will be to your left on a knoll opposite the Petaluma Road. The house is described in the 1976 *Tomales Historic Resource Survey* as a "Greek revival farmhouse with shiplap siding," circa 1850. (The house has now been rebuilt and plastered over.)

A post office using the name "Tomales" was opened in Lower Town in 1854. Present-day Tomales was once called Upper Town and began when Warren Dutton, Keyes's partner, founded his own store here in 1858.

◄ *Church of the Assumption, Tomales.*

Tomales was a productive agricultural community, second in importance only to San Rafael. Large quantities of potatoes, grain, dairy products, hogs, and beef were shipped by schooner from Keys Embarcadero, down Keys and Walker creeks to Keys Estero, a finger of water reaching northeast from Tomales Bay.

Like Bolinas Lagoon, Tomales Bay was soon silted-up because of erosion, and navigation of the creeks and estuary became impossible. When the train service began in 1875, shipping switched from schooner to rail, and products were sent to the ports of San Quentin and Sausalito.

Upper Town prospered and grew, surviving the 1906 earthquake and a devastating fire in 1920. Ten years later the railroad pulled out, leaving the town's future linked to the destiny of the automobile. Few buildings have been added to Tomales since then, and the town still serves the agricultural countryside as it did one hundred years ago.

On your left as you enter the town of Tomales is the Catholic Church of the Assumption, built in 1860. Behind it, just barely visible, is the 1886 Tomales Presbyterian Church located on Church Street. One of the original trustees of this church was George W. Burbank, Luther Burbank's brother. Luther spent time in Tomales with his brother, and while here he developed a potato that he named "Bodega Red."

*Dillon Beach.*

# Dillon Beach

D illon Beach Road heads west from Tomales, ending about four miles away at Marin's northernmost beach. On the way you will pass a picturesque Catholic cemetery, a half-mile out of town on the right, and then some impressive rock formations known as Elephant Rocks (two miles farther). The road curves around them to the left and goes on to Dillon Beach on Bodega Bay.

The bay was named by the Spanish explorer, Bodega, who landed here in 1775. Dillon Beach was founded by an Irish pioneer, George Dillon, who built a hotel here in the late 1800s. The beach prospered as a resort area for many years under Dillon and other owners.

Sylvester Lawson arrived around 1923 and his family now controls local business, including the Lawson Resort Store which carries groceries, apparel, fishing gear, and other supplies.

To reach the bay, follow Beach Avenue. Dillon Beach is a lovely, wide, sandy strip with tall rocks rising dramatically out of the ocean to the north; to the south are the sand dunes covered with sea grass. Rows of old cottages and some modern homes are located to the north on a treeless hill overlooking the area. There is a beach admission fee ($3 per car) and a lot for parking. Public facilities include rest rooms (locked in winter) and picnic tables. The beach is open for day use only and closed entirely in January.

Just beyond is Lawson's Landing. A toll road ($4) leads to a camping area. At the end of the road is a huge trailer park, pier, and boat launch. Overnight camping is $9 per night or $50 per week. (707 878-2443)

Lawson's Landing is at the mouth of Tomales Bay where it flows into Bodega Bay and the Pacific Ocean. The town of Bodega Bay is to the north in Sonoma County.

You may reach Sonoma by continuing north on Highway 1. Here you will find the Russian River resort area, Jack London country (near Glen Ellen) and the beginning of the California wine-growing region.

# Horses

# 12

## Stables

Three popular stables located in Northern, Southern and West Marin provide rental horses and guides for the public. All three facilities are connected to hundreds of miles of spectacular trails making Marin County one of the finest riding areas in the United States.

Other stables, open to the public, have facilities for boarding horses and provide well-trained personnel who specialize in riding and jumping lessons. Many stables also sponsor trail rides and summer camps.

### Northern Marin

**SUNSET CORRAL,** 2901 Vineyard, Novato. 897-8212

This complete horse facility in sunny Novato is owned and operated by Pat and Gail Martin. They offer around twenty horses for rent (more in the summer), plus guides to lead you along the 32 miles of trails through the North Marin Water District, Marin County Open Space and the 125 miles of fire roads adjoining the stables. There are hourly rides, day rides, evening rides and BBQ rides.

The Sunset Corral has about 150 horses (100 boarders), and offers Western and English lessons in both indoor and outdoor arenas. Summer horse day camps run from the end of June through August.

The Martins, who have been in the horse business for 33 years, provide other care for their horses such as shoeing, shots, worming, leg wraps, dentistry and regular vet visits. The actually live on the premises (along with two other families and two hired men), so they can keep an eye on things as well as be available in all emergencies.

Plans for the future include a new roping arena.

The Sunset Corral is open seven days a week from 9:00 A.M. to 5:00 P.M. To get there drive north on Highway 101, take the Atherton Avenue exit; drive west on San Marin Drive which runs into Sutro; turn right (north) on Vineyard Raod.

## Southern Marin

**MIWOK LIVERY RIDING STABLES,** 701 Tennessee Valley Road, Mill Valley. 383-8048

Deni O'Brien and Linda Rubio own the Miwok Livery which

*Krista Nastasuk rides at the Sunset Stables in Novato.*

*Outdoor arena at Miwok Stables in Tennessee Valley.*

is leased from the Miwok Valley Association, a cooperative of horse boarders. The livery provides about 20 horses for guided trail rides through the Marin Headlands and above the Golden Gate Bridge.

One of their most popular events is the four hour "Pelican Inn Ride" which leaves at 10:30 A.M. on weekends. Riders proceed down the Tennessee Valley Trail, then ascend Fox Trail where they have a panoramic view of the Pacific Ocean. Luch is served in the Pelican Inn, an English pub, in Muir Beach. Miwok Livery also sponsors after school classes, adult classes, children's summer courses (Lil' Britches and Junior Britches), summer day camp, a "kids'" overnight ride and an adult overnight ride. Miwok Livery is open Wednesday through Sunday (closed Mon. and Tues.). Take Hwy. 101 to the Stinson Beach exit, turn left on Tennessee Valley Road; follow it to the Golden Gate National Recreation Area parking lot; turn left to reach the stables.

## West Marin

**FIVE BROOKS STABLES,** 1000 State Route #1, Olema. 663-1570 (P.O. Box 567, Point Reyes, CA 94956)

Located in the Point Reyes National Seashore, the Five Brooks Stables offers guided trail rides and hay and buggy rides for

*The stall area at Miwok Stables in Tennessee Valley.*

children, adults, handicapped and the disabled. The rides include one and two-hour, half-day and all-day excursions. Horses may be boarded overnight or by the month. Boarding includes feed, water and "mucking out" the stall or paddock once daily. A tackroom and arena are also available. About 26 horses are available for rent to the public. Trails cover 350 miles and run all the way to the Golden Gate Bridge. During the rainy season, it is suggested that riders telephone first to confirm rides. Hay rides should be reserved at least one week and buggy rides three days in advance. To get to Five Brooks Stables, take Hwy. 101 to the San Anselmo exit; head west on Sir Francis Drake Boulevard to the town of Olema; turn left onto Hwy. 1 and drive approximately 5 miles.

# Riding Academies and Boarding Facilities

**BAYWOOD CANYON,** 3200 Sir Francis Drake, Fairfax, 94930. 454-4564

The horse operation at Baywood Canyon has been leased-out to Marian Nelson who offers training and lessons for beginners through advanced including hunter, jumper and saddle seats. Clinics and horse shows are held in the indoor and outdoor rings. Boarding facilities and tack shop available.

**CANYON OAKS FARM,** 501 Canyon Road, Novato, 94947. 897-2269

Joan Bondoc offers boarding with paddocks, walk-in sheds, stalls, and pastures. Other facilities include a round training pen, sand arena, jumps and facilities for stallions. Canyon Oaks Farm also hosts several 4-H events.

**CROSS ROADS STABLE,** 571 McClay Road, Novato, 94947.

Joan Seebach provides boarding stalls with paddocks which are cleaned daily. Lessons are given in a riding arena. Cross Roads Stable is a private, quiet residence close to open space.

**DICKSON RANCH,** San Geronimo Valley Drive, Woodacre. 488-0454

The historic 50-acre Dickson Ranch, founded in 1855, is still owned and operated by fourth generation family members Grace Dickson Tolson and her husband, Chuck. They offer boarding, lessons and about ten shows a year. Facilities include four arenas including one indoors and a cross country course for beginning jumpers. The Dickson Ranch, Grace explains, originally consisted of 500 acres obtained from the Mailliard family in exchange for a debt. Her great-grandmother built a Vermont style house on the property in 1870 which is still occupied today.

**DOUGHERTY RANCH,** 700 Nicasio Valley Road, Nicasio 94946. 662-2031

Bob and Diana Dougherty raise Arabians and board over 35 horses at their very fine ranch in Nicasio. Facilities include a lighted covered arena, pipe paddocks as well as runs located adjacent to the stables, a four-horse "hot-walker," turn-out paddocks and a large storage area for hay and shavings. Horses are turned out daily to pasture for exercise. The Dougherty Ranch, which provides a resident trainer, offers lessons in halter and performance training, jumping, saddle seat and hunt seat equitation. They can also furnish two stallions for breeding and will foal out mares.

**FRANKLYN TRAINING CENTER,** 404 Gage Lane, Novato, 94947. 892-2737

This ranch is run by Marie and Beve Franklyn and according to Frank Sanders of the Pencil Belly Ranch, Beve Franklyn is the "best trainer around." Franklyn boards forty horses and "trains horses that other people have spoiled!" or does 'just straight training." He also gives lessons and trains student trainers. Facilities include box stalls and pipe corrals plus a big covered arena. No shows.

**GOLDEN GATE DAIRY STABLES** (also known as the "Dairy") 1760 Shoreline Hwy., Muir Beach. 388-8295 (Mailing address: Star Route, Box 250, Sausalito, CA 94965)

Evelyn (Tink) and Dick Pervier, in business for 25 years, board 45 horses in stables near Muir Beach and the Golden Gate National Recreation Area. They provide two rings for dressage and jumping, and teach both English and Western riding. They also sponsor four children's shows a year.

**MAR-GHI ARABIANS** Nicasio Valley Road, Nicasio, 94946. 662-2135

Owned by Mario and Eva Ghilotti who sell feed and tack such as saddles, bridles, blankets and other horse care products.

**MARIN STABLES,** 139 Wood Lane, Fairfax, 94930, 459-9455

Jim McDermott leases land from the Marin Municipal Water District which has excellent riding trails. Facilities include boarding stalls, paddocks and a small covered arena.

**MORNING STAR FARMS,** 885 Sutro Avenue, Novato, 94947. 897-1633

Vicky and Kevin Byars provide boarding, English riding instruction, jumping, dressage, and cross country. They also sponsor shows and clinics in their three arenas.

**OLIVA LOMA STABLES,** 350 Olive Avenue, Novato, 94945. 897-6808

Ruth and Emery Jones offer boarding, and an outdoor arena in their spotless facilities. These are "'quiet adult boarding stables near trails." No lessons or training.

**PENCIL BELLY RANCH,** 1671 Indian Valley Road, Novato 898-0802

Frank and Elaine Sanders board twenty horses, but do not offer lessons or shows. Facilities include covered stalls with paddocks, double-sized pipe corrals and a big open arena. The four-acre ranch borders the Pacheco Open Space District and is near the Indian Valley Riding Club. Families can join the club which offers over 2300 acres for riding, special rides and barbeques. Frank stresses that there are no streets to cross to get into the open space district from the Pencil Belly Ranch and you do not have to trailer your horse.

*Show exhibitor gracefully clears the jump at a San Domenico Schooling Show.* Photo courtesy of San Domenico Riding School.

*Ashley Mangus rides Dolly, a gentle mare with a soft gait at San Domenico Riding School.* Photo courtesy of San Domenico Riding School.

## RANCHO MARIN EQUESTRIAN CENTER, 50 H Lane, Novato, 94947. 897-6885

New owners Joyce Woodruff, Vicky and Kevin Byars who also own the Morning Star Farm, run a large operation here offering boarding, lessons and sales. English and Western pleasure riding also include hunter, jumper and dressage. Facilities are comprised of both a covered and an outdoor arena for clinics and shows.

## SAN DOMENICO RIDING SCHOOL, 1500 Butterfield Road, San Anselmo. Barn, 459-9126 Office, 454-0200

San Domenico School, tucked away in a secluded valley at the end of Butterfield Road in Sleepy Hollow, is surrounded by 550 acres of rolling hills and dedicated open space. The riding school provides boarding stables for students and members of the public, a lighted indoor arena and an outdoor riding ring. Students are encouraged to compete in horse shows throughout California. A "Little Britches" program for children, ages four and five, is held on Saturday mornings at 10:00 A.M. This basic introduction to horses is for mothers and fathers and their children. It is open to the public. Adults ride from 9-11:00 A.M. Sundays are the "horses' day off." Weekly camps held in the summer teach riding, how to groom, saddle and bridle a horse, and good horse care.

**SHADOW CREEK STABLES,** 2980 Sir Francis Drake Boulevard, Fairfax, 94930. 459-0732

Boarding and training plus instruction in Western and English riding. Facilities include a lighted arena and a BBQ area. Trainer Jan Bolds has an excellent reputation in the county according to Grace Dickson Tolson.

**SKY RANCH,** End of Crest Rd., Fairfax, 94930. 459-9925 or 457-4700

Nancy Sandy provides boarding facilities including pasture, paddock and stalls. Boarders enjoy pleasure trail riding all the way to the Pacific Ocean through MMWD lands, Mt. Tamalpais, Pine Mountain, and the Point Reyes National Seashore. Sky Ranch has a common fence line with the Marin Municipal Water District. No lessons are available.

**STEWART RANCH,** 8497 State Route No. 1, Olema, 94950. 663-1362

The Stewart Ranch, operated by Boyd and his daughter, Joanne Stewart, provides a horse camp and boarding adjacent to the beautiful trails in the Point Reyes National Seashore.

**ST. VINCENT'S EQUESTRIAN PROGRAM,** St. Vincent's School, 4900 Redwood Hwy., San Rafael, 94903. 479-8831 or Andre Morrow at 584-1383

This riding program is for a residential treatment facility for boys, ages 7 to 14. It is a non-profit organization, not open to the public.

**WILLOW RIDGE HORSE STABLES,** 30 Knob Hill Road, Pt. Reyes, 94956. 663-1345

Owned and operated by Michael Kaplan who offers boarding facilities, limited instruction, an indoor riding ring and clinics in dressage and the Beau Geste School of Artistic Riding.

**WINDFIELD STATION,** 3431 Nicasio Valley Road, Nicasio, 94946. 662-2232 (Barn, 662-9985)

Owned and operated by Carmen Johnson, Windfield Station boards up to 75 horses in fine facilities built on sixty acres in Nicasio. Classes are held in beginning dressage and hunter/jumper. There are also clinics, schooling shows and rated shows. Facilities include stables, a lighted and covered arena, a large outdoor arena, a dressage court, turn-out paddocks, two extra-large foaling stalls and a storage barn for hay and tack.

*Miwok Stables in Tennessee Valley.*

# Staging Areas *(Hitching Posts and Water Troughs)*

S taging areas are places where groups of riders meet to leave for a ride. Facilities usually include an ample area to park vehicles and horse trailers, hitching posts, water troughs and restrooms.

## Golden Gate National Recreational Area

**Miwok Stables,** 701 Tennessee Valley Road, Mill Valley. Parking, hitching posts, water troughs and privies.

## Marin Municipal Water District - Mt. Tamalpais

*(It is forbidden to ride or water horses in the lakes.)*

**Bear Wallow** - Water troughs and hitching posts

**Lake Lagunitas** - Parking, water, hitching rails, adjacent to picnic areas, restrooms.

**Laurel Dell Fire Road** - Hitching rails (north of Rock Springs)

**Potrero Meadows** - Hitching rails by restrooms

**Rifle Camp** - Water trough (access via Lagunitas/Rock Springs Road next to Potrero Meadows)

**Rock Spring** - Hitching rails and restrooms (north of the Mountain Theater area)

**Sky Oaks Staging Area** - Entrance of the Water District (Lake Lagunitas and Bon Tempe) above Fairfax. Restrooms, and water troughs. $3 fee.

**West Point Inn** - Hitching rails and water troughs (Access via the old Railroad Grade or Eldridge Grade.

## Mt. Tamalpais State Park

**Franks Valley Road** - Horseman's Arena

This special arena was built by Ocean Riders of Muir Beach on State Parks land. For more information contact Superintendent Ron Brean at the Marin Office, 1455-A East Francisco Boulevard, San Rafael 94901.

**Old Mine Trail** - Water trough at the intersection of Old Mine Trail and Old State Road near Pan Toll.

Intersection of the Old State Road and Old Mine Road water trough.

## Point Reyes National Seashore
**Five Brooks Stables,** 1000 State Route 1, Olema

Water troughs, hitching rails, restrooms and good access from State Hwy 1.

# Bay Area Ridge Trail *(Still in planning stages)*

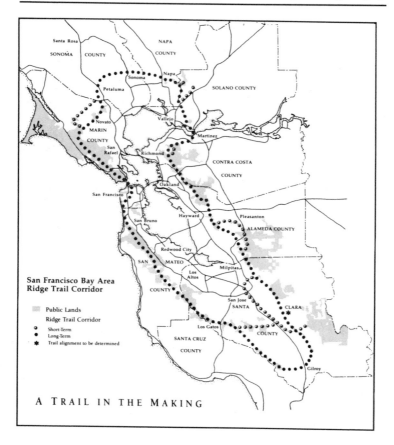

A 400-mile trail link through nine counties will connect parks and open space following the ridges and mountains that circle the Bay Area. Beside horses, the trail corridor will be used by hikers and bicyclists. Alternate parallel routes will be assigned where necessary. This regionwide project was started in 1988, and the first sections were dedicated in 1989. The final phase should be completed by 1992. In Marin, the recreational corridor will run through several parks and water district land. For more information contact: Bay Area Ridge Trail, 116 New Montgomery Street, Suite 640, San Francisco, CA. 94105 (415) 543-4291

## *A Special Marin Ride*
# The Point Reyes Bridge Ride

For the past 13 years, riding enthusiasts in Marin have sponsored a popular three-day ride beginning at Pierce Point Ranch, Tomales Point, and ending at the Golden Gate Bridge overlooking the Golden Gate National Recreation Area Headlands. Riders cover approximately twenty miles per day along the following route: Tomales Bay, Point Reyes, Bear Valley, Bolinas Lagoon, Mt. Tamalpais, Muir Beach and the Golden Gate National Recreation Area.

Much of the trail runs on top of ridges providing stunning views of San Francisco Bay and the Pacific Ocean. Other parts traverse beaches, forests of Douglas fir, redwood trees and fern groves.

The nights are spent at the Olema Campground and Rancho Baulinas. Each rider brings camping gear for personal use. Food and liquid refreshments for horse and rider are provided, and trailer transportation is availalbe. The ride is limited to 50, and it is important that all riders and horses be well conditioned as the trails are mostly up and down hill. For more information on future rides, write Sandra Sullivan, P.O. Box 1536, San Anselmo, CA 94960.

# Horse Clubs

**HALLECK CREEK RIDING CLUB** (For the Handicapped) -
Duane Irving and Joyce Goldstein, Halleck Creek Ranch, Nicasio.
P.O. Box 581, Inverness, CA. 94937, 663-1787.

This riding club of some 400 members began in 1977 as a way
to teach a handicapped child to ride a pony. Now an average of
90 handicapped riders of all ages show up every Saturday morning at 9:30 A.M. to participate. The ninety minute sessions which
include lessons and trail rides, last until 2:00 P.M. There is no
charge.

The Halleck Creek Riding Club also sponsors horseback camping trips, shows, an Easter egg hunt and picnics.

**MARIN COUNTY PONY CLUB** - Sylvia Nagulko, 868-1053.

This pony club currently meets every other week at the
Vanishing Point Ranch in Bolinas. Though members live all over
the county, most are from Bolinas, Pt. Reyes and Nicasio. The
children, ages 6-21 are eligible for membership as soon as they
can walk and trot their pony. They are taught to care for their
ponies or horses, stable management, and are given riding lessons
including dressage, cross country, show and jumping. Many
members go on to compete on regional and national levels. The
children also learn discipline, to work as a team, and to take
responsibility.

**MARIN HORSE COUNCIL,** 171 Bel Marin Keys, Novato, CA
94947, 883-4621 during business hours.

The 150-member Marin Horse Council, formed in 1981, is a
non- profit group which promotes the interests of horse people
and horse-related activities in Marin County. Its members publish
a newsletter, and appear before government bodies such as city
councils, county and state agencies and utilities. The Marin Horse
Council also sponsors educational programs regarding the care
of horses plus their protection and welfare. The twelve-member
Board of Directors meet at the Humane Society Library on the
first Tuesday of each month at 7:30 P.M. Those interested are
welcome to attend.

**MARIN MOUNTED 4-H** - Claudia Rubin, 8 Alvina Avenue, San Rafael, 94901, 457-5814.

The girls and boys who belong to the Marin Mounted 4-H group participate in rides, group lessons, field trips and parades. The field trips are organized to teach members about horse safety, tack and other aspects of horses. Most activities are conducted at the Dickson Ranch in the San Geronimo Valley. Members, ages 8-17, are not required to own their own horses. Claudia Rubin believes that the 4-H activities teach the children how they can be involved with their environment through riding horses.

**MARIN COUNTY SHERIFF'S POSSE** - Skip White, Captain. 897-6280 or 485-3139.

The Marin County Sheriff's Posse, founded in 1942, has about 50 members, both men and women. The main focus of the organization these days is search and rescue for the Marin County Sheriff's Dept. Training sessions are held once a month and practice rescue operations in and out of the county are conducted quarterly. The Posse also raises money for non-profit riding groups such as the St. Vincents Equestrian Program and the Halleck Creek Riding Club for the physically handicapped. Two major rides (by invitation) are held annually: the spring ride and the Frank Monte/Ray Shone Memorial Ride held in the fall. This weekend ride which is conducted in October, includes a Saturday night barbeque. New members are accepted with certain qualifications and orientation rides are held to familiarize them with procedures.

**MIDDLE MARIN HUNT PONY CLUB** - Margot Szabo, 457-7821.

This pony club meets every other Sunday at Shadow Creek Stables in Fairfax where members receive riding lessons and instruction in veterinary care, stable and horse management. The children, ages 8-18, also participate in one or two fox hunts every year out of Windfield Station in Nicasio. The riders chase a scent which has been dragged instead of a live fox. It is not mandatory for members to own their own ponies or horses, but they should have access to one when they want to ride. The club is non-profit and considered quite inexpensive for all the benefits it provides.

**MOUNTED ASSISTANCE UNIT OF THE MARIN DISTRICT, CALIFORNIA DEPARTMENT OF PARKS AND RECREATION** - Debbie Gallagher - 662-2349 or Ranger Mike O'Connel, Samuel P. Taylor State Park - 488-9897

This uniformed group rides patrol through the local state parks: Samuel P. Taylor, Mt. Tamalpais, China Camp and Olompali. Their duties include offering assistance if needed such as giving directions, CPR and other first aid. They also help look for missing people and answer questions. The Mounted Assistance Unit has been in existence for five years and meets two or three times annually.

**NOVATO HORSEMAN'S, INC.**, 600 Bugeia Lane, Novato, 94947. Marianne Gerssing and Ron Lear - 897-7526

Organized in 1944, the 200-member group meets monthly at their own clubhouse located on five acres in Novato. Other facilities include an arena for use by members and guests, and lights for night activities. Activities include weekly roping, cow pennings and monthly rides.

**NOVATO PONY CLUB** - Alba Giomi, 897-5591

The children in this club are ages 8 to 21. Meetings are held the first and third Saturday in Novato from 9:30 A.M. to noon. Activities include riding, trail rides, cross country, dressage, stadium jumping, horse care and safety. Field trips are taken to places related to horses such as the veterinary clinics at the University of California at Davis. Rallies (competitions) are held between pony clubs. Members compete in horse care (such as how to groom), stable management, knowledge of veterinary care, safety and how to improve their riding skills. There are also game rallies. The Novato Pony Club is a member of a national organization called the United States Pony Club, Inc. Members may compete at regional or national levels. They are also rated twice a year. Starting with a "D," a rider may work his or her way up to an "A" rating over a period of six to ten years.

**SLEEPY HOLLOW HORSEMAN'S ASSOCIATION,** 1317 Butterfield Road, San Anselmo, 94960.

This group organizes rides throughout the year plus two clinics dealing with worming and dentistry. The members maintain a public riding ring on the Hidden Valley School grounds in Sleepy Hollow.

**TAMALPAIS TRAIL RIDERS,** P.O. Box 63, San Anselmo, 94960.

Founded in 1939 to protect equestrian usage of trails on Mt. Tamalpais watershed, this club built many of the fine trails enjoyed by horsemen and hikers today on the mountain. The Tamalpais Trail Riders hold day and overnight rides plus a trail test every year.

## Pack Trips

**SPANISH SPRINGS RANCH -** Bob Roberts Spanish Springs Information Center, 1102 Second St., San Rafael, CA 94901. In CA: 1-800-272-8282. Out of state: 1-800-228-0279.

Spanish Springs is comprised of several properties including ranches and historic homesteads located in California's Lassen County and Nevada's Humboldt County. Altogether, they offer horse related activities such as long rides, lessons, cattle drives, wilderness packtrains, team penning, roping, cattle branding, a variety of rodeo events, moonlight hayrides, guided fishing trips, buckboard and sleigh rides in the winter. Facilities include authentic cowboy bunkhouses, private cabins, a large rustic lodge, old homesteads and campgrounds. Hearty, western-style meals are included.

# Marin
# Restaurants

# 13

T here are many outstanding restaurants in Marin, but I will mention only a selection of special ones I have enjoyed over the years plus a few recent arrivals. Call to check on days open, as restaurant hours change.

## Corte Madera

**Il Fornaio,** 223 Corte Madera Town Center. 927-4400

Creative Italian cuisine in an authentic atmosphere. Try the angel hair pasta! Popular Sunday brunch.

**Jade Kitchen,** 5605 Paradise Shopping Center, East Corte Madera. 924-4843 and 924-4842

Really outstanding Chinese food. My favorites include the "Wor Won Ton" soup, beef with asparagus, sweet & sour pork, and shrimp with walnuts. Extensive take-out menu. Reasonably priced.

**La Petite, 1838 Redwood Hwy. 927-1922**

Wonderful homemade soups and sandwiches.

**Marin Joe's,** 1585 Casa Buena Drive. 924-2081 and 924-1500

Italian and continental cuisine, charcoal broiled steak and chops. Try the "Joe's Special." A lot of food for your money and excellent service. Full bar.

**Peppermill,** 1815 Redwood Highway. 924-1830

Open for breakfast, lunch, and dinner (on weekends until 2:30 A.M.). Hamburgers, steaks, pastas and salads.

◀ *Chefs/owners Bob and Harry Ghiringhelli in their kitchen at Deer Park Villa in Fairfax.*

**Savannah Grill,** 55 Tamal Vista, The Market Place. 924-6774

Features mesquite-grilled or smoked meats, fowl and seafood pastas.

**Tony Roma's,** 347 Corte Madera Town Center. 927-7417

This looks like 19th Century Chicago with wood paneling, red brick, banker's lamps and green and burgundy colored booths. Excellent ribs and barbecue chicken. Good shrimp salad.

# Fairfax

**Deer Park Villa,** 367 Bolinas Road. 456-8084

Italian-American cuisine in a relaxed garden setting. Prime rib and veal specialities recommended. Fresh pasta. Dinners only, closed Mondays.

**Ghiringhelli Pizzeria,** 45 Broadway. 453-7472

Great pizza, central downtown location or free delivery. Beer and wine.

**Koffee Klatch,** 57 Broadway. 454-4748

For the early riser, try the delicious full-breakfasts with wide selection of omelets. Hamburgers, sandwiches, chicken, fish or salads for lunch.

**Pucci's Ristorano Italiano,** 35 Broadway. 459-1618

Wonderful Italian food in a friendly neighborhood restaurant at very reasonable prices. Homemade pastas, seafood, chicken and veal. One of my favorites in the county.

**Red Boy Pizza,** 2404 Sir Francis Drake Boulevard. 453-3138

A fun, neighborhood pizza parlor also offering Italian food.

**Spanky's Restaurant,** 1900 Sir Francis Drake Boulevard. 456-5299

Popular with locals. Homemade stews, pasta and prime rib.

# Forest Knolls

**Two Bird Cafe,** 6912 Sir Francis Drake Boulevard. 488-9952

Favorite valley restaurant with American, vegetarian and Italian food.

*Enrico Pucci, in front of his restaurant, "Pucci's," in Fairfax.*

# Greenbrae

**Chevy's Mexican Restaurant,** 302 Bon Air Shopping Center.
461-3203

Popular Mexican dining. Mesquite-broiled fish. High noise level inside, but pleasant outdoor patio. Great salsa.

**LoCoco's, Joe, Ristorante,** 300 Drakes Landing Road. 925-0808

Creative and delicious Tuscan cuisine. Special pasta dishes.

# Ignacio

**Dalecio Ristorante,** Galli Square, 340 Ignacio Boulevard.
883-0960

Like being in Italy. Homemade pasta and fresh seafood. Try the "Capellini con Pomodoro" or Angel Hair Pasta with fresh tomato sauce, garlic and basil. Fantastic! Outdoor dining on the deck under umbrellas. Long bar from old Gallis Restaurant with

*George Brown, Manager of Ristorante Dalecio in Ignacio, stands in front of the antipasto bar.*

an etched mirror illustrating the history of the area. One of Marin's truly great restaurants.

**Maya Palenque,** 349 Enfrente Road. 883-6292.

After remodeling, this restaurant has a great atmosphere and very good Mexican food. Take the Ignacio Road exit.

# Inverness

**Barnaby's By the Bay,** 12938 Sir Francis Drake Boulevard. 669-1114

Seafood, barbeque ribs and oysters.

**Manka's,** Callender Way and Argyle. 669-1034

After 40 years of serving Czech and Viennese dishes, Milan Prokupek and his wife Manka sold in April 1989 to Ben Grade. The new owner has continued to offer Czech food along with some lighter dishes.

**Vladimir's Czechoslovakian Restaurant,** 12785 Sir Francis Drake Boulevard. 669-1021

Another fine Czech restaurant.

# Kentfield

**Half Day Cafe,** 848 College Avenue. 459-0291

Popular with College of Marin and local residents. California cuisine. Now open for dinner. Service could be improved.

**La Lanterna,** 799 College Avenue. 258-0144

Hearty, delicious Italian food with homemade pastas. Fresh fish. Offers a special "healthy heart" menu and fresh fish.

**Pacific Cafe,** 850 College Avenue. 456-3898

One of the best seafood restaurants in Marin. Specialties are pan-fried oysters and seasonal fresh fish dishes. All well-prepared. Reasonable prices.

# Larkspur

**Acapulco,** 801 Larkspur Landing Circle. 461-8044

Delicious Mexican food with a wide choice of selections including seafood.

**Blue Rock Inn,** 507 Magnolia Avenue. 924-5707

An old stagecoach stop, this restaurant features delicious Italian dishes, steak, and prime rib dinners. Homemade pastas, fresh seafood and tasty vegetarian dishes. Full bar with a Monday night TV football special.

**Fabrizio Ristorante,** 455 Magnolia Avenue. 924-3332

Quaint, Italian atmosphere and tasty cuisine which includes seafood.

**The Good Earth,** 2231 Larkspur Landing Circle. 461-7322

Offers a wide selection of vegetarian dishes and sandwiches. Whole-grain bread from in-house bakery. Fish and pasta, brown rice, and low salt selections.

**Lark Creek Inn,** 234 Magnolia Avenue. 924-7766

Bradley Ogden, a famous chef known for his "new wave Americana" cooking at the Campton Place Hotel in San Francisco, moved to Marin in 1989 and reopened the picturesque Lark Creek Inn with what he describes as "American country cooking." The restaurant was an overnight sensation and reservations can take weeks. Satisfied diners rave about the delicious meals and don't seem to mind the high prices.

**Magnolia Food Company,** 1167 Magnolia Avenue. 461-8410

Barbara Camera started this restaurant as a cafe and deli. Today it has emerged as a lunch place containing seating for twenty with an outstanding catering service. Barbara cooks her own turkeys and hams daily, uses all fresh ingredients and offers sumptuous salads and vegetarian sandwiches. For her catering she adds special touches such as fresh flowers, the use of silver and antique baskets.

**Scoma's,** 2421 Larkspur Landing Circle. 461-6161

Delightful decor, sumptuous Italian cuisine. Popular with the business crowd.

**Yet Wah Restaurant,** 2019 Larkspur Landing. 461-3631

Mandarin cuisine with three hundred authentic Chinese dishes; prawns, scallops, spiced beef, musee pork, lemon fried chicken.

# Marshall

**Nick's Cove,** 23240 Highway 1. 663-1033

Seafood restaurant in an old rebuilt herring smokehouse on Tomales Bay. Wonderful place to stop along the coast.

**Tony's Seafood, Highway 1 on Tomales Bay. 663-1103**

Fresh seafood meals. A special treat is barbequed oysters every Saturday and Sunday. The restaurant and bar have a lovely marine view through blue-tinted glass.

# Mill Valley

**Buckeye,** Highway 101. 332-1292
(Near Mill Valley exit traveling north, or Stinson Beach exit traveling south)

German-American cooking at its best. Cocktail lounge.

**Butler's,** 625 Redwood Hwy. 383-1900

Modern American and International cuisine. Overlooks Richardson Bay and Mt. Tamalpais. Try the pan-roasted salmon fillet.

**The Cantina,** 651 East Blithedale. 381-1070 (Blithedale Plaza)

Mexican food, best Margaritas, authentic atmosphere. Patio dining available.

**El Paseo,** 17 Throckmorton Avenue. 388-0741

Located in the El Paseo shopping complex. Excellent French cuisine.

**Giramonti's,** 655 Redwood Highway. 383-3000
(Seminary Drive exit off Highway 101 at the Shelter Bay Office Building)

"Roman Cuisine" with outstanding veal dishes. Try the Cannelloni Rossini or the Lasagna Romana. View of the bay and Mount Tamalpais.

**Hickory Pit (Emil Villa's) The Original,** 205 Strawberry Village. 388-6442

Features barbequed food, especially good spareribs, and fresh berry pies.

**Jennie Low's Chinese Cuisine,** 38 Miller Avenue, 388-8868

Tasty homestyle Chinese cooking. Dim Sum lunch specials.

**La Ginestra,** 127 Throckmorton. 388-0224

Italian cuisine. Every dish is delicious. Try the seafood pasta.

**La Petite,** 33 Reed Blvd. (Behind Strawberry Shopping Center). 381-2336

Sumptuous sandwiches, hearty soups and salads. Outdoor patio with fountain.

**La Veranda,** 163 Throckmorton Avenue. 383-2621

Outstanding Italian food. Patrons enjoy eating outside on the deck within sight and sound of a creek. The gnocci is excellent. Salads are also good.

**Mountain Home Inn,** 810 Panoramic Highway. 381-9000

Enjoy lunch and dinner on top Mt. Tamalpais with fabulous views from the terrace. California cuisine. Weekend brunch.

**Perry's,** 625 Redwood Highway. 383-9300

Popular singles spot. Lunch and weekend brunch spot. American cuisine with a selection of grilled entries and fresh salads.

**Ristorante Lucca,** 24 Sunnyside. 388-4467
A friendly Italian restaurant.

**Strawberry Joe's,** 320 Strawberry Town and Country. 383-1400
Average Italian-American cuisine. Full bar.

# Muir Beach

**Pelican Inn,** 10 Pacific Way. 383-6000
Authentic English pub fare. Sumptuous buffets.

# Novato

**California Diner,** 6090 Redwood Boulevard. 892-0779
A restaurant, bakery and soda fountain plus Sunday brunch.

**Hill Top Cafe,** 850 Lamont Avenue. 892-2222
Nice view of surrounding mountains. Popular with North Marin business crowd. Fresh seafood.

*Roga Patoja, Veronica Cruz and MaElena Patoja enjoy lunch at Las Guitarras, their Mexican and seafood restaurant in Novato.*

**Las Guitarras Inc.,** 1017 Reichert Avenue. 892-3171

Mexican and seafood restaurant. Delightful patio dining with attractive iron garden furniture and a bubbling fountain. Try the tasty tostada.

# Nicasio

**Rancho Nicasio,** 1 Old Rancheria Road. 662-2219

Recently re-opened to the delight of Nicasio residents. Old ranch-style atmosphere. Good wholesome Continential/Italian cuisine. Western style bar and lounge.

# Olema

**Jerry's Farm House,** Highway One. 663-1264

Comfortable old place specializing in family-style lunches and dinner. Seafood, barbecued chicken, and steaks. Closed Mondays.

**Olema Inn,** U.S. 1 and Sir Francis Drake Boulevard. 663-9559

Lunch and dinner are now served in this 1876 restored Victorian hotel. Dinners, Sunday brunch. Picturesque outdoor deck.

# Point Reyes Station

**Chez Madeline,** 10905 State Route 1. 663-9177

Popular Czech restaurant. French cuisine.

**Station House Cafe,** A and Third streets. 663-1515

Fresh seafood, steak, and vegetarian dishes. Great for breakfast.

# Ross

**Alessia,** 23 Ross Common. 925-9619

Italian cuisine. Popular for lunch and dinner. Closed Mondays.

**Ross Garden Restaurant,** Marin Art and Garden Center, Sir Francis Drake Boulevard. 456-7870

International cuisine. Patio open in summer. Run by volunteers and popular for lunch.

# San Anselmo

**Riccardo's Ristorante and Pizzeria,** 411 San Anselmo Avenue. 457-0616

A fine Italian restaurant in the Courtyard. Antipastos, veal, chicken, fish, pasta, and 20 selections of pizza. Take-out service.

**Caffe Alberto,** 208 Sir Francis Drake Boulevard, 453-3025

Chef Alberto Pavanello from Venice, Italy, offers delicious homemade pasta and an extensive menu.

# San Rafael

**Adriana's Ristorante,** 999 Anderson Drive. 454-8000

The hot spot for Marinites who know great Italian food. Pricey.

**Cafe Italia Ristorante,** 1236 4th Street. 459-3977

Wonderful food in a bright airy atmosphere in downtown San Rafael. You can eat at the counter or a table. Reasonable prices and friendly service. Full bar. I recommend the Linguine Alle Vongole.

**Casa Manana,** 711 D Street. 456-6686

Tiny restaurant tucked away among medical offices, but well worth discovering if you appreciate delicious Mexican food. (Also at: 180 Bellam, Ave., San Rafael 456-7345 and 705 Center Boulevard, Fairfax)

**Dominic's Harbor View Restaurant,** 507 Francisco Boulevard. 456-1383

Excellent Italian cooking. Fresh seafood caught in family boats. Weekend brunch and full bar. Large banquet facilities and important art collection. Outside dining with views of San Rafael Canal.

**Gonzales Hacienda,** Corner of 2nd & B. 459-9863

Some of the best Mexican food in Marin at affordable prices. Friendly, prompt service.

**Guido's,** 1555 Fourth Street. 453-7877

Besides the regular Italian menu, Guido's offers dishes with no salt, oil or butter.

*Dominic Pomilia pauses by a table overlooking San Rafael Canal at "Dominic's Harbor View Restaurant in San Rafael.*

**La Petite Auberge,** 704 Fourth Street. 456-5808

French and Continental cooking. Try the delicious crepes suzette.

**Las Camelias Cosina Tradicional Mexicana,** 912 Lincoln Ave. 453-5850

Always good. Several outside tables.

**Las Parrillas,** 812 4th Street. 454-7600

Convenient location with parking lot in back. Casual Mexican dining includes a taco bar.

**Le Chalet Basque,** 405 N. San Pedro Road (Santa Venetia). 479-1070

Basque, French and European cooking. Wide selection of entrees. Full bar. Red-checkered tablecloths, informal atmosphere. Brightly-colored umbrellas for patio dining.

**La Toscana,** 3751 Redwood Hwy. 492-9100.

Flavorful Italian entries from Tuscany. Popular place with the Civic Center crowd.

**Mandarin House Hunan,** 817 Francisco Boulevard, West. 492-1638

Luncheon, dinner, banquets. Live music four days a week.

**Mayflower Inn,** 1533 Fourth Street. 456-1011

Authentic old English pub. Fish and chips and other British offerings. Piano sing-along on weekends. Sponsors the Mayflower Chorus.

**Mimosa,** 901 Lincoln Avenue. 457-2400

Southern French and California cuisine. Homemade pasta. Live music most nights.

*Chefs at San Rafael Joe's Restaurant in San Rafael include Head Chef Chez-Bornia, Peter Zimmerman and Rezinaldo Velasquez.*

**Panama Hotel,** 4 Bayview Street. 457-3993

Older remodeled hotel with lots of atmosphere and delightful patio dining. Excellent service. Try the "Panama Nachos" and "Buffalo Wings." Serves California and French wine and beer. Live music on Tuesday nights.

**Ramona's Mexican Food,** 1025 C Street. 454-0761

Lunches and dinner in a pleasant Mexican atmosphere. Enchiladas, tacos, tamales, combination plates, domestic and imported beer.

**San Rafael Joe's,** 931 Fourth Street. 456-2425

All-around good restaurant and popular bar. Italian food, steaks and seafood at reasonable prices. Makes a good hamburger. Lively piano bar where patrons sometimes volunteer to entertain.

**Villa Romano,** 901 B Street. 457-7404

Italian cuisine. Veal, seafood, pasta and pizza.

# Sausalito

**Alta Mira Hotel,** 125 Bulkley Street. 332-1350

Stunning bay view and terrace. American and Continental cuisine.

**Casa Madrona Restaurant,** 801 Bridgeway. 331-5888

Delicious American cuisine. Try the pan-roasted Cornish game hen. View of Sausalito Yacht Harbor and San Francisco Bay. Light lunches under 500 calories available.

**Flynn's Landing,** 303 Johnson Street. 332-0131

Outstanding seafood. A favorite with Sausalito residents; popular bar and view of yacht harbor.

**Horizons,** 558 Bridgeway. 331-3232

Located in old San Francisco Yacht Club. Fantastic views of San Francisco and the bay. Fresh seafood and California cuisine. Poached or steamed entrees if requested.

**Houlihan's Old Place,** 660 Bridgeway. 332-8512

Dining with panoramic bay view. Try the tostado salad.

**Marina's,** 305 Harbor Drive. 332-0535

This popular artist's hangout is built of natural woods with lots of glass including skylights, a stone fireplace, brick floors and plants everywhere. Good selection of soups, salads and sandwiches plus fresh seafood daily.

**North Sea Village,** 300 Turney. 331-3300

This Hong Kong-style Chinese restaurant overlooking Richardson Bay is so good, it attracts busloads of San Francisco diners. Outstanding North Sea's dim sum. Try the "Barbequed Spareribs" and "Almond Prawns". Prices are very reasonable.

**Scoma's,** 588 Bridgeway. 332-9551
(Also in Larkspur Landing, 2421 Larkspur Landing Circle. 461-6161)

Seafood specialties, salads, and steaks. Pleasant decor overlooking the bay.

**Seven Seas Restaurant,** 682 Bridgeway. 332-1304

Complete seafood selection served in a greenhouse dining area with a retractable roof.

**Spinnaker,** 100 Spinnaker Drive. 332-1500

Popular spot with spectacular views right on the bay. Varied and delicious menu with special seafood dishes.

*Scoma's and Ondine Restaurants in Sausalito.*

**Zack's By The Bay,** Bridgeway and Turney. 332-9779

Juicy hamburgers cooked on an open grill. Deck overlooking the water with a view of yachts and sail boats.

# Stinson Beach

**Parkside Cafe and Snack Bar,** 1 block west of Highway 1. 868-1272

Breakfast and lunch. Specialities are omelets, homemade pies and breads.

**Sand Dollar,** 3458 Shoreline Hwy. 868-0434

Specialties are fresh fish in season, steaks and poultry. Patio dining or drinks by the fireplace.

# Tiburon

**The Caprice,** 2000 Paradise Drive. 435-3400

Continental cuisine. Gorgeous view of the Golden Gate Bridge and San Francisco.

**Guaymas Restaurant,** 5 Main Street, 435-6300

Regional Mexican cuisine with some unique dishes.

**Rooney's Garden Cafe,** 38 Main Street. 435-1911

California cuisine. Garden dining.

**Sam's Anchor Cafe,** 27 Main Street. 435-4527

The oldest restaurant in this area. Fresh seafood served indoors or on an outdoor deck. Gorgeous bay views. Boat docking facilities. A favorite with everyone!

**Servino,** 114 Main. 435-4527

Cozy spot tucked away on Ark Row serving typical Italian specialities. Veal dishes, chicken, fresh seafood and pizza. Friendly staff.

**Tiburon Tommie's,** Pier 41. 435-1229

Restaurant overlooks the bay. Specializes in American-Chinese food. South Pacific atmosphere and an exotic, tropical bar.

# Lodging

# 14

## Hotels, Motels, Inns, Bed and Breakfast Cottages and Homestays Trailer Parks, Campgrounds, Youth Hostels

In the past few years, accommodations have sprung up in the form of bed and breakfast cottages and homestays in Marin residences. Several exchanges have been organized to help people make reservations.

**Bed and Breakfast Cottages of Point Reyes**      927-9445
P.O. Box 644, Point Reyes Station, 94956

They handle eight properties in Inverness and Point Reyes Station.

**Bed and Breakfast Exchange of Marin**      485-1971
45 Entrada Avenue, San Anselmo, 94960

This exchange is owned by Mario and Suellen Lamorte. They specialize in homestays and handle about 25 properties, many of which have private entrances and kitchens. They also have cottages and houseboats, and Suellen personally inspects every property.

**Coastal Lodgings of West Marin**      663-1351
P.O. Box 1162, Point Reyes Station, 94956

This exchange, contracted by the Coastal Lodging Association and operated by Bobbie Stumps, handles eleven properties.

**Inns of Point Reyes**      663-1420
P.O. Box 145, Point Reyes Station, 94956

# Bolinas (94924)

**Blue Heron Inn,** 11 Wharf Road. (868-1102); **Bolinas Bed and Breakfast,** 15 Brighton Avenue (868-1757); **One Fifty Five Pine,** P.O. Box 62 (868-0263); **Round House,** 945 Bolinas-Olema Road. (868-9701); **Thomas' White House Inn,** P.O. Box 132 (868-0279).

# Corte Madera (94925)

**Casa Buena,** 1595 Casa Buena Drive. (924-3570); **Corte Madera Inn—Best Western,** 1815 Redwood Hwy. (924-1502); **Madera Village Inn,** 45 Tamal Vista Boulevard. (924-3608).

# Ignacio (94949)

**Alvarado Inn,** 250 Entrada Drive. (883-5952)

# Inverness (94937)

**Alder House,** Box 644, 105 Vision Road. (669-7218); **The Ark,** P.O. Box 273, (663-9338); **Blackthorne Inn,** 266 Vallejo Avenue, P.O. Box 712 (663-8621); **Dancing Coyote Beach,** P.O. Box 98 (669-7200); **Fairwinds Farm,** Box 581 (663-9454); **Golden Hinde Inn and Marina,** 12938 Sir Francis Drake Boulevard. (669-1389); **Inverness Lodge,** Callendar Way & Argyle (669-1034); **Inverness Motel,** 12718 Sir Francis Drake Boulevard. (669-1081); **Inverness Valley Inn & Tennis Ranch,** Sir Francis Drake Boulevard (669-7250); **The Laurels,** P.O. Box 394 (669-1621); **MacLean House,** 122 Hawthornden Way (669-7392); **Rosemary Cottage,** P.O. Box 619, (663-9338), **Ten Inverness Way,** P.O. Box 63 (669-1648).

# Larkspur (94904)

**Courtyard by Marriott,** 2500 Larkspur Landing Circle (925-1800).

# Mill Valley (94941)

**Fireside Motel,** 115 Shoreline Hwy. (332-6906); **Fountain Motel,** 155 Shoreline Hwy. (332-1732); **Howard Johnson,** 160 Shoreline Hwy. (332-5700); **Mountain Home Inn,** Mt. Tamalpais (381-9000); **TraveLodge,** 707 Redwood Hwy. (383-0340).

## Muir Beach (94965)

Pelican Inn, Shoreline Hwy. (383-6000).

## Novato Area (94947)

Novato Motel, 8141 Redwood Boulevard. (897-7111); Quality Inn, 215 Alameda Del Prado (883-4400); Skylark, 5613 Redwood Hwy. (883- 2406).

## Olema (94950)

Bear Valley Inn, 88 Bear Valley Road. (663-1777); Olema Inn, 10000 Sir Francis Drake Boulevard at junction of Highway 1 (663-9559); Pt. Reyes Seashore Lodge, 10021 Coastal Highway 1, P.O. Box 39 (663-9000); Roundstone Farm Bed and Breakfast, 9940 Sir Francis Drake (663-1909).

## Point Reyes Station (94956)

Arbor Cottage, 1160 Buena Vista, P.O. Box 748 (663-8020); Cricket Cottage, P.O. Box 627 (663-9139); Eureka House, P.O. Box 660 (actually located in Marshall). (663-1784); Ferrando's Hide-Away, P.O. Box 688, 12010 State Route No. 1 (663-1966); Holly Tree Inn, 3 Silverhills Road, (663-1554); Horseshoe Farm Cottage, P.O. Box 332 (663-9401), Jasmine Cottage, P.O. Box 56 (663-1166); Neon Rose, P.O. Box 632 (663-9143); Thirty-Nine Cypress Road, P.O. Box 176, (663-1709); Terri's Homestay, P.O. Box 113 (663-1289).

## San Anselmo (94960)

San Anselmo Hotel, 339 San Anselmo Avenue, (453-3532).

## San Rafael (94901)

Colonial Motel, 1735 Lincoln Avenue (453-9188); Embassy Suites (opening October 1990), 101 McInnis Parkway (499-9222); Panama Hotel, 4 Bayview (457-9339); Villa Inn, 1600 Lincoln Avenue (456-4975); Holiday Inn, 1010 Northgate Drive, San Rafael 94903 (479-8800).

# Sausalito (94965)

**Alta Mira Hotel,** 125 Bulkley Avenue (332-1350); **Casa Madrona Hotel,** 801 Bridgeway (332-0502); **Sausalito Hotel,** 16 El Portal (332-4155).

*A seal sculpture by Peter Allen in front of Seadrift Realty, greets customers who wish to rent beach front homes at Stinson Beach.*

# Stinson Beach (94970)

**Casa del Mar,** 37 Belvedere Avenue (868-2124); **Dipsea House,** 3337 Shoreline Hwy. (868-0806); **Ocean Court Motel,** 18 Arenal Avenue (868-1632); **Seadrift,** Calle del Arroyo and Seadrift Road to gate: a colony of private beach homes, several of which are rented through Seadrift Realty (868-1791).

# Tiburon (94920)

**Tiburon Lodge,** 1651 Tiburon Boulevard (435-3133).

# Recreational Vehicle and Trailer Parks

**Golden Gate Trailer Court,** 2000 Redwood Hwy., Greenbrae 94939 (924-0683).

65 spaces with 45 spaces for overnight trailers. Complete facilities: hookups, showers, laundry rooms.

**Lawson's Landing Campground,** at Dillon Beach (94929) on Bodega Bay (707-878-2443).

500 trailer or camper spaces. No hookups. Summer docking, rental boats, clam digging, rock and pier fishing, and a safe beach.

**Marin Mobile Home & Travel Trailer Park,** 2130 Redwood Hwy., Greenbrae 94904 (461-5199).

270 mobile home and RV sites. Complete facilities: hookups, showers, heated pool, saunas, laundromats. Campers are welcome and tent campsites are available.

**Olema Ranch Campground,** State Route 1, Olema 94950 (663-8001).

150 travel trailer, RV, and tent sites. BBQ pit and picnic table at each site, recreation hall, full hookups, showers, laundry rooms, and RV supplies. Pads at all water/electric sites, firewood, ice, shuffleboard and horseshoes.

# Camp Grounds

**Mount Tamalpais State Park** (388-2070). (Adjacent to Mill Valley on Panoramic Highway)

Individual, family, walk-in campsites are at the Pan Toll Ranger Station (Park Headquarters). Open all year, the campsites are complete with tables, stoves, piped water, and restrooms. There is no vehicular camping, and campsites are available on a first-come, first-served basis. The park provides two other campsites: the six-site backpacker's camp along the Coast Trail and the Alice Eastwood Group Camp near Mountain Home which can handle up to 75 people.

**Samuel P. Taylor State Park** in Lagunitas. (488-9897).

There are 60 campsites within the redwood groves and two group camps located in the Madrone Group area which have a combined capacity of 75 people.

Facilities in the park include restrooms, hot shoers, picnic tables and barbecue pits.

Devil's Gulch Camp is maintained for horsemen and other groups using the state riding and hiking trails. The camp has a corral, hitching racks, watering troughs, and a cleared camping area for up to 25 people and their horses.

For reservations phone MISTRIX at 1-800-444-7275.

**Point Reyes National Seashore** (663-1092), Recorded Weather (663-9029)

Entrance to the Bear Valley Camping area is at the Point Reyes National Seashore Headquarters, a quarter mile west of Olema on Bear Valley Road.

There are four backpack camps in this region: Skycamp, Coast Camp, Glen Camp, and the Wildcat Campground. Coast and Wildcat Camps are used for groups. There are hitching rails, drinking water, and restrooms.

Reservations are recommended two months in advance and sites are available on a first-come, first-served basis when not reserved. Each campsite will accommodate a maximum of eight persons; at the Wildcat Group, each site will accommodate twelve people.

Camping permits are required and are available without charge at the Bear Valley Visitor's Center. Camping is limited to four nights using any combination of the sites. No woodfires, fireworks, or dogs are permitted.

# Youth Hostels

**Golden Gate Hostel** (or the Marin Headlands Hostel) is located within Fort Barry, in the Marin Headlands. Open all year, facilities include 60 beds, a common room, kitchen, family room and laundry. Reservations may be made by writing Golden Gate Hostel, Building 941, Ft. Barry, Sausalito, CA 94965 or telephoning 331-2777.

**Point Reyes Hostel** is located off Limantour Road in the Point Reyes National Seashore. Open all year, accommodations include sleeping for 45 people, hot showers, a kitchen, dining room, and common room. Reservations may be made by writing Point Reyes Hostel, P.O. Box 247, Point Reyes Station, CA 94956 or telephoning 663-8811.

# Transportation, Tours, Fishing Trips and Entertainment 15

## Transportation

**G**olden Gate Transit operates daily buses within Marin and to nearby San Francisco and Sonoma County, with modified services on weekends and holidays. The fares vary according to the distance traveled, and various discounts are provided to regular commuters, students, senior citizens, and handicapped persons.

Golden Gate Ferries operate from Sausalito and Larkspur terminals. During the week there are commute trips daily between Larkspur and the San Francisco Ferry Building, and between Sausalito and the Ferry Building.

Golden Gate "feeder" buses operate from all the communities in Marin to the Sausalito and Larkspur terminals.

For bus schedules and information call: 332-6600 (from Southern Marin) or 453-2100 (from Northern Marin). For information on the ferries, call 982-8835.

**Greyhound Bus** provides through service from Third and Tamalpais in San Rafael (453-0795).

**Angel Island State Park Ferry** (435-2131) leaves Tiburon for Angel Island every Saturday and Sunday from 10 A.M. to 4 P.M., every hour on the hour. The return trips to Tiburon are a quarter-after-the-hour, every hour. In summertime the ferries are run daily from 10 A.M. to 4 P.M.; weekends from 10 A.M. to 6 P.M.

---

◄ *Candy Ireton at Muir Woods National Monument.*

**Marin Airporter** offers daily shuttle service to and from Marin County and the San Francisco International Airport. The bus departs from stations and stops in Larkspur, Mill Valley and Sausalito. A connecting bus serves Terra Linda, Ignacio and Novato.

The busses run every half hour between 5:00 A.M. and midnight. The main office is located at 300 Larkspur Landing Circle, Larkspur (461-4222).

# Tours, Commuting & Fishing Trips

## Sightseeing by Boat

One of the best ways to see Marin County is to sail the bay on a San Francisco Bay Cruise. Ships of the **Blue and Gold Fleet** leave Pier 39 in San Francisco daily (starting at 10 A.M. and 11:00 A.M. in December, January and February).

The ships are smooth-riding and offer glass-enclosed lower decks, open-air top decks, and snack bars. The cruise lasts about one-and-a-half hours and is narrated by tour guides. The ship passes many San Francisco landmarks, sails under the Golden Gate Bridge and past Sausalito, Belvedere, Tiburon, and Angel Island.

For schedule and fare information call 781-7877.

**The Red and White Fleet** offers ferry commute service weekdays to Tiburon and other places around the bay area. It is located at Pier 41 in San Francisco. Call 546-2815 for schedules.

## Fishing Trips

Daily boat trips from Sausalito provide deep-sea sport fishing; bay fishing for salmon, bass, and rock cod; or planned cruises for whale and bird watching.

The rates vary. Reservations for open parties or charter must be made in advance. Reels, tackle, live bait, lunches, rental equipment, licenses, and free parking are available.

Individual captains or sport fishing centers may be found in the Yellow Pages under "Fishing Parties."

# Entertainment

## Marin Center

**Marin County Civic Center,** San Pedro Road, San Rafael.

Booking Information: Jim Farley, 499-6396

Event and Ticket Information: Marin Center Box Office, 472-3500

Annual entertainment offerings in the Exhibition Hall, Showcase Theater and Veterans Memorial Auditorium include: Marin Symphony concerts, Marin Ballet "Nutcracker," Golden Gate Geographic Travel Film Series, Marin Opera Company fall and spring seasons, and the Novato Music Association.

*Johnny Mathis.* Photo by Skip Heinecke. Photo courtesy of Jim Farley, Marin Center.

318 TRANSPORTATION, TOURS, FISHING TRIPS AND ENTERTAINMENT

Exhibit shows and festivals include: Antique Show and Sale (March and November), Sir Francis Drake Kennel Club All Breed Dog Show (April and September), Home Show (June), Marin County Fair and Exposition (Fourth of July weekend), Quilt and Needlecraft Show (Labor Day weekend), Ski Swap (October), Christmas Antiques Fair (December), Western States Crafts Jamboree (April and November), and Antique Doll Show (April, October and December).

The Marin Center also sponsors an amazing array of international performers. The shows are billed as 'Live! At Marin Center!' Guests have included the Red Army Chorus, Vienna Boys Choir, the "Chieftains" from Ireland, Jose Greco and Company, a Switzerland mime group called "Mummenschanz," the Peking Acrobats, Soviet Acrobats and other performers from Asia, Europe, Africa, South America, the Soviet Union and Eastern Europe.

The Marin Memorial Auditorium closed on January 9, 1990 for earthquake seismic reinforcement work. It will open again in January 1991.

## Marin Community College District

College of Marin and Indian Valley Colleges sponsor professional-quality stage productions. Actors Robin Williams, David Dukes and Kathleen Quinlan are College of Marin theater alumni.

There is also an interesting selection of guest lectures with such diversified personalities as Gloria Steinem, and Isaac Bashevis Singer. In addition, the colleges sponsor films, art exhibits, concerts, dance programs and poetry readings.

**College of Marin:** Sir Francis Drake Boulevard, Kentfield. Box Office & Events Information: 485-9385

**Indian Valley Colleges:** 1800 Ignacio Boulevard, Novato. Information: 883-2211

## Dominican College

Grand Avenue and Acacia, San Rafael. 457-4440 or 485-3228 for the Dominican Conference Center.

Dominican offers dramatic and musical productions in the Angelico Auditorium and the Forest Meadows Amphitheater plus art exhibits, lectures, concerts and dance exhibitions.

When it became known that the County of Marin would have

to close the Veterans Memorial Auditorium for earthquake seismic reinforcement, Jim Farley, Public Events Manager, decided to move some of their scheduled performances to Angelico Hall. The county joined Dominican College in completely refurbishing this facility which now has 850 new seats, refinished hardwood floors, a new stage, curtains, a vastly improved lighting system, and other updated equipment. The county, in cooperation with Dominican, is currently managing Angelico Hall.

## Marin Art and Garden Center
Sir Francis Drake Boulevard, Ross. 454-5597.

Includes the Frances Young Gallery (continuing art and sculpture shows operated by the Marin Society of Artists), Northgate Summer Group luncheons and fashion shows, Northgate Group's table decor and tea display, and Ross Valley Players productions (456-9555).

## Marin Community Playhouse
27 Kensington Road, San Anselmo. 456-8555

This is a non-profit theater rental facility. Community groups in Marin sponsor a variety of musical and dramatic productions, film series, lectures, dance concerts, and music concerts.

## Marin Theater Company
397 Miller Avenue at La Goma Street, Mill Valley. 388-5208

The 23-year-old Marin Theater Company operates a school for children and adults and produces new plays.

# Further Reading on Marin

Arnot, Phil, *Exploring Point Reyes*. San Carlos, Ca., Wide World Inc., 1976.

Arnot, Phil, *Point Reyes, Secret Places and Magic Moments*, San Carlos, Ca., Wide World Publishing/Tetra, 1988.

Bingham, Helen, *In Tamal Land*. San Francisco, Ca., The Calkins Publishing House, 1906.

Both Sides of the Track, *A Collection of Oral Histories From Belvedere and Tiburon*, Shirley Mitchell, editor, San Francisco, Ca., Scottwall Associates, 1985.

Chan, Gordon I., *A Survey of Marine Life on the Pt. Reyes National Seashore Park*. Kentfield, Ca., College of Marin, no date.

Conrotto, Eugene L., *Miwok Means People*. Fresno, Valley Publishers, 1973.

Dalby, Alice F., *A Visitor's Guide to Point Reyes National Sea shore*. Riverside, Connecticut, The Chatham Press, 1974.

Dekker, Mary Case and Elizabeth Mulryan, *Recycling History, New Lives for Old Buildings*. San Rafael, Ca., Marin Heritage in cooperation with the Marin County Board of Realtors, 1976.

Dines, Glen, *Drake in Marin: Fact and Fancy*. San Rafael, Ca., Marin County Free Library, Civic Center, 1975.

Dines, Glen, *Kit Carson's Black Deed and Other True Stories from Marin's Lively Past*. Nicasio, Ca., Academy Press, 1968.

Donnelly, Florence G., *Early Days in Marin, a Picture Review*. San Rafael, Ca., Marin County Savings and Loan Association, 1960.

Dunham, Tracy, *Discover Marin State Parks*, Marin County, Ca., 1987.

Fairley, Lincoln, *Mount Tamalpais, A History, San Francisco, Ca.*, Scottwall Associates, 1987.

Ferber, Richard, *Exploring Coastal Marin*. Stinson Beach, Ca., Curlew Press, 1969.

Gardiner, Dorothy, *"San Rafael's First Century,"* San Rafael Centennial Souvenir Program, 1874-1974.

Geary, Ida, *Marin Trails, A Natural History Guide to Marin County*. Fairfax, Ca., Tamal Press, 1969.

Gilliam, Harold, *Island in Time, The Point Reyes Peninsula*. San Francisco, Ca., Sierra Club, 1962.

Green, Aaron G., F.A.I.A., with Donald P. De Nevi, *An Architecture for Democracy*, Frank Lloyd Wright, The Marin County Civic Center, San Francisco, Ca., Grendon Publishing, 1990.

Harlan, George H., *San Francisco Bay Ferryboats*. Berkeley, Howell-North Books, 1967.

Hart, John, *San Francisco's Wilderness Next Door*. San Rafael, Ca., Presidio Press, 1979.

Hayden, Mike, *Exploring the North Coast from the Golden Gate to the Oregon Border*. San Francisco, Ca., Chronicle Books, 1976.

Heller, Miranda, *The Coast Miwok at Miller Creek*. San Rafael, Ca., Bank of Marin and the Miwok Archeological Preserve of Marin, 1974.

Hoffman, George, *Saucelito-Sausalito, Legends and Tales of a Changing Town.* Corte Madera, Ca., A Woodward Book, 1976.

Hurd, Edith Thacher and Clement Hurd, *The Blue Heron Tree.* New York, The Viking Press, 1968.

Iacopi, Robert, *Earthquake Country.* Menlo Park, Ca., Lane Books, 1969.

Killion, Tom, *Fortress Marin.* San Rafael, Ca., Presidio Press, 1977.

*Larkspur Past and Present, A History and Walking Guide.* Nancy Curley, editor, Larkspur, Ca., The Larkspur Heritage Committee, 1979.

Lueck, David and Claire Villa, *Self-Guiding Walking Tour of Downtown San Anselmo.* San Anselmo, Ca., San Anselmo Historical Commission, 1979.

*Marin County Almanac, Resident and Newcomer's Orientation Guidebook. Novato, Ca.,* A Thatcher Publication for the Marin County American Revolution Bicentennial Commission, 1976.

*Marin County Parks and Recreation Facilities Inventory, an Element of the Marin Countywide Plan.* Pierre Joske, editor. 1978.

*Marin People,* Volumes 1, 2, and 3. San Rafael, Ca., Marin County Historical Society, 1971, 1972, and 1980.

Mason, Jack, in collaboration with Helen Van Cleave Park, *Early Marin.* Petaluma, Ca., House of Printing, 1971.

Mason, Jack, *Earthquake Bay, A History of Tomales Bay, Ca.* Inverness, Ca., North Shore Books, 1976.

Mason, Jack, in collaboration with Thomas J. Barfield, *Last Stage for Bolinas.* Inverness, Ca., North Shore Books, 1973.

Mason, Jack, in collaboration with Helen Van Cleave Park, *The Making of Marin (1850-1975).* Inverness, Ca., North Shore Books, 1975.

Mason, Jack, *Point Reyes Historian,* Volume 4, Number 1. *Ben's Auto Stage.* Inverness, Ca., North Shore Books, Summer 1979.

Mason, Jack, *Point Reyes, The Solemn Land.* 2nd edition. Inverness, Ca., North Shore Books, 1972.

Mason, Jack, *Summer Town, the History of Inverness, California.* Inverness, Ca., North Shore Books, 1977.

Murdock, Dick, *Point Bonita to Point Reyes, Outdoor in Marin,* Ross Ca., May-Murdock Publications, 1989.

Munro-Fraser, J. P., *History of Marin County, Ca.* New York, Alley Bowen & Co., 1880. Republished by Charmaine Burdell, 1972.

Nelson, John Olaf, Richard A. Lawman, and Dan Lee Peterson, *Tomales, California Historic Resource Survey.* Novato, Ca. North Marin County Water District, 1976.

*Old Marin with Love,* James D. Adams, editor. Marin County American Revolution Bicentennial Commission, 1976.

Olmsted, Nancy, *To Walk with a Quiet Mind, Hikes in the Woodlands, Parks and Beaches of the San Francisco Bay Area.* San Francisco, Sierra Club Books, 1978.

Pepper, Marin Waterhouse, *Bolinas, A Narrative of the Days of the Dons.* New York, Vantage Press, 1965.

*Pictoral History of Tiburon, A California* Railroad Town, James Heig, editor, San Francisco, Ca., Scottwall Associates, 1984.

Pfeiffer, Bruce Brooks, *Global Architecture, Frank Lloyd Wright, Solomon R. Guggenheim Museum, New York City, N.Y. 1943-59, Marin County Civic Center, California, 1957-1970.* Yukio Futagawa, editor. Tokyo, Japan, A.D.A. EDITA Tokyo, Co., Ltd., 1975.

Pomada, Elizabeth, *Places To Go With Children In Northern California.* San Francisco, Ca., Chronicle Books, 1973.

Radford, Dr. Evelyn Morris, *The Bridge and the Building.* Carlton Press, Inc., A Hearthstone Book, 1974.

Raymond, Lee and Ann Rice, *Marin Indians.* Sausalito, Ca., Pages of History, Box Six, 1957.

*Redwood Empire Visitor's Guide* (annual magazine). San Francisco, Redwood Empire Association, 1980.

*Saint Mary's Church, Nicasio, California, 1867-1979.* Nicasio, Ca., Parishioners of St. Mary's Church, 1979.

*"San Rafael, 1874-1974,"* Marin County Historical Bulletin, Vol. 5, Oct. 1973.

Secchitano, Jean, *The Golden Days of Fairfax, 1831-1931.* Fairfax, Ca., Fairfax Central P.T.A., no date.

*Self Guided Walking Tour of San Anselmo's Seminary Area.* San Anselmo, Ca., San Anselmo Historical Commission, 1978.

*Shark Point, High Point, An Illustrated History of Tiburon and Belvedere, Marin County, Ca.* Belvedere-Tiburon, Ca., Reed School, 1970.

Slaymaker, C., *Culture of Coast Miwok.* Miwok Archeological Preserve of Marin, 1977.

Strauss, Joseph B., *The Golden Gate Bridge.* San Francisco, Golden Gate Bridge District, 1938.

Teather, Louise, *Discovering Marin.* Fairfax, Ca., The Tamal Land Press, 1974.

Teather, Louise, ed. *Glimpses of Belvedere and Tiburon, The Early Decades,* Volume II. Belvedere-Tiburon, Ca., The Landmarks Society, 1978.

Teather, Louise, *Place Names of Marin,* San Francisco, Ca., Scottwall Associates, 1986.

Terwilliger, Elizabeth, *Sights and Sounds of the Seasons.* Tiburon, Ca., The Elizabeth Terwilliger Nature Education Foundation, 1979.

Tierney, Robert J., Joseph W. Ulmer, Leonard J. Waxdeck, Harris N. Foster, and John R. Eckenrood, *Exploring Tidal Life along the Pacific Coast with Emphasis on Point Reyes National Seashore.* Fourth Printing, Oakland, Ca. OECOLOGOCA, 1969.

Tracy, Jack, *Sausalito, Moments in Time,* Sausalito, Ca., Windgate Press, 1983.

*West Marin Directory.* Olema, California, West Marin Publishing Company, 1980.

Whiteley, Barbara, *Gerstle Park, An Environmental Walk.* San Rafael, Ca., A San Rafael Schools Early Retirement Project, 1977.

Whitnah, Dorothy L., *An Outdoor Guide to the San Francisco Bay Area.* Berkeley, Ca., Wilderness Press, 1978.

Whitnah, Dorothy L., *Guide to The Golden Gate National Recreation Area.* Berkeley, Ca., Wilderness Press, 1978.

Wurm, T. G. and A. G. Graves, *The Crookedest Railroad in the World. History of the Mt. Tamalpais and Muir Woods Railway.* Berkeley, Howell-North Books, 1960.

*Yabroff, Lawrence, Miwok Indians of Marin.* San Francisco, Ca., Sausalito Teacher Education Project, San Francisco State College, 1967.

# Acknowledgments

As I compiled the facts for this book, hundreds of people helped me by answering questions, reading portions of the manuscript for accuracy, and making intelligent suggestions. I especially want to thank my editor at Presidio Press, Joan Griffin, whose faith in the book from the first proposal sustained me through the final rewrite. Also of tremendous assistance was Louise Teather who volunteered her time to read the entire manuscript and check for historical accuracy. Diane Van Renselaar provided much needed field assistance, and Mary Ann Shaffer compiled information and helped me meet deadlines. Directors, officers, and employees of historical societies, chambers of commerce, and national, state, and county parks were of immeasurable assistance.

I would particularly like to thank:

Sarah Allen, field researcher on marine mammals; Adele Anthony, San Francisco Theological Seminary; Frank Archibald, San Geronimo Valley Water Treatment Plant; Bob Armstrong, park technician, Corps of Engineers Bay Model, Sausalito; Peter R. Arrigoni, former Marin County supervisor; Lynn Bagley, aide to Congressman John Burton; William T. Bagley, former Marin assemblyman; Thomas J. Barfield, Marin historian and writer; Peter Behr, former state senator; Sheila Berg, Dixie Schoolhouse Foundation; Woody Binford, founder of first Marin airport; Don Brittson, Marin County Farm Advisor; Le Roy Brock, chief ranger, Point Reyes National Seashore; Mary Bruce, typist; Charmaine Burdell, Marin historian; Cassie Burke, ranger at Angel Island State Park.

Carney Campion, Golden Gate Bridge, Highway and Transportation District; Gordon L. Chan, Biology Department, College of Marin; Margaret Coady, Novato historian; Nancy Curley, Larkspur Heritage Committee; Mary Case Dekker, curator of Falkirk Community Cultural Center; Don Dimitratos, Marin County Parks and Recreation Department; Carla Ehat, Marin Oral History Program; Dr. Eliot Evans, Angel Island historian; Jim Farley, auditorium manager, Marin Center, Marin County Civic Center; Fred Faude; Roy Flatt, ranger at Mt. Tamalpais State Park; Francis T. Fogarty, manager, Marin County Chamber of Commerce and Visitor's Bureau; Alan Freeland, lawyer.

Betty Gardner, West Marin historian; Gary Giacomini, Marin County supervisor; Dan Goltz, former San Anselmo planning commissioner; Charles Grasso, Fairfax historian and police chief; Harry Hearfield, Golden Gate Bridge, Highway and Transportation District; Burr Heneman, executive director, Point Reyes Bird Observatory; Marvin Hershey, site manager, Muir Woods National Monument; Jean Hitchock, Mill Valley Public Library; Dave Hodgson, Sausalito Historical Society; Ken Hough, Golden Gate Bridge, Highway and Transportation District; Don Hunter, director of parks and recreation for Mill Valley.

Pierre Joske, director, Marin Parks and Recreation Department; Robert Kane, publisher, Presidio Press; Alice C. Katzung, executive director, Marin Wildlife Center; Anne T. Kent, Marin Oral History Program; Marty Kent; Helen Lamb Marin Art and Garden Center; Bobbie Lawrence, researcher; Emma M. Lawson; Bunny Lucheta, aide to Senator Barry Keene; William S. Mailliard, former Marin congressman; Paul S. Marcucii, historian for San Francisco Yacht Club; Adrianne Marcus; Marin County Builders Exchange; Jack Mason, historian and writer; Charles Mastin, College of Marin Reference Room; Paul Maxwell, director, Yosemite Institute.

Elsie P. Mazzini, president, Marin County Historical Society; William McCluskey, Marin Academy; Don McCune, ranger, Tomales Bay State Park; Eric McGuire, Marin Municipal Water District; Ulla McLean, executive secretary, Coastal Parks Association; Barbara Melville, Humane Society of Marin; Ralph Moreno, Reference Room, Mill Valley Public Library; Phil Murphy, St. Vincent's School.

James Neider, California State Parks; Beth Olivier, Marin County Chamber of Commerce; Steve Olsen, district ranger, Marin Headlands; Larry Perkins, ranger, China Camp; David Plant; Kristy S. Powell, manager, Corinthian Yacht Club; Tom Price, former Marin County supervisor; Inez Purser; Earl Reink, Mill Valley Library volunteer; Mark Reisenfeld, Marin County Planning Department; Leonard Richardson, headmaster, Katharine Branson/Mt. Tamalpais School; Patrick L. Robards, ranger, China Camp; Liz Robinson, Sausalito Historical Society; Robert Roumiguiere, Marin County supervisor.

Alice Sagar, Fairfax historian; Phil Schaeffer, former director, Western Education Center, Richardson Bay Wildlife Sanctuary; Vera Schultz, former Marin County supervisor; Darrell Scott, general manager, Vindar Aviation; Ruth Scott; Dick Shaler; Susan Shea; Nancy Skinner, College of Marin hiking instructor; Mark Smith, Golden Gate Baptist Theological Seminary; Marion Spillman; Carol Staley, assistant Marin County clerk; Sally Stanford, life-time vice-mayor, Sausalito; Boyd Stewart; Madeline Stiver, Miwok Archeological Preserve.

Louise Teather, writer and historian; Elizabeth Terwilliger, naturalist and writer; Silvia Thalman, Miwok Archeological Preserve; Bill Thomas, Golden Gate National Recreation Area; Thompson family, Marin French Cheese Company; Jack Tracy, founder, Sausalito Historical Society; Ron Treleven, publicist, College of Marin and Indian Valley Colleges; Claire Villa, San Anselmo Historical Commission and Historical Society; Ken Watts, Marin Rod and Gun Club; Brian Wittenkeller, Marin County Parks and Recreation Department; Maureen Woods, National Marine Fisheries Service; Michael Wornum, former Marin assemblyman and Larkspur City councilman; Mel Zell, Marin Rod and Gun Club; Clerin Zumwalt, Audubon Society.

# Acknowledgements —
## 1990 Edition

A special thanks to the following people:

Bill Allen, President, Fairfax Historical Society; Ron Angier, Mt. Tamalpais State Park; Beverly Bastian, The Landmarks Society of Belvedere and Tiburon; Dory Bassitt, Mill Valley Historical Society; Connie Berto, consultant on horses and trail maps; Pat Briggs, Bay Conference Center; Carney Campion, General Manager, Golden Gate Bridge, Hwy. and Transportation District.

Katherine Coddington, San Anselmo Historical Museum; Carol Dahlman, Larkspur Recreation Department; Robert E. David, Golden Gate Bridge District Staff; Peter Dreyfus, Mill Valley Library; Carla Ehat; James Farley, Manager, Marin Center; Al Fleming, Marin City Development Corp.; Glen Fuller, Muir Woods National Monument; Carl Harrington, Golden Gate Ferries; Brian Hubbard, Richardson Bay Audubon Center and Sanctuary.

Betty Krause, Larkspur historian; Dan Mohn, Golden Gate Bridge; Dewey Livingston, Pt. Reyes National Seashore; Eric McGuire, Marin Municipal Water District; Alison Murphy, Bay Area Discovery Museum; Gayle Murphy, San Domenico Riding School; Doug Nadeau, Golden Gate National Recration Area; Alice Sagar, Fairfax historian; Jane Sheeks, Fairfax Librarian; Marcy Shone, consultant on horses; Nancy Skinner, historical photographs.

Jane Toops, historical photos; Anita Torres, Marin Art and Garden Center; Louise Teather, Marin historian; Silvia Thalman, Miwok Archeological Preserve; Diane Van Renselaar, editor; Lt. White, San Quentin; Barbara Weitz, horse information; Ranger Mike Whitehead, Angel Island State Park.

# The Author

**P**atricia Arrigoni has written about Marin County since 1965 when when she joined the staff of the Ross Valley Reporter, contributing feature articles, photographs, and a weekly column. A graduate of Dominican College in San Rafael, she worked there for a time as director of public information.

As a free-lance writer she has published in many Bay Area newspapers and magazines and for several years wrote a weekly travel column for the *Marin Independent Journal*. She was also syndicated with Gannett News Service for four years writing travel and supplying photographs. She has had a one-woman photography show at the Marin County Civic Center and showings in several businesses in Marin and San Francisco.

She continues now to write articles on travel on a free lance basis for magazines and newspapers.

Patricia is married to Peter Arrigoni, whose family moved to Marin after the 1906 earthquake and fire in San Francisco. The Arrigonis have both been active on the Marin political scene; Peter, now with the Marin Builders Exchange, served for eight years as a member of the Board of Supervisors, four years on the Fairfax City Council and many years on various regional boards including the Golden Gate Bridge, Highway and Transportation District, Association of Bay Area Governments, the California Coastal Commission and the Bay Area Air Pollution Control District. He currently serves on the boards of the Marin Community Foundation, the Marconi Conference Center Board of Directors and the Marin Peace Conversion Commission.

The Arrigonis have two children, James and Robert, and a daughter-in-law, Trudy, married to James.

# Index

# Order Form

For **MAKING THE MOST OF MARIN**                    $15.95
By mail from the publisher:
**Travel Publishers International**
P.O. Box 1030, Fairfax, CA 94930

Company Name:  _____

Name:  _____

Address:_____

City:_____ State: _____ Zip: _____

Please make checks payable to: **Travel Publishers International**

|                                      | QTY. | COST | TOTAL |
|--------------------------------------|------|------|-------|
| **MAKING THE MOST OF MARIN**         | _____ | _____ | _____ |

Sales tax: (In CA. add 6¼%. $1.00 per book)                    _____ _____

Shipping:
  Book Rate: Add $1.75 for the first
  book and 75¢ for each additional book                 _____ _____
  (Surface shipping may take 3-4 weeks.)
  Air Mail: $4.00                                        _____ _____

      TOTAL FOR BOOK(S), SALES TAX & SHIPPING:          _____

Payment: *(Please check box)*
  ☐ Check ☐ Money Order
  ☐ Credit card: ☐ VISA  ☐ MasterCard

     Card Number: _____

     Expiration Date:_____ /_____

     Name on Card:  _____
                              please print

Signature:  _____

Telephone orders:
  Book Passage, (415) 927-0960. Open until 10:00 P.M. daily.

# Order Form

For **MAKING THE MOST OF MARIN**          $15.95

By mail from the publisher:

**Travel Publishers International**
P.O. Box 1030, Fairfax, CA 94930

Company Name: _____

Name: _____

Address:_____

City:_____ State: _____ Zip: _____

Please make checks payable to: **Travel Publishers International**

|                                                   | QTY. | COST | TOTAL |
|---------------------------------------------------|------|------|-------|
| **MAKING THE MOST OF MARIN**                      | _____ | _____ | _____ |

Sales tax: (In CA. add 6¼%. $1.00 per book)          _____ _____

Shipping:
  Book Rate: Add $1.75 for the first
  book and 75¢ for each additional book          _____ _____
  (Surface shipping may take 3-4 weeks.)
  Air Mail: $4.00          _____ _____

        TOTAL FOR BOOK(S), SALES TAX & SHIPPING:          _____

Payment: *(Please check box)*

  ☐ Check  ☐ Money Order
  ☐ Credit card:  ☐ VISA   ☐ MasterCard

        Card Number: _____

        Expiration Date:_____ / _____

        Name on Card: _____
                                        please print

Signature: _____

Telephone orders:
  Book Passage, (415) 927-0960. Open until 10:00 P.M. daily.

MAP:
Horse Trails of MARIN

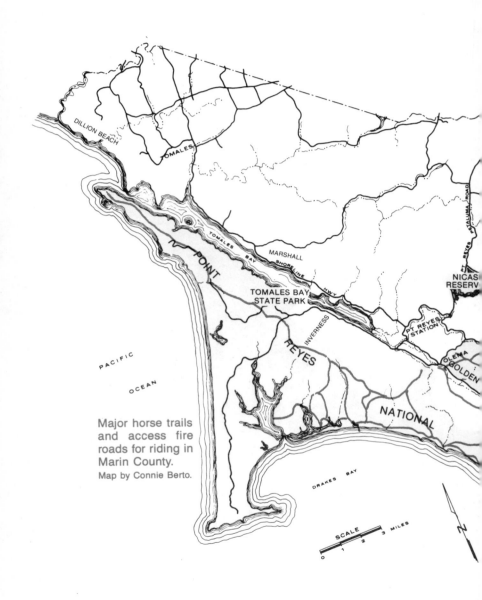

DILLION BEACH

TOMALES

POINT

TOMALES BAY

MARSHALL

SHORE LINE HWY

TOMALES BAY
STATE PARK

INVERNESS

REYES

PT REYES
STATION

PACIFIC

OCEAN

NICAS
RESERV

PT REYES PETALUMA ROAD

OLEMA
GOLDEN

NATIONAL

Major horse trails
and access fire
roads for riding in
Marin County.
Map by Connie Berto.

DRAKES BAY

SCALE    MILES
0   1   2   3

N